OECD Economic Surveys:
Poland
2012

OECD

This document and any map included herein are without prejudice to the status of or sovereignty over any territory, to the delimitation of international frontiers and boundaries and to the name of any territory, city or area.

Please cite this publication as:
OECD (2012), *OECD Economic Surveys: Poland 2012*, OECD Publishing.
http://dx.doi.org/10.1787/eco_surveys-pol-2012-en

ISBN 978-92-64-12728-9 (print)
ISBN 978-92-64-12729-6 (PDF)

Series: OECD Economic Surveys
ISSN 0376-6438 (print)
ISSN 1609-7513 (online)

OECD Economic Surveys Poland:
ISSN 1995-3542 (print)
ISSN 1999-060X (online)

The statistical data for Israel are supplied by and under the responsibility of the relevant Israeli authorities. The use of such data by the OECD is without prejudice to the status of the Golan Heights, East Jerusalem and Israeli settlements in the West Bank under the terms of international law.

Photo credits: Cover © David Bank/Flickr/Getty Images.

Corrigenda to OECD publications may be found on line at: *www.oecd.org/publishing/corrigenda*.

Table of contents

This Survey is published on the responsibility of the Economic and Development Review Committee of the OECD, which is charged with the examination of the economic situation of member countries.

The economic situation and policies of Poland were reviewed by the Committee on 6 February 2012. The draft report was then revised in the light of the discussions and given final approval as the agreed report of the whole Committee on 21 February 2012.

The Secretariat's draft report was prepared for the Committee by Hervé Boulhol and Balázs Égert under the supervision of Peter Jarrett. Statistical assistance was provided by Patrizio Sicari.

The previous Survey of Poland was issued in April 2010.

This book has...

**A service that delivers Excel® files
from the printed page!**

Look for the *StatLinks* at the bottom right-hand corner of the tables or graphs in this book.
To download the matching Excel® spreadsheet, just type the link into your Internet browser,
starting with the *http://dx.doi.org* prefix.
If you're reading the PDF e-book edition, and your PC is connected to the Internet, simply
click on the link. You'll find *StatLinks* appearing in more OECD books.

BASIC STATISTICS OF POLAND, 2010

LAND

Area (sq. km)	312 679
Arable land (in per cent of total area)	35

PEOPLE

Population (million, mid-year)	38.2	Employment (million)	16.0
Rural population (% of total, mid-year)	39.0	Employment by sector (% of total):	
Life expectancy at birth: Male	72.1	Agriculture	12.9
Female	80.6	Industry (including construction)	30.2
Infant mortality (per thousand)	5.0	Services	56.9
Labour force survey unemployment (% of labour force)			9.6
Number of pensioners (million)			9.2

PARLIAMENT

Bicameral Parliamentary system

Sejm membership (lower house)	460
Senate membership (upper house)	100
Number of political parties in Sejm	6

PRODUCTION

GDP (Zl billion, current prices)	1 414.5
GDP per capita (US$, market exchange rate)	12 292.0
Gross fixed capital formation (% of GDP)	19.7

PUBLIC FINANCE

General government budget balance (% of GDP)	−7.9
General government revenues (% of GDP)	37.5
General government expenditures (% of GDP)	45.4
General government debt, Maastricht definition (% of GDP)	54.9

FOREIGN TRADE AND FINANCE

Exports of goods and services (% of GDP)	42.3
Imports of goods and services (% of GDP)	43.5
Official reserves assets (US$ billion, end-year)	93.5
Total external debt (US$ billion, end-year)	315.3

CURRENCY

Monetary unit: zloty

Currency units per:	US$	€
Average: 2011	2.9634	4.1198
January 2012	3.3884	4.3775

Executive summary

Poland has been the best growth performer within the OECD through the global economic crisis. *However, with its planned fiscal retrenchment and the European economy grinding to a halt, real GDP growth is projected to slow to 2¾-3 per cent in 2012 and 2013. That should be sufficient to ease inflation pressures, implying that the current somewhat accommodative monetary policy stance is appropriate, even though inflation risks are currently tilted to the upside. Yet, Poland is not immune to contagion risks from its European trading partners. Despite sound prudential regulation and a comparatively solid financial system, the banks' large foreign-currency liabilities and the reliance on potentially volatile portfolio inflows represent potential sources of instability in the event of a deeper liquidity crisis. Under a scenario of a sharper-than-projected slowdown, Poland would have policy space to cushion the shock by easing monetary conditions, provided that the zloty does not weaken substantially. On the other hand, automatic fiscal stabilisers should be allowed to work within the constraints imposed by the constitutional debt rule.*

Fiscal consolidation is the best way to reduce vulnerabilities in the economy. *Lowering the deficit will help to limit price pressures, keep external debt under control and enhance fiscal credibility, all of which will alleviate contagion risks. The government looks capable of meeting its deficit target of 2.9% of GDP in 2012. Detailed measures to reduce the deficit to about 2% of GDP in 2013 (a surer way station on the route to achieving the European Union's Medium Term Objective of 1% of GDP in 2015 than the government's current goal for 2013 of 2.5% of GDP) should be announced quickly, focusing on: cutting tax expenditures, reforming the farmers' social security system, removing pension privileges for selected occupations and continued tightening of eligibility criteria for disability support. Worthy changes that would help in the longer term include: enhancing public-sector efficiency, opting for less distortive taxes and raising and equalising retirement ages for men and women. Now that the government has its second electoral mandate, it is also time to formulate and implement a broad range of product- and labour-market reforms to boost economic performance.*

Health-care reform could ease the substantial limitations in access to care and reduce persistent inequalities in health outcomes. *The health status of the population remains relatively poor, though in line with Poland's level of economic development. The health-care system is characterised by low spending, tight budget constraints and a thin private insurance market. Widening the health-care contribution base would help secure an adequate level of financing to limit heavy out-of-pocket payments, shorten waiting times and address growing health-care needs, while improving labour-market performance. Private health insurance might allow expanded resources and make the system more responsive, but it should be designed carefully so as not to exclude low-income households. Current resources should be re-allocated from the hospital sector into both primary care, through strengthening the gate-keeping function and developing a more integrated treatment approach, and long-term care. Improving health-care efficiency and equity can also be achieved by: providing hospitals with clear incentives to rationalise the use of financial resources; streamlining responsibilities between the National Health Fund and central and local governments; and better regulating doctors working in both public and private facilities.*

Poland's potential for cutting greenhouse gas emissions is substantial and should be realised in a least-cost fashion, which is crucial given the country's high expected overall abatement costs. An economy-wide single carbon price is key to minimising abatement costs, but present explicit and implicit carbon prices vary widely across sectors. It is important to further pursue electricity market liberalisation in line with EU Directives. Public ownership in electricity generation and the lack of effective separation between producers and distributors may curtail responsiveness to the price signal provided by the EU-ETS by curbing new entry and limiting the role of the organised wholesale electricity market. Integrating the Polish electricity market with its neighbours' would help to spread climate-change efforts more efficiently across the continent. The current uniform and thus cost-efficient support to renewable sources of power should be maintained, but incentives to encourage investment in new generating capacity should be enhanced. Finally, government policies to increase the production of nuclear power and natural gas from shale formations should take fully into account tail risks and the short- and long-term environmental costs of the use of the former and fully consider environmental risks related to extraction of the latter.

Assessment and recommendations

Towards a soft landing?

A star growth performer within the OECD

Since 2007, Poland has been the best economic performer within the OECD as measured by real GDP growth (Figure 1). As a result, Poland has caught up on average 2 percentage points of its GDP-per-capita gap with the EU15 annually since 2005, more than double the rate achieved in the first half of the 2000s. This strong performance can be explained by substantial inflows of EU funds (which have contributed to modernising transport infrastructure), stimulus from domestic macroeconomic policies (through 2010), exchange-rate depreciation and effective prudential regulation of the comparatively solid financial system. In contrast, despite improved business-sector profitability, private capital outlays were weak until 2010 (Figure 2). In 2011, real GDP, mainly driven by private consumption and public investment, especially in the construction sector, is estimated to have grown by 4.3%, exceeding OECD estimates of potential growth of about 3-3.5%. However, the sustainability of high growth is open to question, unless a broad range of reforms are undertaken to deal with underlying imbalances and to overcome structural weaknesses. With the government having received its second electoral mandate, now is the time to formulate and implement a reform programme that will promote continued rapid catch-up and solidify the confidence of financial markets in Poland's economic future.

Figure 1. **Poland has outperformed OECD countries in GDP growth outcomes**

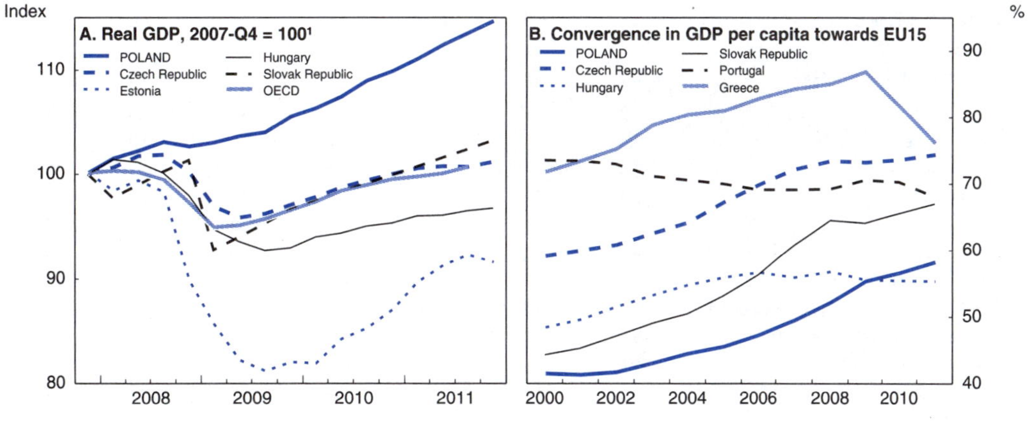

1. Preliminary estimates for 2011Q4.
Source: OECD, OECD Economic Outlook 90 Database and OECD updates.

StatLink http://dx.doi.org/10.1787/888932583939

Figure 2. **Diverging dynamics in public and private investments**

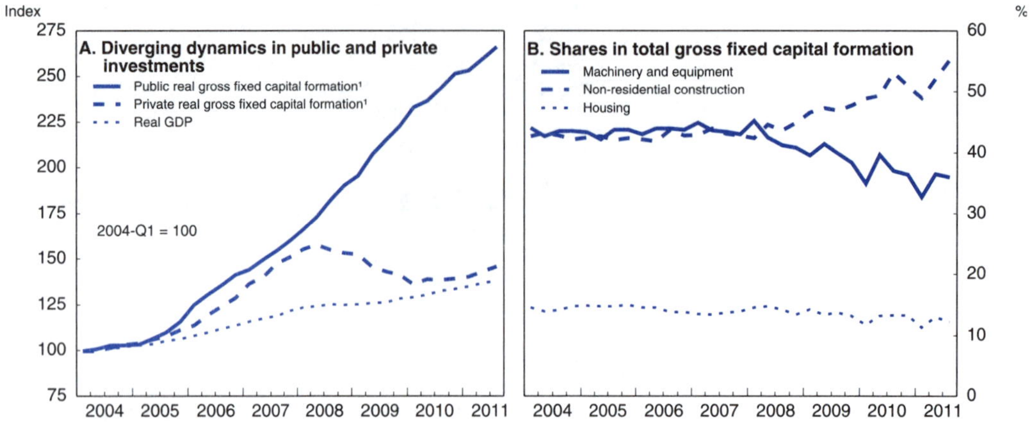

1. Deflated by the gross total fixed capital formation deflator; estimates for 2011.

Source: OECD Economic Outlook 90 Database; National Bank of Poland, *Quarterly Macroeconomic Indicators.*

StatLink 🔗 http://dx.doi.org/10.1787/888932583958

Overheating pressures were reduced, but not completely eliminated, by the Great Recession, and a substantial fiscal expansion helped to sustain activity in the 2008-09 downturn (Table 1 and Figure 3). The general government deficit rose from 1.9% of GDP in 2007 and peaked at 7.8% of GDP in 2010 and the Maastricht definition of the debt-GDP ratio increased from 45% in 2007 to an estimated 57% in 2011.

Table 1. **Recent trends and outlook**

Year-on-year percentage change, volume

	Average 2000-07	2008	2009	2010	2011[1]	2012[1]	2013[1]
GDP at market prices	4.1	5.0	1.6	3.9	4.3	3.0	2.7
Private consumption	3.5	5.3	2.3	3.1	3.4	2.3	2.1
Government consumption	3.6	6.7	2.5	3.8	0.1	0.1	0.0
Gross fixed investment	4.0	9.7	−1.2	−0.2	7.2	5.0	4.6
Stockbuilding[2]	0.3	−1.3	−2.1	1.9	0.4	0.0	0.0
Total domestic demand	3.7	5.1	−0.5	4.5	3.9	2.0	2.1
Exports of goods and services	11.4	5.9	−6.0	12.1	6.8	3.6	4.4
Imports of goods and services	9.3	8.0	−12.7	13.8	5.5	3.3	3.5
Trade balance[2]	0.2	−0.6	2.7	−0.7	0.4	0.5	0.4
Consumer price	3.4	4.2	3.5	2.6	4.2	3.3	2.5
Unemployment rate	16.8	7.1	8.2	9.6	9.6	10.0	10.2
Total employment	0.4	3.7	0.4	0.6	1.0	−0.2	0.0
Labour productivity	3.8	1.2	1.1	3.4	3.4	2.6	2.6
Current account[4]	−4.0	−6.5	−3.9	−4.5	−4.5	−4.5	−4.1
General government net lending[4]	−4.3	−3.7	−7.4	−7.9	−5.5	−3.2	−2.0
Cyclically adjusted government net lending[3]	−4.1	−4.2	−7.2	−8.0	−6.1	−3.6	−2.2
Public debt, Maastricht definition[4]	43.6	47.1	51.1	54.9	56.8	57.1	56.2
Public debt, national definition[4]	44.4	46.9	49.9	52.8	53.8[5]	–	–
Potential output	4.2	4.5	3.6	2.8	3.0	3.2	3.2

1. Projections.
2. Contribution to GDP volume growth.
3. As a percentage of potential GDP.
4. As a percentage of GDP.
5. Government estimates for 2011.

Source: OECD, *OECD Economic Outlook 90 Database* and OECD updates.

Figure 3. **Excess demand and weakened public finances**

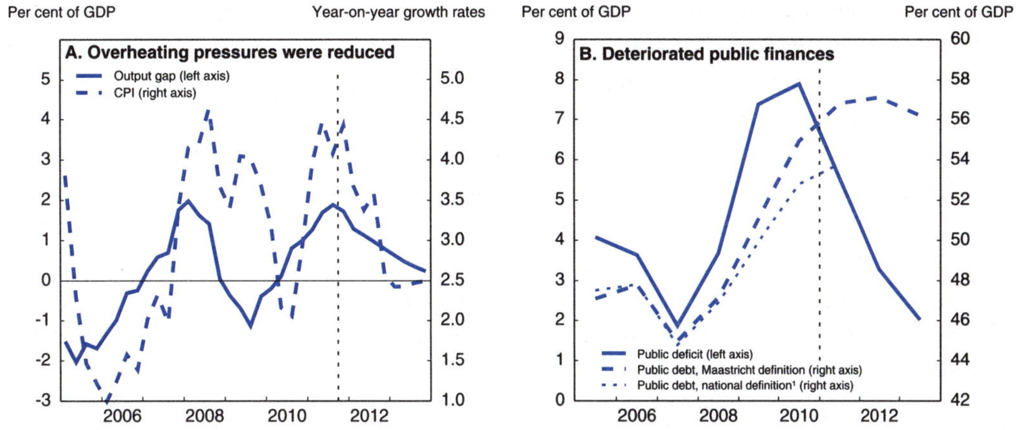

Per cent of GDP   Year-on-year growth rates   Per cent of GDP   Per cent of GDP

A. Overheating pressures were reduced

— Output gap (left axis)
— · CPI (right axis)

B. Deteriorated public finances

— Public deficit (left axis)
— · Public debt, Maastricht definition (right axis)
— · · Public debt, national definition[1] (right axis)

1. Government estimates for 2011.

Source: OECD, *OECD Economic Outlook 90 Database;* GUS.

StatLink http://dx.doi.org/10.1787/888932583977

The constraining 55% intermediate public-debt threshold, which is an early ceiling that is intended to prevent the constitutional debt limit of 60% of GDP from being reached, did not trigger corrective mechanisms because, according to the separate national definition, the debt-GDP ratio has remained below 55% (Panel B). The government is committed to reducing the general government deficit from an estimated 5.6% of GDP in 2011 to 2.9% in 2012 and 2.5% in 2013. Structural measures, including the partial redirection of new pension contributions from the second to the first pillar and an increase in disability contributions, should bring the 2012 deficit to 3.2% of GDP, so long as the global economy does not suffer an especially deep recession. If the new expenditure regime for local governments is implemented as planned, the 2.9% target might be reached. A further fiscal effort should be made, however, to continue fiscal consolidation at an appropriate pace in 2013; specific policies should be announced quickly to reach a deficit of some 2% of GDP, which would strengthen credibility. Additional tightening will then be needed to bring the structural deficit to the Medium Term Objective of 1% of GDP.

The economy is likely to slow down

Against the backdrop of an OECD-wide slowdown and the planned fiscal retrenchment, real GDP growth is projected to fall to about 2¾-3 per cent in 2012 and 2013 in the baseline scenario (Table 1), although activity should be supported by the 2012 European football championship and investments financed by EU funds, which increased sharply to about 2.7% of GDP in 2011 and should rise to some 4% of GDP in 2012 and 2013. The unemployment rate should stay high at about 10%, while headline and core inflation should converge towards the middle of the inflation target band of 2.5 ± 1%, given muted wage pressure and the sustained slightly accommodative monetary policy stance. Given recent inflation outcomes with headline inflation at 4.1% year-over-year in January 2012, risks to these inflation projections are tilted to the upside, although this would be tempered by any unexpected weakening of activity.

There are significant downside risks for the economic outlook

Serious downside risks to the baseline scenario stem from negative events that could lead to an intensification of concerns about the robustness of the global banking system, contagion from euro-area sovereign debt markets and current macroeconomic stress faced by Hungary, and an excessively tight fiscal policy in the United States due to political gridlock (OECD, 2011). The Polish economy is not insulated from the specific problems affecting some euro-area countries, and mounting uncertainties led to a 13% depreciation of the zloty relative to the euro in the second half of 2011. Contagion can arise through the trade channel as export markets shrink, the foreign-investment channel as emerging markets tend to be especially affected when risk premia increase, the financial channel as most Polish banks are foreign owned and the exchange-rate channel due to the burden of liabilities denominated in foreign currencies.

The sizeable current account deficit has been increasingly financed by potentially unstable inflows

At over 4.5% of GDP, the current account deficit has shrunk from its 2008 peak of close to 7%, thanks to strong export performance and growing migrants' remittances (Table 2). The sharp depreciation of the zloty in 2008, moderate wage pressures and hefty productivity gains have contributed to improved price competitiveness. While the current account is almost entirely financed by EU capital transfers (included in the capital account) and foreign investment, the structure of inward investment flows shifted from direct to portfolio investment, especially in the form of debt securities, between the beginning of 2009 and mid-2011, as in some other Central and Eastern European countries (CEECs) (Table 2). The share of non-resident holdings of zloty-denominated government bonds has doubled over the last three years and has reached a record level of over 30% (Figure 4), higher than in most other large emerging economies. This trend may have been driven by the substantial interest-rate premium resulting from both extraordinarily easy monetary conditions in most developed countries and some tightening in Poland, as well as the depth of the Polish financial markets, which allows global investors to take a regional position by focusing on Polish securities (IMF, 2011). Although such flows might reflect sound economic prospects, they could at the same time become problematic, because they are more speculative in nature and, as such, could reverse course quickly.

Table 2. **Current account and selected balance of payments items**

Per cent of GDP

	2005	2006	2007	2008	2009	2010	2011[1]
Current account	**−2.4**	**−3.8**	**−6.2**	**−6.6**	**−3.9**	**−4.7**	**−4.1**
Goods and services	−0.8	−1.9	−3.3	−4.8	−0.6	−1.8	−1.5
Income	−2.2	−2.8	−3.8	−2.4	−3.8	−3.6	−3.8
Current transfers	0.6	0.9	1.0	0.6	0.6	0.8	1.1
Capital account	**0.3**	**0.6**	**1.1**	**1.1**	**1.6**	**1.8**	**2.2**
Financial account	**5.0**	**3.9**	**8.8**	**7.1**	**7.8**	**8.1**	**4.9**
Direct investment	2.3	3.1	4.3	2.0	1.9	0.7	1.6
Portfolio investment	4.1	−0.8	−1.5	−0.6	3.3	5.4	3.1
Net errors and omissions	**−0.2**	**0.1**	**−0.8**	**−2.4**	**−2.3**	**−2.0**	**−1.8**

1. 2011 is based on monthly estimates up to December.
Source: National Bank of Poland (2011).

Figure 4. **Strong appetite for Polish government bonds despite an increase in risk aversion**

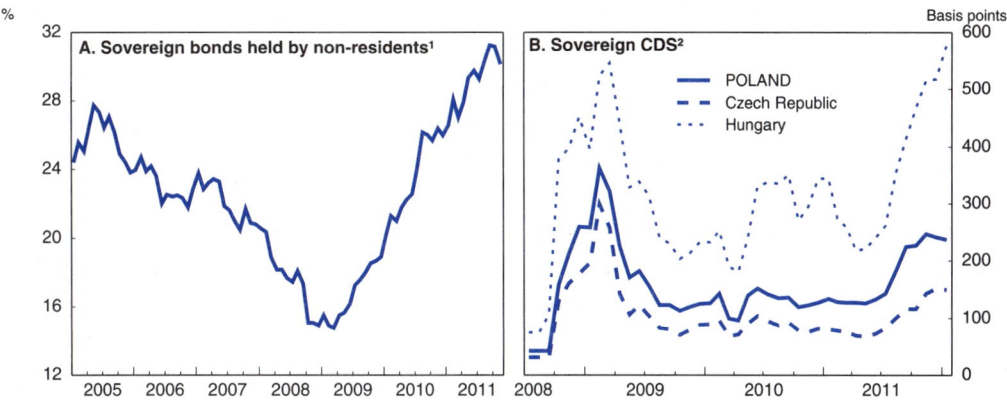

1. As a share of outstanding Polish zloty-denominated government bonds.
2. 5-year sovereign bonds

Source: National Bank of Poland (2011); OECD, *OECD Economic Outlook 90 Database*; Datastream.

StatLink http://dx.doi.org/10.1787/888932583996

Notwithstanding this specific risk factor, external vulnerabilities seem to be fairly well contained (Table 3). External debt is limited compared with other CEECs, although it has been growing rapidly since 2008, and the share of short-term external debt – at about 25% – is lower than in most other countries in the region. Inflows on the financial and capital accounts have helped build up official reserves, which amount to 20% of GDP. That seems to be broadly adequate. Nevertheless, the IMF cautions that they fall short of short-term debt at remaining maturity plus the current account deficit, suggesting that additional accumulation might be desirable (IMF, 2011). A Flexible Credit Line with the IMF provides Poland with an additional insurance of USD 30 billion, if needed.

Table 3. **External vulnerabilities**

End of 2010

Measure (per cent of):	Domestic FX loans stock to private sector	FX credit	Total external debt	Gross reserves		Banking system		
						Total assets	State-owned banks	Foreign-owned banks
	GDP	Total loan stock	GDP	GDP	Short-term debt	GDP	Total assets	Total assets
Poland	**18.2**	**34.6**	**66.6**	**19.7**	**122.2**	**76.8**	**22.9**	**70.5**
Estonia	1.4	1.5	117.6	13.9	24.1	135.0	0.0	97.9
Hungary	35.6	61.1	143.3	34.5	66.8	103.7	–	–
Slovak Republic	13.5	0.9	75.4	0.9	1.1	83.1	0.9	91.8
Slovenia	4.5	5.4	115.2	2.3	8.5	139.9	18.9	28.7

Source: EBRD and NBP.

The financial system seems sound

According to the central bank (NBP, 2011a), the condition of the banking sector has been steadily improving since the end of 2009. Interest margins have been restored, thereby boosting the sector's profitability. In turn, on top of new capital raised through share issuance, a higher propensity to retain earnings, following recommendations of the Financial

Supervision Authority (KNF), has helped to lift capital-adequacy ratios. They reached an average of 13.2% in the third quarter of 2011, lower than the peak of about 14% reached in the first quarter, but well up on the 11-12% registered in 2008-09, with Tier 1 capital exceeding 90% of the total. As a result, the loss-absorption capacity of Polish banks is fairly strong.

The Polish banking system weathered the preceding 2008-09 crisis relatively well, as the fears of massive credit-line withdrawals by foreign parent banks generated tensions but did not in fact materialise. While Polish banks are not directly exposed to credit risk in European periphery countries, the banking system is deeply integrated with international (especially euro-area) banks: foreign investors control almost three-quarters of the sector's capital. The results of the 2011 NBP stress tests suggest that reduced dependence on funding from foreign parent entities would be favourable for the stability of the financial system in the current context (NBP, 2011a), even though this is less clear over the long term (OECD, 2010a). In this context, capitalisation needs of euro-area banks, which could be substantial, may squeeze credit supply in Poland.

With the strength of the local economy, credit growth has been more buoyant than in other CEECs (Figure 5, Panel A), but the credit-GDP ratio remains low by OECD standards. The 2011 monetary tightening has had a limited impact on the appetite for housing loans, because it was only partly reflected in long-term rate increases and because some of those loans are still denominated in foreign currencies. Despite the resilience of the economy, in a context of rising unemployment the quality of loans to the non-financial sector has worsened since 2009 across the board (Panel B), although in 2011 loan-quality indicators broadly stabilised.

Figure 5. **Credit developments**

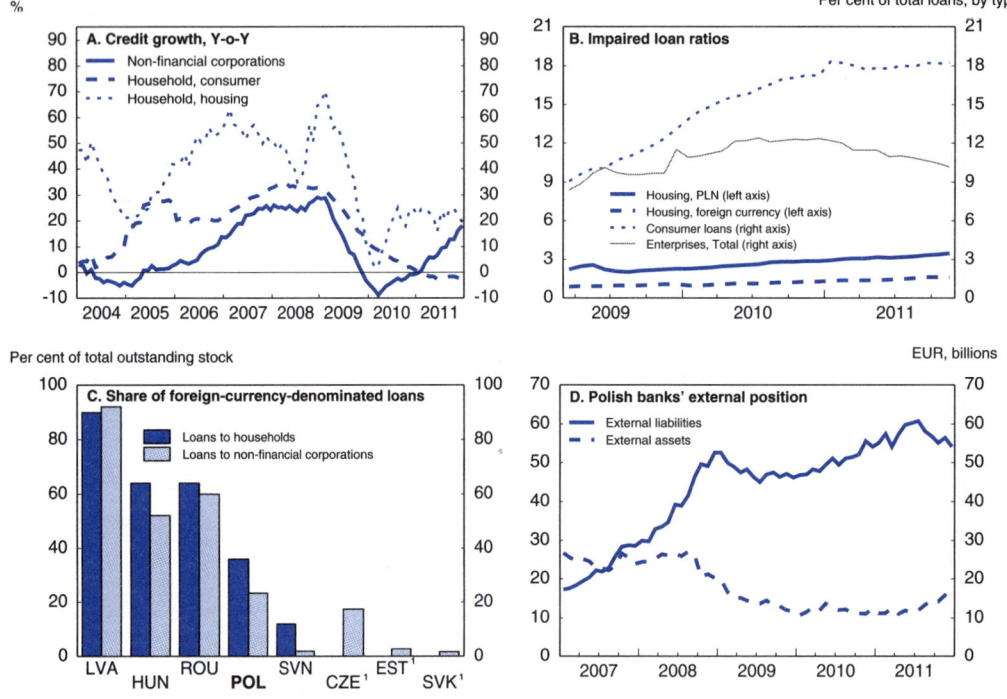

1. Foreign-currency-denominated loans to households are close to nil in these countries.

Source: National Bank of Poland; IMF, *International Financial Statistics Database*; ECB; European Systemic Risk Board (ESRB).

StatLink ⟡ *http://dx.doi.org/10.1787/888932584015*

Currency mismatches raise specific concerns

Some Polish banks have accumulated significant liabilities with non-residents (Figure 5, Panel D), which would be more difficult to roll over in the event of a liquidity crisis than their domestic counterparts and exceeded the liquidity reserve level for about a quarter of all banks as of April 2011 (NBP, 2011b). Intensified market turmoil might thus translate into potential liquidity problems, especially in foreign currencies, and into higher financing costs. Even if banks typically hedge their exchange-rate exposure with off-balance-sheet transactions, they might encounter difficulties in rolling over both their swap transactions covering foreign-currency open positions as well as other forms of market funding (NBP, 2011b). In case of heavy capital outflows triggered by renewed global difficulties in accessing liquidity, foreign-currency refinancing for banks would need to be secured through swap arrangements between the NBP and foreign central banks.

In order to curb household borrowing and discourage loans in foreign currencies, the KNF has tightened lending regulations for mortgage and consumer loans over the last few years by setting limits for debt service as a share of monthly income, imposing maximum loan-to-value ratios and introducing more stringent risk weighting to raise capital requirements for foreign-currency loans. Tighter lending policies have helped to restrain the share of new foreign-currency-denominated housing loans to 20-30% since 2009, against 70% in 2008, but foreign-currency lending is increasingly concentrated among banks (NBP, 2011b). While in the short term the main risks are related to the drying up of liquidity, should financial markets return to normal, these measures may be insufficiently restrictive, as suggested by buoyant housing credit growth (Figure 5, Panel A). Macro-prudential policies, such as dynamic provisioning and counter-cyclical capital buffers based on total credit growth, as well as moving to a less favourable tax treatment of owner-occupied housing, could help head off a credit boom in that case.

High unemployment is weighing on wage gains

Despite robust growth in 2010-11, the unemployment rate has been edging up to nearly 10%, equal to its cyclical peak reached at the beginning of 2010, which is also close to its estimated structural level (NAIRU) (Figure 6). The moderate increase in employment has not been enough to match the sharp rise in the participation rate of about 3 percentage points over the past three years (albeit from a very low level in international comparison). Increasing participation is attributable to the tightening of early-retirement schemes and cohort effects related to the baby boom of the 1980s, while return migration has not been large, despite strong growth in Poland. The robustness of labour force participation and the freeze in public-sector wages have helped to contain wage pressure.

Despite subdued wage gains, inflation bounced back from its mid-2010 trough and accelerated in the last quarter of 2011 (Figure 2, Panel A). Year-on-year CPI inflation (according to the national definition) peaked at about 4.6% in December 2011, well above the target band of the National Bank of Poland (NBP), due in part to higher commodity and drug prices, the VAT-rate hike from 22 to 23% and the zloty depreciation in the second half of 2011. However, inflation decelerated to 4.1% in January 2012. Core annual inflation also moved up above 3% in December 2011. Headline inflation has persistently exceeded the underlying measure (which excludes food and energy prices) since 2004 (Figure 7), much more so than in most other OECD countries; this is partly explained by the relatively high share of food and energy in Poland's CPI basket, the highest in the OECD at about 38% compared with 23% on average. This suggests that such a core measure might not be a good proxy for underlying price pressures and that the associated external supply shocks were more of a permanent than a temporary nature.

Figure 6. **High unemployment weighs on wages**

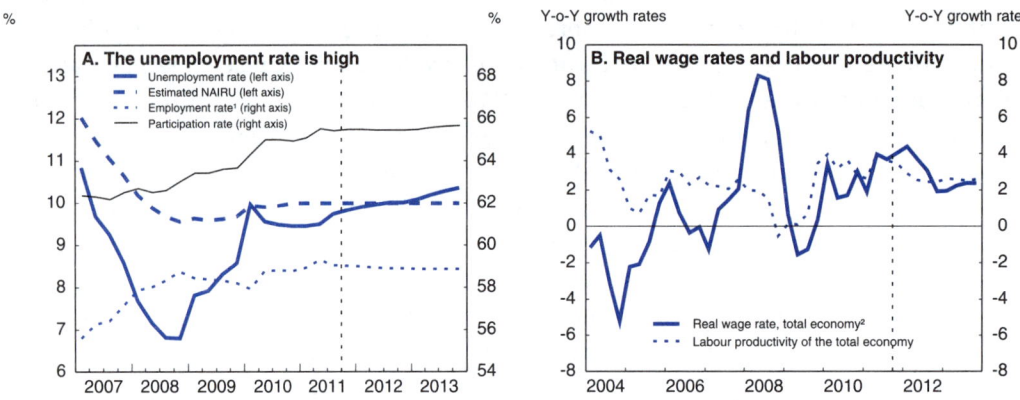

1. Ratio of 15-64 total employment to census-based working-age population.
2. Deflated by the GDP deflator; projections from 2011Q3.

Source: OECD, *OECD Economic Outlook 90 Database.*

StatLink http://dx.doi.org/10.1787/888932584034

Figure 7. **Monetary policy has tended to be accommodative**

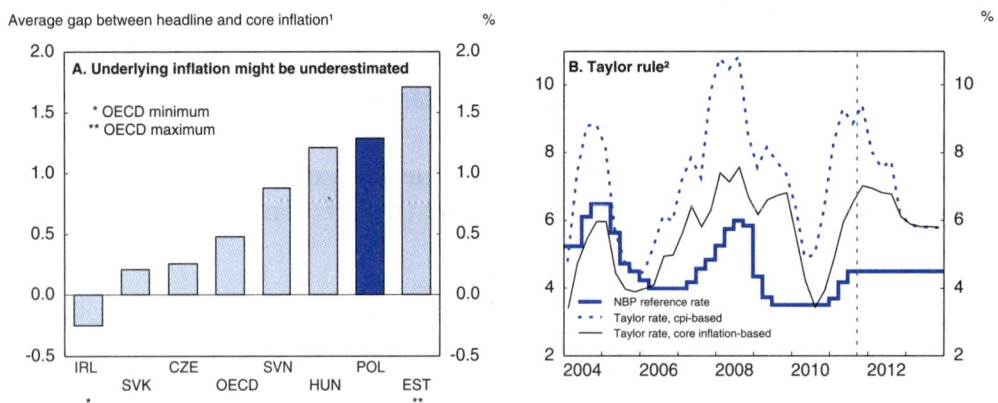

1. Year-on-year growth rates, 2004Q1-2011Q3.
2. The Taylor-rule rate is the sum of equilibrium real interest rate (proxied by the growth rate of potential output), actual inflation (here either CPI or core), half of the output gap and half of the gap between actual inflation and the mid-point of the inflation target (2.5%).

Source: National Bank of Poland (2011); OECD, *OECD Economic Outlook 90 Database*; Datastream.

StatLink http://dx.doi.org/10.1787/888932584053

The macroeconomic policy mix is appropriate in the baseline scenario

After keeping its key rate stable at a low of 3.5% between mid-2009 and end-2010, the NBP entered a tightening phase in 2011, raising the main reference rate in stages to 4.5% in June. Although it is *ad hoc* in many respects, a Taylor rule applied to Poland suggests that monetary policy remains somewhat accommodative (Figure 7, Panel B). On the other hand, medium-term government bond yields declined between March and September 2011, suggesting that market players did not consider that the NBP was "behind the curve". Given the projected slowdown, the deceleration in energy and food prices and the removal of the continuing effect of the VAT hike on annual inflation, both headline and core inflation are expected to converge towards the middle of the target band, assuming an unchanged policy interest rate. Hence, the current stance of monetary policy is appropriate. But disappointing core and headline inflation outcomes may have caused an upward shift in inflation expectations and generated upside risks to the inflation outlook.

As discussed in past *Surveys*, to increase the effectiveness of the monetary-policy decision-making process, it would be useful to address the insufficient continuity of monetary policy. This is due to a lack of overlapping terms in appointments of Monetary Policy Committee (MPC) members, as the whole MPC (other than the NBP Governor) turns over at virtually the same time (every six years). In particular, the current approach suffers from a periodic severe loss of human capital, experience and institutional memory that cannot easily be conveyed to new MPC members.

In 2010, the general government deficit and the public debt rose to 7.8% and 54.9% of GDP (Maastricht definition), respectively. In an attempt to keep public debt below the 55%-of-GDP intermediate ceiling (according to the domestic definition), and subject to the European Union's Excessive Deficit Procedure, the government committed itself to reducing the general government deficit to 5.6% of GDP in 2011, 2.9% in 2012 and 2.5% in 2013. On top of expected proceeds from privatisation, this would put Poland's gross general government debt-GDP ratio on a declining path (Figure 2). This pace of fiscal consolidation is appropriate for 2012, but is not sufficiently ambitious for 2013 in view of the pace of projected growth, as it delays consolidation efforts to achieve the Medium Term Objective of a deficit of 1% by 2015, just prior to parliamentary elections. Fiscal consolidation should be helpful in reducing remaining imbalances in the economy by curtailing current price pressures and boosting national saving, thereby diminishing the current account deficit and keeping external debt under control. Another key benefit of enhanced fiscal discipline would be to limit contagion risks from the euro-area sovereign-debt crisis through improved credibility.

The 2011 deficit target is likely to have been met on the back of a number of consolidation measures (VAT rate increase, restraint in central government expenditures, dividends from state-owned companies) and buoyant corporate income tax revenues due to strong growth. Most importantly, the government also decided in 2011 to reduce contributions to the second, funded defined-contribution pension pillar (which is outside the government sector) from 7.3 to 2.3% of gross salary and to credit the difference to notional sub-accounts in the pension system's first pillar (which is within it). This reduced the budget deficit by an estimated 0.6% of GDP in 2011 and will reduce it by 1.2% in 2012 and around 1% in 2013 as the contributions going to the second pillar rebound from 2.3 to 2.8% of gross salary. Based on OECD estimates that assume no change in risk-taking behaviour within the second pillar (Box 1), this will also most probably reduce public debt in the long run, though at the cost of lower replacement rates.

Achieving the 2012 deficit target of 2.9% of GDP seems to be a realistic task, provided that all planned measures including the new expenditure rule for local government are duly implemented. On top of the existing temporary spending rule for the central government wage bill and the remaining effect of the 2008 bridge pension reform, the government indeed plans to tighten its grip on the budgets of local governments. But the bulk of the consolidation comes from the revenue side, including a rise in employers' disability insurance contribution rate, excise tax increases, a new mining tax, a freeze in nominal personal income tax brackets, an increase in dividends from state-owned companies and a reduction of tax expenditures.

> **Box 1. The weakening of the second pension pillar will probably lower public debt and already low replacement rates**
>
> Simulations show that the reform will permanently reduce both the pension system's deficit and the public debt compared to the no-change scenario, though it might not resolve the fiscal sustainability problem (Figure 8; Égert, 2012). Simply put, fiscal sustainability improves at the cost of reduced future replacement rates, which might become socially unsustainably low (Jarrett, 2011). As part of the reform, the government offered a tax break on savings going to the voluntary third (funded) pension pillar. In fact, if one accounts for the extra costs of tax breaks and the existence of minimum social pensions, the pension system's deficit may become higher around 2050 compared to the no-change scenario, even though permanent gains in debt reduction remain thanks to important upfront savings. Indeed, a pessimistic scenario (including lower wage growth and more rapid population ageing) shows that costs related to the third-pillar tax breaks and minimum social pensions may even offset upfront gains and lead to higher implicit debt after 2070.
>
> **Figure 8. Impact of the 2011 change in the pension system on long-term fiscal sustainability**
>
>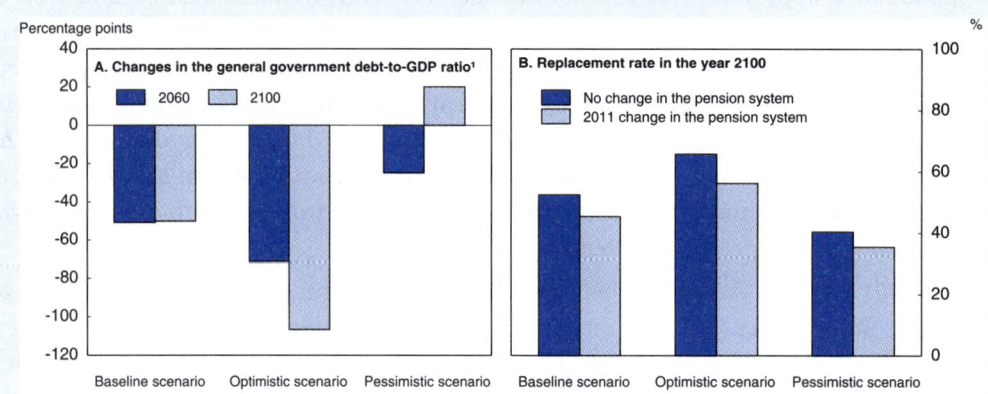
>
> 1. Percentage point difference in the changes in the ratio of the general government debt to GDP (no-change scenario *minus* 2011-change scenario).
> *Source:* OECD calculations.
>
> *StatLink* ￼ http://dx.doi.org/10.1787/888932584072

On the other hand, bringing the deficit to about 2% in 2013 will require additional measures, which should be disclosed quickly. In his speech to the Parliament in November 2011 after his re-election, Prime Minister Tusk touched upon a number of measures that could potentially help attain the 2013 target: i) reforming KRUS, which provides farmers with pension and health-care benefits without any corresponding meaningful contributions; ii) limiting pension privileges of uniformed services, judges and miners; and iii) further cutting tax expenditures, officially estimated at 5% of GDP in 2010. A number of these measures will shortly be submitted to Parliament, but passage is not ensured. Specific tax expenditures that could be reduced in Poland include: the child tax credit (as planned), which is not well targeted at the poor; joint taxation of spouses, which lowers female labour-force participation rates; exemption of farmers from income tax; reduced VAT rates; and exemptions from excise taxes. In addition, green and property taxes, particularly low in international comparison, could also be increased. Tightening further the eligibility criteria in the generous disability pension system (which had more than 2 million beneficiaries in 2009), broadening tax bases and shifting the tax burden towards those taxes that are the least distortive or correct negative externalities (property and environmental taxes) could help increase potential growth and reduce the public debt.

But policy can and should be eased, should a sharper economic downturn ensue

The conduct of macroeconomic policy is being complicated by the euro-area sovereign debt crisis and the possibility of scenarios that might dramatically affect the world economy. In particular, fulfilling the fiscal consolidation at the aforementioned pace in 2012 and 2013 might become difficult and even undesirable in such a context. A significant deterioration of economic conditions beyond what is currently projected could be met by interest-rate cuts. However, the monetary policy space might be constrained by the weakening of the zloty in such a case. As mentioned above, a general increase in risk premiums, renewed stress on euro-area banks and the volatility of portfolio investment flows could worsen liquidity access in CEECs, including Poland. If these risks materialise, automatic stabilisers should be allowed to function within the fiscal limits allowed by the Polish debt rule.

The exchange-rate rule for the conversion of foreign-exchange-denominated debt should be changed

As mentioned, the zloty weakened sharply in the third quarter of 2011 following the resurgence of euro-area financial tensions. According to current accounting rules, the year-end level of the exchange rate determines the zloty value of the external debt. This explains why the government, through the BGK (a large public investment bank), intervened at the end of both 2010 and 2011 in order to lower the zloty value of the near 30% of public debt denominated in foreign currencies. A period average for the exchange rate used for the conversion of foreign-exchange-denominated public debt would avoid the temptation by the government to undertake such potentially costly market interventions at year end. The depreciation of the zloty also spurred exchange-market interventions by the NBP. In this instance, this was consistent with the inflation target, as a strengthening of the zloty would help bring inflation back to the target band. Such interventions by the NBP have been and should remain exceptional. Otherwise, doubts would necessarily arise regarding whether monetary policy is truly targeting the inflation rate (as, in the long term, it cannot target both inflation and the exchange rate).

The fiscal framework should be strengthened and made more transparent

Although the Maastricht debt-GDP ratio is estimated by the OECD to have further increased to 57% in 2011, the corrective mechanisms associated with the 55% threshold have not been triggered, because, according to the national definition, the debt-GDP ratio has remained below 55%. This is because the government shifted public infrastructure spending to the National Road Fund and more recently the BGK, both of which are excluded from the domestic definition. According to official projections contained in *Public debt management strategy for 2012-15*, the difference between the two definitions will increase from 0.2 percentage point in 2008 to more than 3.5 percentage points in 2012 (see also Figure 3, Panel B). Harmonising the domestic definition of debt with its Maastricht counterpart would clarify the debt ceiling and make it a harder constraint on fiscal policy, less open to manipulation.

In any case, however, the existing fiscal framework, which comprises the debt rule and temporary spending rules in central government, should be enhanced. The government should aim to reduce the public-debt-to-GDP ratio in the medium term. This could be achieved by adopting an explicit medium-term deficit target – in this case the EU Medium Term Objective of 1% of GDP – that avoids pro-cyclicality, which in turn could be made operational by multi-year spending and revenue norms coupled with pay-go rules. This would lead to a significant decline in government indebtedness.

The fiscal framework also needs to be improved by extending budget discipline beyond the central government to other levels of general government. Central-government spending accounts for only about one third of the general-government total, thus allowing slippages by local authorities and social security. The government's plan to introduce deficit and debt limits for local authorities would be a step in the right direction. Mandatory safety buffers should be included in the central-government budget to account for local governments' slippages (since their budgets are not fully controlled by the central government) and for unexpected negative shocks and revenue shortfalls. This could effectively amount to a substitute for the Swiss debt-brake approach (OECD, 2009, p. 32).

An independent fiscal council, in line with the EU Directive of 8 November 2011, composed of high-profile national or international fiscal-policy experts, would be helpful in strengthening the fiscal framework. The council should monitor fiscal plans and outcomes relative to the debt, deficit and spending targets. In Austria, the Netherlands, Sweden and the United Kingdom, an independent body in addition either prepares or approves the macroeconomic projections underlying the budget. A fiscal council could also be mandated to provide a non-partisan analysis of current and planned fiscal changes (such as the pension reform) on long-term debt sustainability, although this would involve considerably more resources. The Netherlands Bureau for Economic Policy Analysis (CPB) and the US Congressional Budget Office are examples of institutions that evaluate the impact of planned measures.

There are many possible avenues for further fiscal consolidation in the medium term

Beyond 2013, further savings could be achieved by: i) equalising the retirement age of men and women currently at 65 and 60 years, respectively; the government plans to raise them to 67, phasing in the increase until 2020 for men and 2040 for women; ii) linking the legal retirement age to projected gains in life expectancy; and iii) enhancing cost efficiency in public administration, which is among the lowest in the OECD (OECD, 2010b). Implementing some of these key measures may be politically difficult, as the two coalition parties differ with respect to a number of them.

Growing health-care needs will require some fiscal adjustments. Given Poland's relatively low level of and its tight grip on public health-care spending (see below), there is a risk that fiscal pressures could lead to insufficient provision of health-care services. As needed and beyond efficiency gains, extra resources should therefore be financed by savings on other public expenditures and possibly by additional revenues, which should be based on taxes that are least detrimental to economic performance. The scope of current health contributions, which are indexed to wages, should also be broadened by: increasing health contributions on employees whose currently freely co-insured spouses are not employed, which would improve work incentives (albeit at the cost of taxing marriage in some cases); and ensuring that revenues from all temporary contracts contribute to health care financing. In addition, farmers' contributions for health care (and pensions) should be raised far more substantially than the government currently envisages for 2012

(PLN 107 million) by better linking them to individual incomes, especially as mean agricultural incomes have improved sharply relative to the national average since 2005, in large part because of the adoption of the EU Common Agricultural Policy.

Box 2. **Main macroeconomic policy recommendations**

Monetary, prudential and exchange-rate policies

- In the event of greater than projected weakness, utilise the monetary policy space that exists to lower official interest rates, which are otherwise appropriate in the medium term.

- Reduce currency mismatches in banks' balance sheets by appropriately calibrating liquidity requirements to strengthen their funding structure and diminish the reliance on foreign funding. In due course, as the euro area recovers from its current crisis, preventing a credit boom might require further restricting credit to households by cutting the maximum loan-to-value and debt-service-to-income ratios, and by introducing macro-prudential policies such as counter-cyclical capital buffers.

- Introduce staggered terms for Monetary Policy Committee members' appointments to ensure continuity of monetary policy.

Fiscal policy and the budgetary framework

- Announce quickly the detailed measures needed to reduce the general government deficit to about 2% of GDP in 2013 and 1% in the medium term. These should include: cutting tax expenditures and opting for less distortive taxes, further tightening eligibility criteria in the generous disability pension system, enhancing the efficiency of public administration, reforming the farmers' social security scheme, eliminating pension privileges for certain occupations, and equalising retirement ages for men and women at 67 as currently planned.

- Let the automatic stabilisers function within the debt ceiling constraints, if the economy slows more than projected.

- Strengthen the fiscal framework by: introducing a deficit rule, putting in place detailed multi-year budgeting and spending ceilings, creating an independent fiscal council at least to monitor fiscal performance relative to targets, and harmonising the domestic and Maastricht definitions of government debt.

- Use some sort of period-average exchange rates, rather than end-of-year values, for the evaluation of foreign-currency public debt.

- Accommodate growing health-care needs, beyond efficiency gains, by savings on other public expenditures and raising resources as needed through: the use of less distortive tax bases; an increase in employee health contributions when a freely co-insured spouse does not work; an extension of the social insurance contribution base to uncovered earnings; and a rise in farmers' contributions.

Structural reforms can boost economic performance

Improving labour-market performance

Except in 2008, wage increases have not matched the pace of productivity gains (Figure 6, Panel B). As a result, labour's share of national income has never recouped the ground lost at the beginning of the 2000s (Figure 9, Panel A), so workers do not seem to have fully benefited from economic growth. Moreover, economic inequalities have

Figure 9. **Labour market structural indicators**

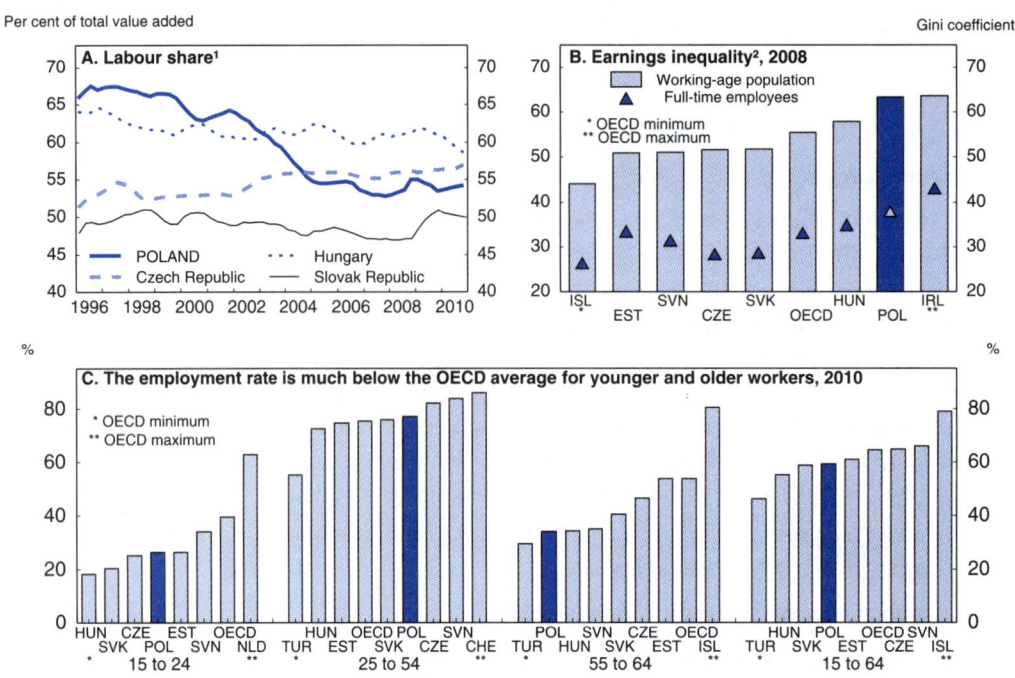

1. The labour share is calculated as the ratio of employees' compensation to GDP less indirect taxes.
2. Gini coefficients for different population subgroups, 15-to-64 year-olds.

Source: OECD, *OECD Economic Outlook 90* and *Labour Force Statistics Databases*; *Going for Growth 2011*; Eurostat, *European Union Statistics on Income and Living Conditions* (EU-SILC).

StatLink http://dx.doi.org/10.1787/888932584091

increased substantially since the end of the 1990s across a broad array of inequality measures (Brzezinski and Kostro, 2010), and earnings inequalities are marked (Panel B). Hoeller *et al.* (2012) show that Poland belongs to a group of countries in which individual labour earnings are concentrated, with redistribution taking place within families, while taxes and transfers seem to have little redistributive impact. For Poland, beyond tax-based redistribution the best options to reduce wage inequality rest with reforms that boost employment and educational attainment.

Indeed, a low employment rate remains one of Poland's major structural economic weaknesses (Panel C), even though between 2003 and 2008 it drifted upward. Along with diminished possibilities for early retirement, one area of progress is the tightening of criteria in the disability pension scheme which led to a fall of 10% in the number of disability pensioners in 2011 (see Annex). Also, the labour tax wedge has been reduced (through lower personal income tax) toward the OECD average level, though the decision to increase disability contributions in 2012 will work the other way. In contrast, specific weaknesses remain with respect to: limited active labour market policies; the poor quality of transport infrastructure and insufficient housing supply for the private rental market in urban areas (on which no progress has been made; see Annex), which heavily restrict labour mobility (OECD, 2012); the insufficient development of childcare institutions and pre-school arrangements, which, despite improved access over the last few years (European Commission, 2011a), still penalises female employment; and farmers' and other special pension regimes with lower contribution rates and retirement ages, which limit the labour force participation of those in these occupations.

Poor employment performance is particularly striking for older workers. While the incentives built into the pension system imply only a low implicit tax on continued work at older ages, female participation beyond the age of 55 might still be influenced by the legal retirement age of 60, which tends to shape social norms in terms of working at older ages. The statutory female retirement age is lower than its male counterpart, a feature that persists in only a small and diminishing number of OECD countries. Such structural weaknesses are especially problematic, as the total population has already begun to decline. Moreover, the Central Statistical Office projects that between 2010 and 2035 total and working-age population will fall by 6 and 16%, respectively, thereby reducing potential output growth.

The gap between the skills needed by firms and those provided by the education system remains significant despite rising educational attainment, as argued in the previous *Economic Survey of Poland* (OECD, 2010a). The 2011 reform of tertiary education is a first step to develop vocational education through the introduction of "practical" programmes. Yet, more efforts are needed to promote vocational education as a distinct and important sector so as to provide a strong orientation towards meeting employers' needs within local labour markets. Also, a comprehensive and flexible lifelong-learning strategy should be developed. Finally, while the 2011 reform of higher education goes in the right direction (Annex), quality assessment of higher education institutions should be further improved.

Additional priorities for structural reform

Previous *Economic Surveys* recommended that the administrative burden of doing business should be reduced to boost productivity gains. A recent OECD study showed that Poland has the largest potential in the OECD to increase productivity by improving product market regulations in network industries (Bouis and Duval, 2011). Entrepreneurship has also suffered from a number of barriers (OECD, 2010b). The government estimates the administrative burden imposed upon business by regulation at more than 5% of GDP a year and has launched a programme aiming at reducing it. In 2011, several significant improvements to economic law and business registration procedures were implemented. They aim to cut red tape for setting up and running businesses by simplifying information requirements via replacing around 200 certificates issued by public administration by self-certification, and by reducing the documents needed for starting a business. The number of information obligations required to run a business has been also reduced. While new firms have been able to be registered on the Internet since mid-2011 and the time needed for the registration of businesses run by individuals is now one day, the registration time for companies to take effect is still long. The government's plans to further ease the administrative burden in 2012 by continuing to implement simplification measures and by reducing the paperwork related to tax regulation and contacts with the social security system are welcome.

The state still plays an important role in the economy, despite ongoing privatisation. Previous *Economic Surveys* (OECD, 2010b) and *Going for Growth* (OECD, 2012) have recommended that state ownership should be reduced by implementing the government's ambitious privatisation plan, which was launched in 2008 and targets the sale of around 800 companies. The process accelerated in 2010, as privatisation proceeds increased from 0.2% of GDP in 2008 to 1.0% of GDP in 2011, and additional revenues of about 0.5% of GDP per year are expected by the government between 2012 and 2014. The government should go further: the state should withdraw from the potentially competitive segments of network industries, and there is no reason why it should retain controlling stakes in financial institutions, airport operators, and mining and chemical companies.

The case for direct government involvement in the energy industry is also weak. There are good reasons for effective ownership separation of vertically integrated utilities in the gas and electricity industries, as vertical integration hinders third-party access to the network. This impedes competition, given that the network operator of a vertically integrated company will always be tempted to favour a supplier belonging to the same holding company. First steps to open up the wholesale gas market to competition were made in 2005, when the gas transmission network system operator, Gaz-System, was separated from the gas supplier, Polish Oil and Gas Company (PGNiG). Although the Treasury has a controlling stake in both, a third-party access rule to the network was introduced. The legal unbundling of gas distributors is well advanced, even if most of these companies remain in the PGNiG group (Office of the Energy Regulator, 2011). Despite legal unbundling, improved third-party access and increasing interconnection capacities to neighbouring countries, the incumbent PGNiG still controls 98% of the gas sector (including production, imports, storage, wholesale and retail sale, and distribution) (Energy Regulatory Office, 2011). To increase competition, the government should consider further encouraging entry to gas production and its wholesale and retail distribution and potentially separating the ownership of: i) gas production from transmission, and ii) gas production and wholesale sale from distribution. Parts of network industries, which are natural monopolies, need to be overseen by a sector regulator that would simulate a competitive environment via incentive regulation with a view to forcing the incumbent operator to reduce inefficiencies. To boost investment, the sector regulator should be a politically independent body of experts, solely responsible for determining regulated prices in accordance with transparent procedures.

Box 3. **Main structural policy recommendations to improve economic performance**

- Promote labour mobility by continuing to upgrade transport and communication infrastructure and reforming housing policies, such as through the mandatory release of zoning plans by municipalities (OECD, 2008).

- Reduce the skills mismatch in the labour market by: improving the training system and developing a flexible lifelong learning system; promoting a clearly distinct system of vocational education at the tertiary level; and encouraging internships as a way to strengthen the links between firms and education institutions (OECD, 2010a).

- Improve tertiary education by allowing public higher education institutions (HEIs) to introduce cost-related tuition fees for all students, developing student loans and reinforcing HEI quality assessment (OECD, 2006).

- Continue efforts to further ease the administrative burden on businesses (OECD, 2010a).

- Continue the privatisation of state-owned companies in the financial, mining, chemical and airport sectors, and network industries (OECD, 2010a).

- Pursue gas and electricity market liberalisation by fully complying with EU regulations and possibly by implementing ownership unbundling in those sectors (OECD, 2012).

Improving the health-care system

Health outcomes are relatively weak, related spending low and the budget constraint tight

Long-term growth can also be spurred by better health, which boosts productivity and education performance, reduces absenteeism, extends working life and raises the incentive to acquire human capital. However, the causality also runs the other way, as greater affluence enables nations to devote more resources to health care. In the 1980s, Poland suffered from a health crisis characterised by high mortality rates of working-age men. But since the transition period the country has matched improvements in health outcomes of the most developed countries, although without catching up the ground previously lost. As a result, the health status of the population remains relatively poor, while inequalities are pronounced, especially amongst men (Figure 10). However, after controlling for per capita GDP, health outcomes are only slightly below the OECD average. In that sense, and also based on other analysis described later in this *Survey*, the efficiency of the Polish health-care system is average in cross-country comparison. Against this background, Poland spends relatively little money on health care (Figure 11). Total health-care expenditures represent 7.4% of GDP, with related public spending reaching 5.3% of GDP, against 9.7 and 6.9%, respectively, on average across OECD countries.

Figure 10. **Poland's health outcomes are rather mediocre**

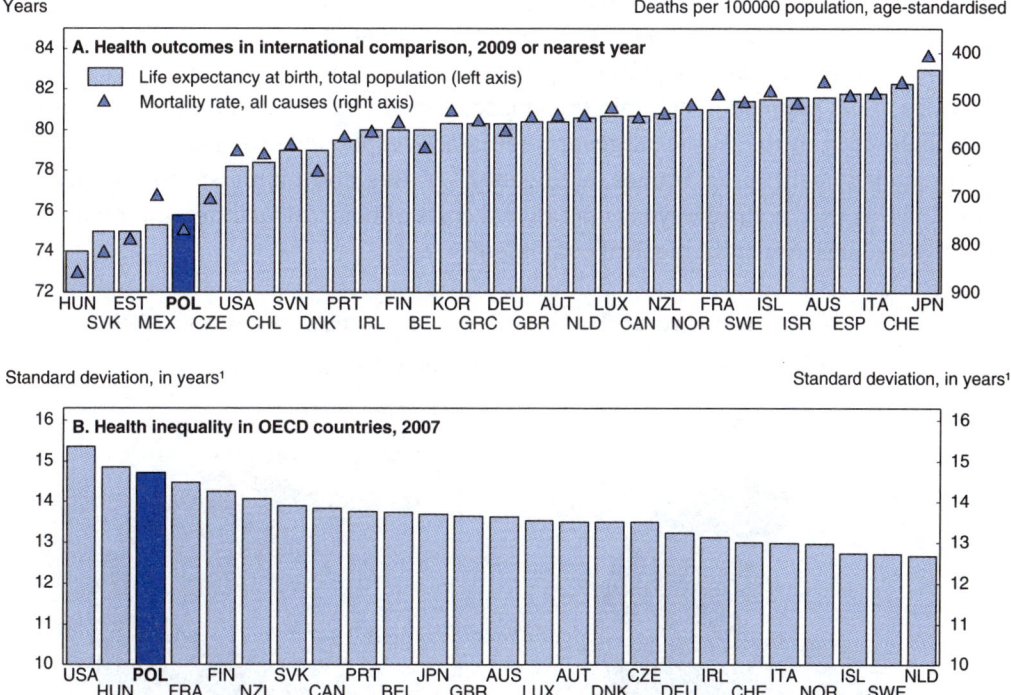

1. Standard deviation in mortality ages for population older than 10.

Source: OECD, *OECD Health Data 2011* for Panel A; Joumard, I., C. André and C. Nicq (2010), "Health Care Systems: Efficiency and Institutions", *OECD Economics Department Working Papers*, No. 769, OECD Publishing, for Panel B.

StatLink 🔗 http://dx.doi.org/10.1787/888932584110

Poland shares with a group of other OECD countries the following characteristics related to its health-care system: a heavily regulated public system in which the budget constraint is stringent; significant provider choice for patients; restricted sub-national

Figure 11. **Health expenditures are modest but consistent
with Poland's economic development level**

2009 or closest year available

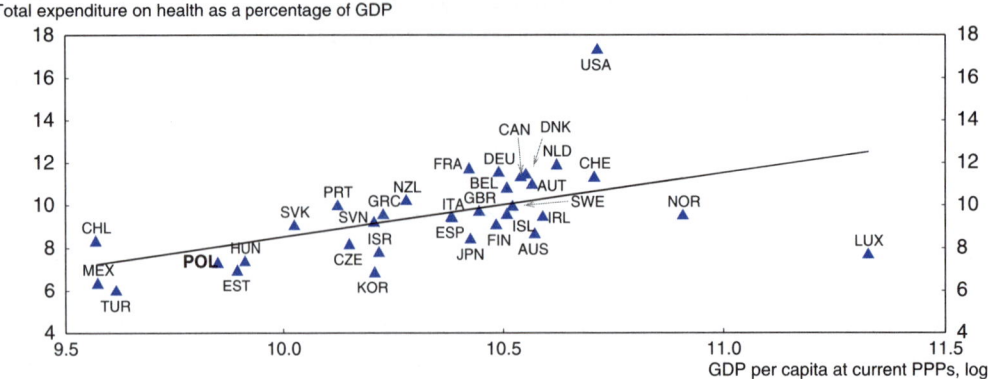

Source: OECD, *OECD Health Data 2011* and *National Accounts Database 2011*.

StatLink 🔢 http://dx.doi.org/10.1787/888932584129

government autonomy and thin private insurance markets (OECD, 2010c). In addition, private financing is mainly in the form of out-of-pocket expenses covering pharmaceuticals and specialist medical services, while private insurance does not formally exist (Figure 12). The National Health Fund (NFZ), which is financed by social contributions, is the main source of public funding, representing about 90% of the public purchase of health-care services. Besides covering the health-insurance premium for selected categories of the population and reimbursing costs of health services for certain groups of the uninsured, central and local governments are responsible for partial financing of specific public health programmes, emergency services and highly specialised medical procedures, as well as the everyday operational costs of hospital facilities, maintenance of buildings and investment in medical equipment.

Figure 12. **Structure of the health-care system's revenues, 2009**

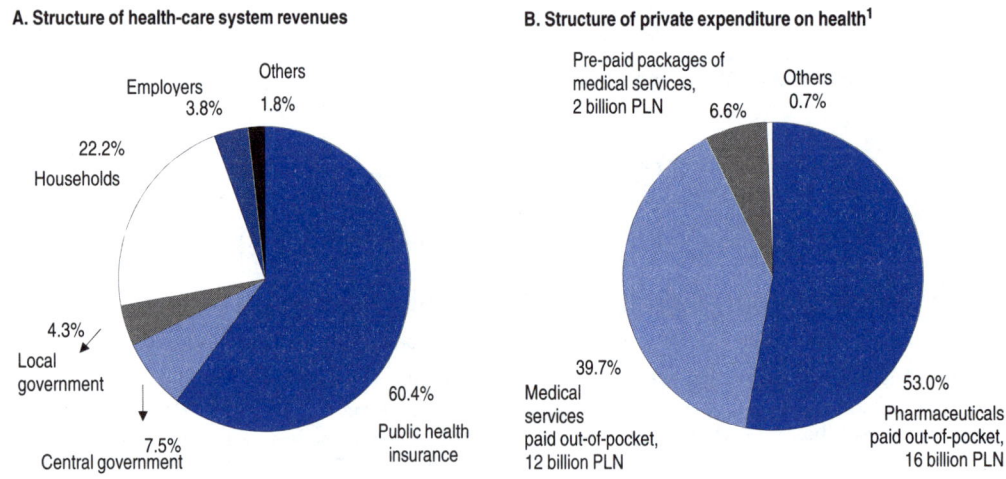

1. Per cent of total private expenditure on health.

Source: OECD, *OECD Health Data 2011* (Panel A); Ministry of Health, 2011 (Panel B).

StatLink 🔢 http://dx.doi.org/10.1787/888932584148

Growing health-related needs will exert manageable strains on public finances

Public health-care spending is very likely to increase in the longer term, given increasing demands for health and long-term care as well as technological developments. Like most CEECs, Poland's population is expected to age rapidly: within the EU, the fertility rate is now one of the lowest, and by 2060 the effective old-age dependency ratio is projected to be the highest. On the other hand, healthy ageing and reduced needs for outlays on education and unemployment benefits might partially offset these budgetary pressures.

According to recent OECD and European Commission estimates, public spending on health and long-term care is projected to increase by 3.6 percentage points of GDP over 2005-50 and 1.7 points over 2007-60, respectively, similar to the average across countries. Provided budgetary discipline prevails in the long term, the induced fiscal pressure is likely to prove manageable, given the currently low level of public spending and the tight grip on the supply of health services. Realising available efficiency gains in the health-care sector, which are estimated by the OECD at about 1.5% of GDP for public spending in Poland (OECD, 2010c), would help the government to face these ageing challenges. However, growing health-care needs and welcome improvements in the health-care system should also be accommodated by savings on other public expenditures and possibly by additional revenues (see above).

Access to care is inequitably restricted

Substantial limitations in access to care need to be addressed. While about 98% of the population is covered by public health insurance (though insurance status is poorly verified due to a lack of any public insurance card), access is unsatisfactory, given lengthy waiting times, which restrict access to specialist care in particular, non-means-tested co-payments for drugs and only basic dental coverage by public insurance. Large out-of-pocket payments and long waiting times have resulted in the development of duplicative unregulated private "insurance" schemes to jump the queue, both of which generate serious equity concerns. The absence of trade-offs across countries between improving average health outcomes and reducing inequalities in health status (Koske et al., 2012) reinforces the call to limit such dispersion.

Waiting times should be shortened...

Surveys suggest that Poland is the European country in which waiting times restrict access the most (Figure 13, Panel A), and long queues seem to result mainly from insufficient funding and poor co-ordination of patient treatment. Long waiting times have encouraged informal payments, even though the government has taken anti-corruption measures since 2005 that seem to have reduced their prevalence. Private duplicative schemes generate an inappropriate utilisation of public resources due to a lack of transparency in delineating public and private employment: specialists running private practices can refer a patient to a public hospital in which they also work, thus avoiding the queue. Bringing down waiting times should be achieved by: targeting additional funding to delivering extra activity specifically aimed at reducing waiting times; enhancing computerisation; and, more generally, realising efficiency gains (see below). In any case, physicians being employed in both the public and private sectors, if allowed at all, should be made more transparent to ensure equality of access.

Figure 13. **Access to care is restricted, 2009 or closest year**

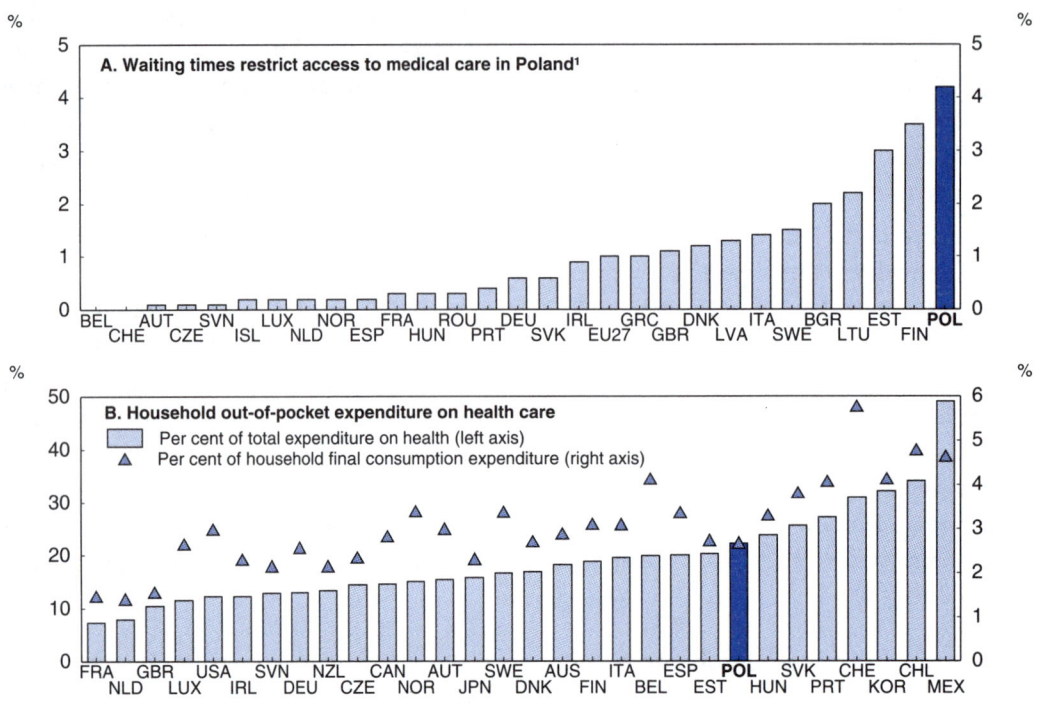

1. Unmet needs in medical care due to excess waiting, as a percentage of population aged 16 and over.
Source: Eurostat, *SILC Database* (Panel A); OECD, *OECD Health Data 2011* (Panel B).

StatLink ᴍˢᴾ http://dx.doi.org/10.1787/888932584167

... and out-of-pocket payments reduced, at least for the those on low incomes

Access is also restricted by out-of-pocket payments. Poland has one of the highest shares of such outlays in total health-care expenditure (though not as a share of total household consumption; Figure 13, Panel B). More specifically, private spending for pharmaceuticals is essentially all out of pocket (rather than through private insurance) and represents 62% of total drugs spending, with non-prescription over-the-counter (OTC) drugs and co-payments on reimbursable drugs purchased in pharmacies representing about two thirds and one third of this, respectively. In no other European country does the private exceed the public share. Limiting the negative equity impacts of large out-of-pocket payments can be achieved by introducing an income-contingent cap on such payments; such a scheme exists in many OECD countries, while in Poland social assistance includes benefits for drugs in the most extreme cases only. Furthermore, the reimbursement list was reduced (in 2004), which might have limited accessibility for the poor (Luczak, 2010). On the other hand, Poland has by far the highest share of generic drugs' market penetration in the OECD. Broadening the range of prescribed drugs eligible for reimbursement and/or extending insurance, potentially through the creation of private complementary and supplementary health insurance (*i.e.* covering cost-sharing and items not included in the basic coverage, respectively), would also help reduce out-of-pocket payments. While public insurance should widen its coverage of dental services, co-payments for medical care could be introduced along with the creation of private complementary insurance schemes. Such insurance should be carefully designed to be affordable for low-income households. In contrast, the government recently had plans to introduce mostly duplicative (private) health insurance, but the project is now on the back burner.

Allocation of resources to hospitals should be streamlined and management skills strengthened

There is a case to reallocate resources away from the hospital sector toward primary care (especially using integrated delivery models) and long-term care (see below). In-patient care represents about one-third of health spending and is a potential source of significant efficiency gains. Over the past decade some progress has been made. While the total number of hospitals has been broadly stable, the number of hospitalisations has increased by about 30%, and the mean length of stay has been cut by about 30%. At the same time, the average occupancy rate has fallen, which might signal persistent overcapacity. Also, hospital admission rates are high for diseases for which costly hospitalisation could be avoided, judging by practices elsewhere. Additional priorities should be to provide clearer incentives to hospitals to rationalise their use of financial resources and to improve managerial competencies and co-ordination among the various stakeholders.

Indeed, persistent hospital indebtedness has plagued the Polish health-care system over the past 20 years. Recurrent public interventions to clear liabilities have provided practitioners with confusing incentives and might have induced some resource misallocation, since well managed hospitals have not been rewarded. Financial difficulties have been generated by a paradoxical combination of tight supply limitations by the NFZ and *ex post* reimbursement of providers who exceeded their contracted provision of services, inevitably generating moral hazard. Management inefficiencies and a vague division of responsibilities among the various stakeholders compound these weaknesses. Clearer incentives should be provided to rationalise both the allocation of resources across and their use within institutions. Responsibilities should be streamlined between the NFZ and central and local governments in order to improve consistency. Also, hospital-management skills are insufficiently developed and should be promoted via remuneration incentives. This applies especially to university hospitals where financial control should be reinforced, while the payment system should be adjusted to account for the severity of cases they handle.

The 2011 *Law on Therapeutic Activity* aims to improve hospitals' cost efficiency through enforcing financial accountability and stimulating changes in their operational framework and ownership status, extending similar efforts taken since 2009. Hospitals may be privatised or transformed into state-owned enterprises regulated by the code of commercial companies (corporatisation, or "commercialisation" in official Polish parlance) in order to introduce corporate management techniques. The government agreed to partially assume the debts of those hospitals willing to go through that process until the end of 2013. Corporatisation might indeed promote better management and quality improvements. Yet, this process should be carried out carefully to avoid threatening equal access to care across regions.

A broad strategy for long-term care is needed

Families traditionally supply most elderly care, which tends to penalise formal female labour force participation. Long-term care institutions are underdeveloped, as formal health-related long-term care expenditure, publicly funded in full, represents just 0.4% of GDP. A comprehensive long-term care strategy would be helpful, given the prospect of rapid population ageing, which would otherwise create an increasing gap between the number of elderly in need of care and the actual supply of relevant (informal) services. The following measures should be considered: a separate insurance scheme covering long-term care risks (as in Japan); making social services offered to the elderly dependent on their degree of incapacity, rather than their income; developing geriatric specialisation among physicians; and financially supporting informal, family-provided care.

Human resources should be used more efficiently and expanded

Poland lacks health-care human resources (Figure 14, Panel A). This comes from both the supply and demand sides of the specific labour markets, as public policies and unattractive career prospects have limited numbers. Thought should be given to measures that expand the number of physicians, whether through boosting salaries, increasing medical school places or

Figure 14. **Health professionals are lacking**

2009 or closest year

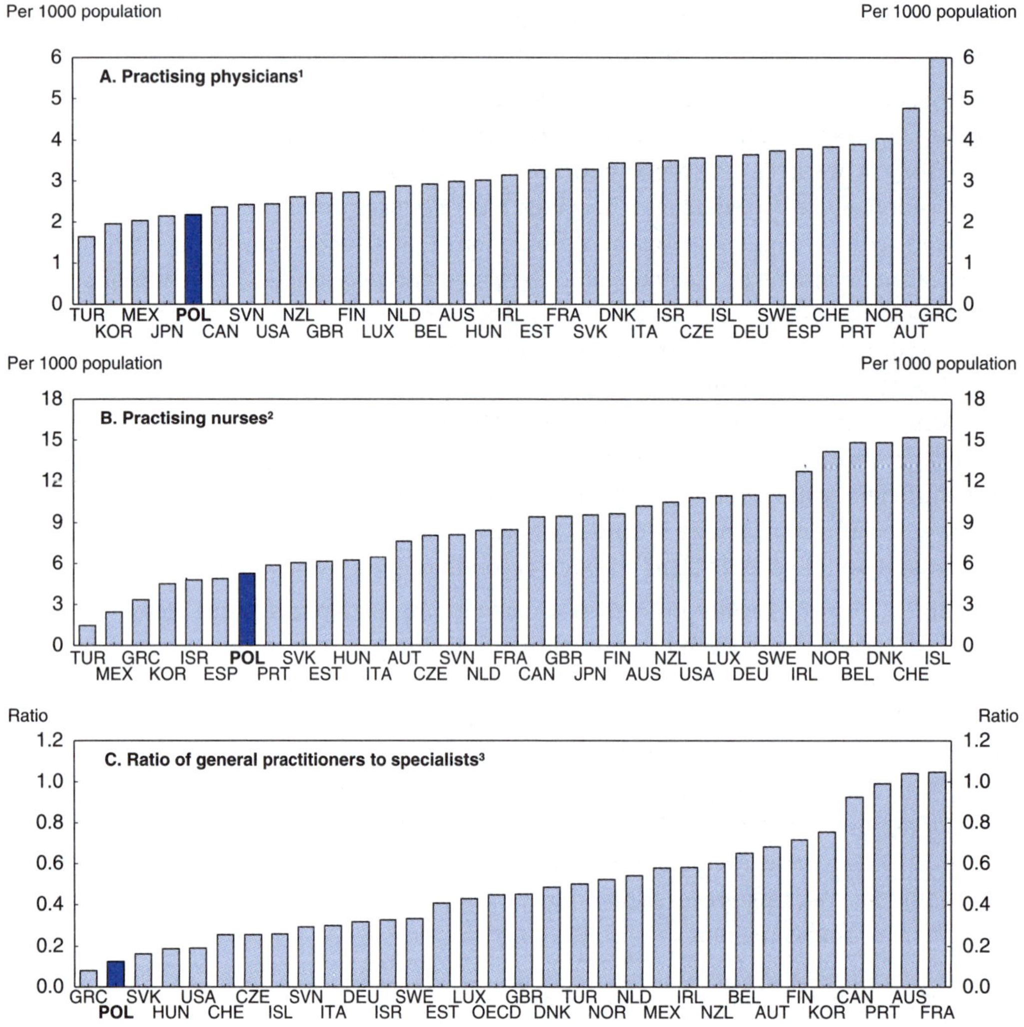

1. Professionally active physicians for Canada, France, Ireland, Mexico, Netherlands, Slovak Republic, Sweden and Turkey. Physicians licensed to practice for Portugal.
2. Professionally active nurses for France, Greece, Portugal, Slovak Republic, Sweden and Turkey. Nurses licensed to practice for Belgium and Italy.
3. Doctors are classified in either of three categories: General Practitioners (GPs), Specialists and Other Physicians. For Poland, most of the "Other physicians" might actually be GPs. If these two categories are merged into "GPs", then the ratio of GPs to specialists increases from 0.12 to 0.30 for Poland. Specialists include paediatricians, obstetricians/gynaecologists, psychiatrists, medical specialists and surgical specialists.

Source: OECD, *OECD Health data 2011.*

StatLink ⟪⟫ *http://dx.doi.org/10.1787/888932584186*

other measures to limit shortages. Productivity should also be improved by linking pay to performance. Finally, the gate-keeping role played by primary-care doctors should be strengthened. The ratio of generalists to specialists is low (Panel B), which suggests that gate-keeping does not function well. Generalists are paid based purely on capitation, but rates have been set at modest levels. Hence, cases tend to be pushed to the more expensive outpatient specialist or hospital segments. Moreover, no referral is required to access a long list of specialists. It follows that primary medicine should be promoted more heavily: an activity-based component should be incorporated into doctors' remuneration, and, if necessary, training efforts should be enhanced to avoid unnecessary specialist consultations.

Box 4. Main policy recommendations regarding health-care provision

- Broaden access to care and reduce inequality by: targeting extra resources to shorten waiting lists; extending dental services covered by public insurance, introducing co-payments on medical services while imposing a means-tested cap on the level of out-of-pocket payments; carefully designing a complementary/supplementary private insurance system; and increasing transparency of dual physician employment in the public and private sectors.

- Improve the allocation and use of current resources by: shifting resources from hospitals to primary and long-term care, potentially by integrated health-care delivery models; strengthening the gate-keeping role of primary medicine; providing clearer incentives to hospitals to make them respect their financial commitments and rationalise the use of their resources; promoting the development of hospital management skills; and streamlining the responsibilities of the NFZ and central and local governments.

- Expand human resources and implement policies to avoid labour shortages.

- Develop a comprehensive strategy to address growing long-term care needs, thereby facilitating female labour force participation.

Climate-change policies: minimising the costs of GHG emissions reduction

Economic transformation-related cuts in GHG emissions followed by relative stability

Poland is set to meet its international greenhouse gas (GHG) emissions commitments. It has reduced such emissions by more than 30% relative to the 1988 Kyoto base year (Figure 15), chiefly thanks to the sharp decline of inefficient Communist-era industry. It is also on track to meet the EU 2020 target for sectors not included in the EU's tradable permits system (EU-ETS). However, current Polish energy policy, whose focal points are energy security and competitiveness, implies little reduction in overall GHG emissions by 2030. In early 2011 the European Council (that is, EU member states) set the ambitious objective of an EU-wide emissions reduction from 1990 levels of 80-95% by 2050 in order to help restrict global warming to below 2 degrees Celsius (European Council, 2011), and the implications for individual countries are currently discussed by EU member States based on the *Low Carbon Roadmap 2050* (European Commission, 2011b). If such a roadmap were adopted, Poland would have to design a comprehensive climate-change policy package to contribute more substantially to the overall long-term EU effort to achieve GHG emissions reduction involving all EU countries. It has also to be recognised that given the global nature of the negative externalities related to GHG emissions, the EU's emissions reduction will be efficient only if accompanied by a world-wide reduction effort.

Figure 15. **Observed and officially projected GHG emissions in Poland, 1988-2030**
(1988 = 100)

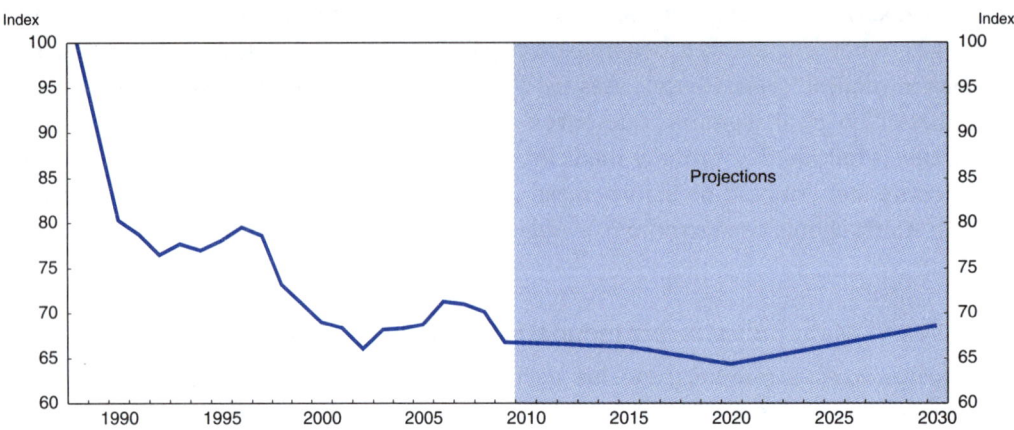

Source: UNFCCC data and Polish government projections.

StatLink http://dx.doi.org/10.1787/888932584205

Poland's GHG emissions-reduction potential is substantial

Per capita emissions are higher in Poland than in 11 other EU member countries with higher per capita income (out of 21 more developed EU countries). Hence, the usual justification for allowing less affluent countries to cut GHG emissions less than their wealthier counterparts does not seem to hold for Poland. It is based on equity considerations: poorer countries tend to emit less GHGs on a per capita basis, and as real convergence progresses they should be allowed to move towards the per capita emissions levels of their richer partners. Poland's elevated per capita energy-related emissions are due to its highly carbon-intensive electricity and heat production (Figure 16). Therefore, the country's potential to cut GHG emissions further at relatively low marginal cost (by EU standards) is substantial. The Polish authorities are worried that a large reduction in GHG emissions reduction will imply substantial overall costs for the Polish economy, because of additional investments in low-carbon technologies and losses in the country's

Figure 16. **Carbon intensity of electricity and heat production and electricity and heat intensity of GDP**

2009, OECD median = 100

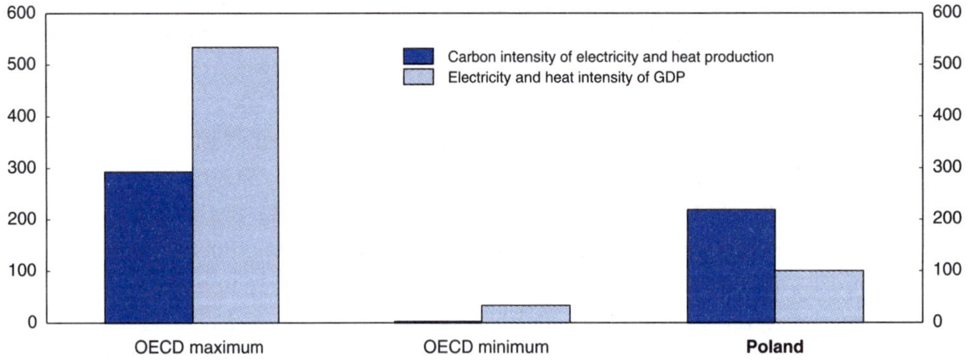

Source: OECD calculations.

StatLink http://dx.doi.org/10.1787/888932584224

price competitiveness position, and might threaten energy security. A recent World Bank report suggests that cutting emissions in line with EU objectives would lower the level of real output by about 1% by 2030, which is about two to three times higher than for the EU average (World Bank, 2011).

Minimising the costs of emissions reduction requires a single carbon price

A single carbon price is required for a cost-efficient emissions reduction, as it provides incentives to cut where it is the cheapest to do so; the resulting savings are not trivial: perhaps on the order of a half per cent of GDP for a moderate amount of emissions reduction. In any case, the adverse effects of higher energy prices on poor households calls for some direct compensation, perhaps in the form of lump-sum cash payments, which could be financed by additional tax revenues related to a higher effective carbon price. A carbon price is currently being imposed in Poland via: i) the EU-ETS for the power and heavy energy-using industries; ii) an explicit but only symbolic Polish carbon tax for sectors outside the EU-ETS; and iii) a differentiated excise tax on fossil energy products. However, natural gas as a heating fuel, liquefied natural gas and heavy industrial oil for agricultural use and for electricity and heat generation are untaxed, although the exemptions for electricity and heat generation are justified by their coverage by the EU-ETS. While this year Poland introduced a tax on coal used outside the EU-ETS, it is very limited in both size and coverage, as it is only applied to companies' own heat production and not to household heating. As a result of these various measures, implicit carbon prices vary significantly across different fossil-energy products (Figure 17). Hence, to promote least-cost abatement, implicit and explicit carbon taxes should be equalised for sectors outside the EU-ETS and aligned to the EU-ETS prices with a view to imposing a unique carbon price for the whole economy. Exemptions from the excise duty for coal and gas for household use should be progressively eliminated, and taxes on petrol and diesel adjusted to fully internalise the costs of negative local externalities such as air pollution and congestion.

One place where there is great potential for emissions reduction is Poland's extensive district heating network, the most carbon intensive in Europe. Its efficiency can be raised by the use of cogeneration (combined heat and power or CHP plants), and it can accommodate a variety of low-emissions energy sources and production methods. Also, compared to individual heating devices, district heating systems represent a limited number of emission points. These can be easily fitted with modern filters to radically lower both air pollutants and GHGs by cutting black carbon/soot particulate emissions, which have a global-warming potential 600 times higher than CO_2. An economy-wide carbon price (applied also to individual heating) would stimulate investment in the construction and modernisation of CHP plants producing low-carbon electricity. Given the monopolistic nature of district heating networks, incentive regulation based on benchmarking could help simulate market competition and improve efficiency, and thus boost the attractiveness of the technology.

Minimising abatement costs also calls for boosting the response to the EU-ETS carbon-price signal

The EU-ETS is the cornerstone to sizeable emissions reductions by 2050, as it is the main means to almost fully decarbonise the energy industries covered. Ideally, the EU-ETS would promote least-cost abatement in electricity generation, as firms that can cut emissions at a lower cost than the market price will sell their emissions permits to

Figure 17. **Explicit and implied carbon prices, after adjustment for negative local externalities[1]**

EUR/tonne of CO_2, 2011Q1

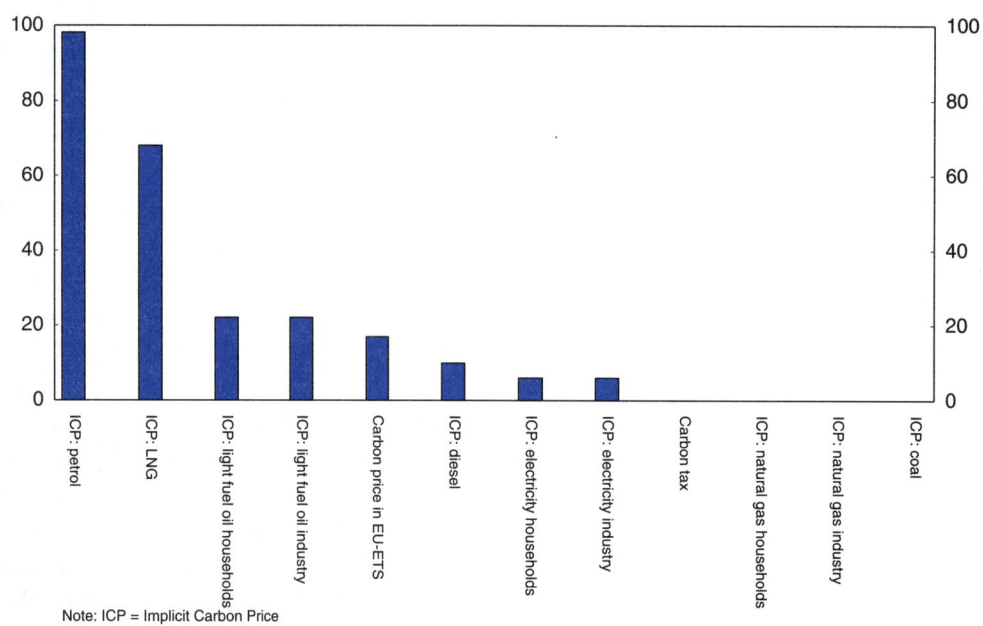

Note: ICP = Implicit Carbon Price

1. The implicit carbon price for diesel and gasoline is obtained by subtracting the external costs of negative local
   externalities from the carbon price implied by excise taxes.

Source: OECD calculations.

StatLink http://dx.doi.org/10.1787/888932584243

companies with above-market-price marginal abatement costs. In Poland, however, investment decisions in generation capacity are not fully private decisions, which could potentially blur the response to the price signal, because: i) electricity generation is dominated by state-owned firms, mostly joint-stock companies, with minority shares traded on the Warsaw Stock Exchange; ii) investment decisions in generation capacity are subject to the expansion of the distribution or transmission grids, owned and supervised by state-owned companies; and iii) the organised wholesale electricity market is small (but developing), as an important share of Poland's electricity transactions is based on bilateral contracts between electricity producers and distributors belonging to the same holding company. The Treasury holds controlling stakes in three out of the four major electricity companies. Proceeding with privatisation, accompanied by an appropriate regulatory framework that would ensure competition in electricity generation and simulate competitive conditions in electricity distribution, would render the sector more responsive to the carbon-price signal. Poland has gone a long way in legally unbundling vertically integrated companies in the energy sector, as required by the EU, and the Polish government seems to be satisfied with the results. But grid development is a major bottleneck for connecting new generation capacity to the grid. In this context, distribution system operators may tend to favour their own new production capacities over those of independent producers. Full ownership separation could eliminate any such potential bias. The recent push to deepen the organised wholesale electricity market is very encouraging and has raised its share of total wholesale electricity sales from about 5% in 2010 to roughly 15% in 2011. Yet, this level remains insufficient to substantially weaken the link between state-controlled producers and distributors.

A better integration of the Polish electricity market with neighbouring markets would also help

In a fully integrated continental electricity market, the price of electricity, corresponding to the cost of the marginal unit, *i.e.* the highest price in the market, would encourage the deployment of low-emissions and low-cost generation capacity all over Europe. Nevertheless, the Polish electricity market is isolated from its neighbours because of important bottlenecks resulting from a lack of international interconnections. Therefore, the EU-ETS' price signal, if the response to it is strong enough, will allow low-cost abatement only domestically and not in Europe more broadly, because of different energy prices across countries, which will result in Poland bearing more of the cost than other countries. The government plans to expand cross-border connections to increase trade in electricity with neighbouring countries to about 20% of electricity consumption by 2020. Even greater electricity openness would certainly decrease the burden of abatement on Poland.

The cost-efficiency advantage of uniform support to renewables via green certificates should be retained

Actively supporting electricity generation using renewable energies is required if Poland is to meet its renewables targets set at the EU level, but it may also have external benefits including learning by doing and scale effects. The government plans to replace the existing quota system for renewables, which is combined with tradable "green" certificates, by a support scheme accounting for technology-specific investment costs. That will lead to an outcome that is more diversified across alternative green technologies but come at the expense of higher abatement costs. While measures to support renewables may overlap with price signals provided by the EU-ETS, if the government wishes to maintain specific support for such sustainable forms of energy, it should do so in a cost-efficient and technology-neutral manner: specific technologies should be awarded the same amount of support per tonne of CO_2 avoided. Therefore, the government should preserve the uniform feed-in tariffs implied by the existing green certificate system (Figure 18). In order to encourage investment in renewables, the government plans to

Figure 18. Abatement costs associated with explicit and implicit feed-in tariffs, 2011

EUR/tonne of CO_2 equivalent[1]

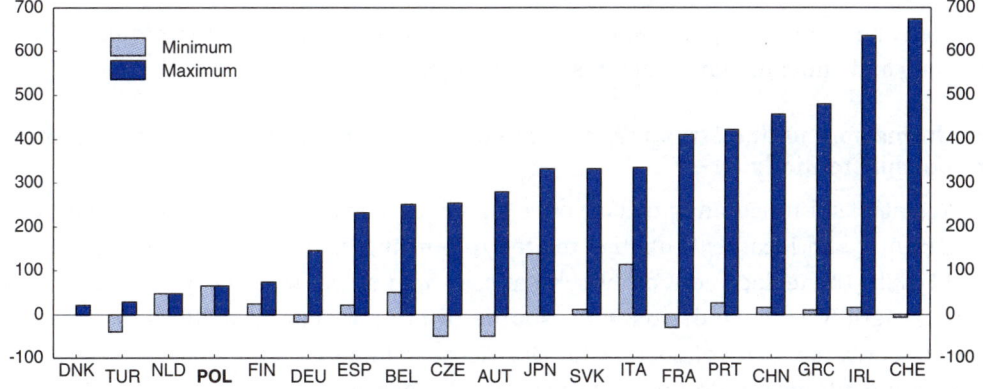

1. Abatement costs are computed using the lower and upper bound feed-in tariffs in excess of wholesale electricity prices and the amount of avoided CO_2-equivalent emissions. Benchmark = coal fired power plants (EUR/tonne of CO_2 equivalent)

Source: OECD calculations.

StatLink http://dx.doi.org/10.1787/888932584262

reduce uncertainty for new investment by extending the time horizon of the existing quota scheme. New investment is crucial, given that co-firing of biomass, accounting for the biggest chunk of renewables, takes place in old, coal-fired power plants, which will have to retire by 2020 according to EU regulation. Against this backdrop, the planned changes also include a strong differentiation between existing and new generation capacities, in favour of the latter. As the production of biomass may increase overall GHG emissions via direct and indirect land use change, the government should pay attention to its over-the-lifecycle GHG balance and enforce the sustainability criteria proposed by the European Commission. To remove barriers to wind energy production, thus far under-utilised, administrative and grid-access barriers should be eased by: reducing the time needed to get a construction permit; opening one-stop shops for contacts with public administration; and increasing incentives for investment in the distribution grid by putting in place a transparent long-term price-setting framework.

Energy-efficiency policies should focus on market failures that cause low carbon-price responsiveness

Poland's official energy-efficiency targets, reflecting the EU's goal of a 20% improvement by 2020, include a constant-energy scenario that brings its energy intensity to the average EU15 level by that year. In principle, a (single) carbon price will not only reduce GHG emissions cost-efficiently, but will also improve, as a side effect, energy efficiency. Energy-efficiency measures should complement carbon pricing if market failures (including credit-constrained households and asymmetric information) substantially reduce responsiveness to the carbon-price signal and, as such, should be directly linked with CO_2 reduction. How energy efficiency measures implemented by the government are targeted at low-response economies sectors is not clear. If the planned "white" certificate scheme will cover sectors not subject to explicit or implicit carbon pricing, it would be better aimed directly at CO_2 reduction rather than energy savings. To reduce asymmetric information, energy-performance certificates for buildings should also show CO_2-emissions performance in a transparent way. Financial support should be targeted at credit-constrained households and should be awarded based on CO_2 performance by encouraging investments with low abatement costs. An action plan is urgently needed to implement strict emission standards for new buildings, given their long lifetimes, and compliance should be enforced more rigorously. Also, more co-ordination between the numerous government entities and agencies involved is required for the planning and implementation of emissions standards.

Any framework with a strong response to the carbon price signal will cut reliance on coal substantially

A single and functioning carbon price signal, especially if carbon prices were to rise significantly and local externalities related to burning coal were internalised properly, would make the replacement of today's old coal-fired power stations with new ones and more generally the use of coal as a source of energy economically less appealing. Consequently, the share of coal in the electricity and energy mix, which is very high by OECD standards, would decline; otherwise, the burden on the economy of achieving any given overall GHG emissions-reduction target would be considerably higher, because of the reliance on more expensive abatement options.

The government can currently largely determine the country's electricity mix. It plans to increase nuclear power from 0 to 15% of electricity supply by 2030 and to increase the share of renewable-energy sources in the total energy mix, in accordance with the country's EU commitments. This will imply a decline in the sector's carbon intensity from 0.95 tonne of CO_2/MWh in 2008 to around 0.6 tonne/MWh by 2030. This latter figure is higher than the current OECD and European average of 0.5 and 0.4 tonne of CO_2 per MWh, respectively. Replacing old, inefficient coal-fired plants with more efficient modern power stations would also help. Carbon-free electricity production is possible due to investment in technologies including nuclear power, renewables, and, more speculatively, coal- and gas-fired plants combined with carbon capture and storage.

Energy prices should include the full cost of nuclear energy, and environmental risks related to the extraction of gas from shale formations be closely monitored

A shift to a low-emissions electricity mix needs to be designed carefully. Investment choices in new power generation capacity should be backed by transparent cost-benefit analysis. The government has decided to go ahead with building multiple nuclear power plants by 2030, the first of which by 2020. For such power, all global and local negative externalities should be accounted for in prices and strict safety environmental standards should be imposed and enforced to minimise tail risks. The current legal framework enforces proper provisioning for the estimated costs of future decommissioning and long-term waste disposal. The president of the National Atomic Energy Agency proposes, on the basis of expert evaluation, the amount of provisions per unit of electricity produced that the nuclear industry has to set aside. The government (Council of Ministers) then assesses and approves the expert evaluation. To maximise transparency, the government's approval should be only an administrative step that verifies that the correct procedures were followed, without involving any judgement. The independence of the president of the Agency, who can be dismissed by the prime minister, should be strengthened by a fixed-term nomination going beyond political cycles and during which he or she cannot be removed. The government is also supportive of private-sector efforts to explore for and produce natural gas from shale formations. Given the potential availability of substantial domestic shale-gas deposits, vigilance is warranted for environmental risks, especially with respect to underground water pollution and methane leakages.

Towards a more efficient organisation of the transport sector

Increased pollution and fuel consumption, due in part to the intensive imports of older-model, second-hand cars, could be mitigated, on top of existing fuel taxes, by an annual vehicle tax calibrated to vehicles' environmental performance, instead of the existing one-off registration fees and taxes. Such an annual tax would reduce myopic behaviour and asymmetric information, which prevent consumers from fully appreciating over-the-life-cycle carbon savings. Moreover, the modal transport split is strongly biased in favour of roads because of massive under-investment in railroad infrastructure, especially regarding its maintenance. Allowing for more efficient private-sector involvement, coupled with a truly independent sector regulator and a pricing system ensuring operating and perhaps also capital-cost recovery could help railways to emerge as an alternative to roads, both for passenger and freight transport.

> ### Box 5. **Main recommendations regarding climate-change policies**
>
> - Equalise implicit and explicit carbon prices across sectors outside the EU-ETS, and align them to prices prevailing in the EU-ETS, first by progressively eliminating tax exemptions for coal and gas for household use. Provide lump-sum cash compensation for the poor and ensure that the costs of all negative global and local externalities are fully internalised by taxes on petrol, diesel and other fossil fuels.
>
> - Strengthen the price signal for investment by deepening the wholesale electricity market, improving cross-border interconnections and implementing a long-term plan for grid development to allow new installed capacity to be quickly connected, and potentially by privatising electricity generation capacity.
>
> - Retain the cost-efficiency advantage of uniform support to renewables via green certificates.
>
> - Create a sustainable regulatory environment including: i) effective competition in electricity generation and simulating competitive conditions in distribution; ii) easing administrative burdens associated with connecting new generation capacity to the grid; iii) insulating the approval of the expert evaluation of the costs of future decommissioning and long-term waste disposal from political influence and strengthening the independence of the nuclear energy regulator by a fixed-term nomination going beyond political cycles and during which he or she cannot be removed; iv) imposing and enforcing strict safety and environmental standards to minimise tail risks of nuclear energy; and v) effective monitoring of environmental risks connected with the extraction of natural gas from shale formations.
>
> - Target energy-efficiency measures at areas with low responsiveness to the carbon price signal. Ensure that energy-performance certificates for buildings show CO_2 performance. Strengthen co-ordination between the numerous government entities and agencies responsible the country's energy-efficiency strategy.

Bibliography

Bouis, R. and R. Duval (2011), "Raising Potential Growth After The Crisis", *OECD Economics Department Working Paper*, No. 835.

Brzesinski, M. and K. Kostro (2010), "Income And Consumption Inequality In Poland, 1998-2008", *Bank i Kredyt*, Vol. 41, No. 4.

Égert, B. (2012), "The Impact Of Changes In Second Pension Pillars In Central And Eastern Europe", *OECD Economics Department Working Paper*, No. 942.

European Commission (2011a), *Council Recommendation On The National Reform Programme 2011 Of Poland*, SEC(2011)824.

European Commission (2011b), *A Roadmap For Moving To A Competitive Low Carbon Economy In 2050*, Brussels, 8.3.2011, COM(2011)112 final.

European Council (2011), 4 February 2011 conclusions, Brussels, 8 March 2011, *www.consilium. europa.eu/uedocs/cms_data/docs/pressdata/en/ec/119175.pdf*

Hoeller, P., I. Joumard, M. Pisu and D. Bloch (2012), "Less Income Inequality And More Growth – Are They Compatible? Part 1: Mapping Income Inequality Across The OECD", *OECD Economics Department Working Paper*, No. 924.

IMF (2011), "Staff Report For The 2011 Article IV Consultation", *IMF Country Reports*, No. 11/166.

Jarrett, P. (2011), "Pension Reforms In Poland And Elsewhere: The View From Paris", *CASE Network Studies and Analyses*, No. 425/2011, Warsaw.

Luczak, J. (2010), "Financial Burden Of Drug Expenditures In Poland", *Erasmus University Rotterdam*, School of Economics thesis, June.

NBP (2011a), *Financial Stability Report*, National Bank of Poland, Warsaw, December.

NBP (2011b), *Financial Stability Report*, National Bank of Poland, Warsaw, July.

OECD (2006), *OECD Economic Surveys: Poland*, OECD Publishing, Paris.

OECD (2008), *OECD Economic Surveys: Poland*, OECD Publishing, Paris.

OECD (2009), *OECD Economic Surveys: Switzerland*, OECD Publishing, Paris.

OECD (2010a), *OECD Economic Surveys: Poland*, OECD Publishing, Paris.

OECD (2010b), *OECD Economic Surveys: Hungary*, OECD Publishing, Paris.

OECD (2010c), *Health Care Systems, Efficiency and Policy Settings*, OECD Publishing, Paris.

OECD (2011), *OECD Economic Outlook*, Vol. 2011/2, No. 90, OECD Publishing, Paris.

OECD (2012), *Going for Growth*, OECD Publishing, Paris.

World Bank (2011), *Transition to a low-emissions economy in Poland*, Washington, DC, February.

ANNEX

Progress in structural reform

This annex reviews action taken on recommendations from previous *Surveys*. Recommendations that are new in this *Survey* are listed in the relevant chapter.

Recommendations	Action taken since the previous *Survey* (April 2010)
Product market competition and competitiveness	
Increase competition in mining, electricity, gas and telecommunication.	The government plans to partially privatise electricity and mining companies and to open up the wholesale gas market to competition. Further liberalisation of wholesale electricity market is planned, in particular by increasing the share of exchange trading in electricity production. Additional measures are needed to reduce vertical integration between electricity producers and distributers (within the same group).
Deepen financial development through a consolidation of co-operative banks and an improved legal framework for collateral.	No action.
Develop broadband internet by further reinforcing the power of the regulator, proceeding with the functional separation of the incumbent, ensuring effective unbundling of local loops, and defining a transparent cost-based wholesale pricing scheme.	No action.
Reduce the administrative burden of doing business.	A number of 2011 legal changes reduce red tape for setting up and running firms by simplifying information requirements via replacing official certificates by self-certifications, and by reducing the number of documents needed for starting a business and to run a business. The government plans to further ease the administrative burden in 2012.
Ease competition-restraining regulations by reducing public ownership in the potentially competitive segments of network industries and scaling down regulations in professional services regarding both educational requirements and licensing.	No action.
Reduce state ownership by implementing the government's ambitious privatisation plan in a transparent way.	The Privatisation Plan for the years 2008-11 considerably accelerated the privatisation process. Yet, further privatisations will still be beneficial following its implementation.
Transport infrastructure	
Elaborate and publish a precise and comprehensive top-down strategy for the transport sector, addressing long-term prospects and interrelations among projects, based on cost-benefit analysis.	The government is currently working on a transport development strategy.
Charge passenger cars for using expressways; determine in a transparent way the level of tolls on EU- and state-funded high-capacity roads; consider the introduction of an explicit congestion tax.	Road pricing for heavy vehicles and buses was introduced in July 2011 on selected motorways, expressways and other national roads.
For providing regional rail services, implement competitive tendering procedures and consider creating independent system operators to plan traffic and rail connections.	No action.
Split the Polish Airports State Enterprise (PPL) into different entities, consider their privatisation, and introduce a formula for the transparent calculation of caps on take-off and landing fees.	The government plans to transform the Polish Airports State Enterprise into a joint stock company.

Recommendations	Action taken since the previous *Survey* (April 2010)
Streamline the legal framework related to public procurement, issuance of building permits, environmental impact assessments and archaeological research.	Amendments to the Law on Public Procurement, enacted between 2008 and 2010, aim to streamline the contract award procedure.

Labour markets

End the 50% target for the ratio of the legal minimum to average wage and refrain from further increasing the ratio. Consider differentiating the minimum wage across regions depending on local labour-market conditions.	Minimum wages were increased by 8% in 2012, compared to recent rises of average wages of around 4½ per cent.
Restrict the disability scheme to those who are truly incapable of work, re-evaluate the stock of beneficiaries, and make such pensions time-limited.	The number of disability pensioners was reduced by more than 10% from 2010 to 2011 by tightening eligibility criteria and better verifying the health status of the beneficiaries.
Facilitate labour-market access for foreign workers through the issuance of work permits tailored to meet specific project needs. Provide easier access to foreign workers from a broader range of countries than those on the eastern border.	Since 2010, foreigners working for international sporting events organised by international sports organisations and doctoral students are exempt from work-permit requirements.

Fiscal sustainability

Set a ceiling on the structural general government deficit of 1% of GDP in law consistent with the Stability and Growth Pact's medium-term objective.	Progress is being made, but much more remains to be done. The government is currently working on a permanent expenditure rule, which aims to stabilise the general government deficit at the MTO level of 1% of GDP.
Adopt a medium-term budgetary framework with an explicit expenditure rule.	The 2009 Public Finance Act introduced a multi-year financial plan for the state on a rolling four-year horizon (current and three years ahead), medium-term plans at other levels of government and elements of performance-based budgeting. Yet, only annual budgets are truly binding. The government is currently working on a permanent expenditure rule, which aims to stabilise the general government deficit at the MTO level of 1% of GDP.
Make consistent the domestic definition of the public debt with Eurostat's, notably by including the debt of the National Road Fund.	No action. The National Road Fund and the state-owned bank BGK have been increasingly used to shift public debt outside the national definition.
Create an independent fiscal council.	No action.
Reduce subsidies to the farmers' social security scheme (KRUS) and work towards merging it with the general system. Income from farming should be treated the same as that from other types of activities.	A law imposing a health-insurance premium of 1 PLN per hectares per insured person for all those with more than 6 hectares of land was passed in February 2012, and will apply from April to December 2012.
Continue the pension reform by making pension schemes for soldiers, police officers and miners closer to actuarial fairness and neutrality.	The government is considering increasing the minimum contribution period from 15 to 25 years and imposing a minimum retirement age for new members of uniformed services.
Increase efficiency and reduce expenditure in the public sector by diminishing the payroll and linking promotion more closely to performance.	The central government's wage bill is frozen nominally in 2011 and 2012. No explicit action on the wage bill borne by local governments. The government plans the introduction of a new expenditure rule for local governments.

Tax policies

Redesign and increase the least distortive taxes, by establishing market-value-based property taxes, taxing capital gains on rented properties, eliminating the tax discrepancy between diesel used as a motor fuel and that used as heating oil, and implementing an economically meaningful carbon tax.	No action.
Further reduce the tax wedge on labour income by lowering social security contributions. The reductions should be both significant and targeted at the low end of the distribution.	The disability pension contribution was reduced from 13% in 2006 to 6% in 2008 (but is being boosted back to 8% in 2012) and PIT rates were simplified and lowered in 2009. Yet, the tax wedge remains one of the least progressive in the OECD.
Broaden tax bases by making revenues from farming activities liable to the income tax, introducing cash registers for all professional services to improve VAT collection, significantly tightening eligibility for the lump-sum income tax, and linking social security contributions of the self-employed to actual earnings. These measures should be accompanied by tighter enforcement.	Based on the legislation on VAT, the Ministry of Finance has been reducing exemptions from keeping records through cash registers.

Recommendations	Action taken since the previous *Survey* (April 2010)
Consider introducing an earned-income tax credit to encourage labour market participation of marginal groups.	No action.

Monetary policy management	
Introduce overlapping terms in appointments of MPC members to ensure the continuity of monetary policy.	No action.
Strengthen macro-prudential regulation by introducing a dynamic provisioning for banks and increasing their capital buffer. Consider adopting limits on loan-to-value and loan-to-income ratios	Recommendations T and S require maximum limits on the monthly instalments-to-earnings ratio for foreign currency and consumer loans and recommend loan-to-value ratios of 80% to 90% for mortgage-based loans. Risk weights for foreign currency mortgages will be increased to 100% as from June 2012.

Education	
Reduce the skill mismatch in the labour market. Improve the training system and develop a flexible lifelong learning system; promote a clearly distinct vocational education at the tertiary level with separate mission and staff from the other education institutions; raise students' interests in science and technology; and encourage internships as a way to strengthen the links between firms and education institutions.	The government has been developing a national strategy for lifelong learning. An amendment to the School Education Act passed in 2011 allows vocational schools to be integrated into the continuous education system, which will make it easier to obtain qualifications outside the school-based system. The New Core Curriculum emphasises core competencies development, including mathematics, science, technology and the use of ICT at schools. The reform of tertiary education includes measures to strengthen the collaboration between higher education institutions and the private sector. The government has launched a programme to attract students to economy-relevant areas, including information technology, chemistry, mathematics, construction and biotechnology.
Expand provision of free pre-school education at ages 3 to 5, focusing particularly on poor and rural areas.	Pre-school education for five-year olds became compulsory in September 2011. Six year-olds may still choose whether to stay in pre-school or move on to primary school until 2014/15 when they will be obliged to receive their education in primary schools.
Reinforce quality assessment of higher education institutions (HEIs) through the State Accreditation Commission. Ensure that career structures in tertiary education are based on open competition and transparent promotion criteria.	Some progress has been made. Following the higher education reform of 2011, the Polish Accreditation Committee is authorised to carry out evaluations of HEIs. The quality assessment procedure has been strengthened by underlining the importance of learning outcomes and quality of research. HEIs are required to fill research and teaching vacancies competitively, with job openings published online.
Consider allowing public HEIs to introduce cost-related tuition fees for all students. Reform the system of student loans to allow repayment along with income tax once graduates are employed.	No action.

Housing	
Remove fiscal incentives supporting the residential sector	No action.
Introduce escrow accounts to protect buyers' advances against the risk of developers' bankruptcy.	The Act of 16 September 2011 on the protection of the rights of the purchaser of a dwelling or a detached house, which comes into force on 29 April 2012, sets forth the principles of procedures involving the financial resources of buyers in the event of bankruptcy of the developer.
Make the release of municipal zoning plans mandatory.	No action.
Publish official composite house price indexes for the country as a whole as well as different market segments.	No action.
Work towards further easing of controls on rent increases.	No action.

Chapter 1

Improving the health-care system

Since the transformation following the Communist era, Poland has matched improvements in health outcomes of the most developed OECD countries, although without catching up the ground lost during the 1970s and 1980s. The health status of the population remains relatively poor, although after controlling for per capita income health outcomes are only slightly below the OECD average. The Polish health-care system is characterised by low spending, a heavily regulated public system with a stringent budget constraint, restricted sub-national government autonomy and a thin private insurance market. Heavy out-of-pocket payments and long waiting lists generate inequalities in access to care. The most pressing issues to be addressed concern: easing the substantial limitations in access to care; reducing persistent inequalities; carefully designing new private health insurance; better coordinating among major public actors; improving hospital management; strengthening the gate-keeping function played by generalists; and developing a comprehensive long-term-care strategy.

With the post-Communist transformation Polish health outcomes have improved at about the same pace as in most developed countries, therefore without making up the ground lost during the preceding decades. Hence, despite this improvement, health status appears weak in cross-country comparison. Poland spends a relatively low share of its GDP, about 7.4%, on health care, and this share, although on the rise over the past 20 years, has increased less than in most OECD countries (Figure 1.1). However, once per capita incomes are taken into account, Poland's health-care aggregate inputs and output performance are broadly in line with the average (see Figure 1.2 and below).

Figure 1.1. **Long-term trends in health expenditure**

As a percentage of GDP

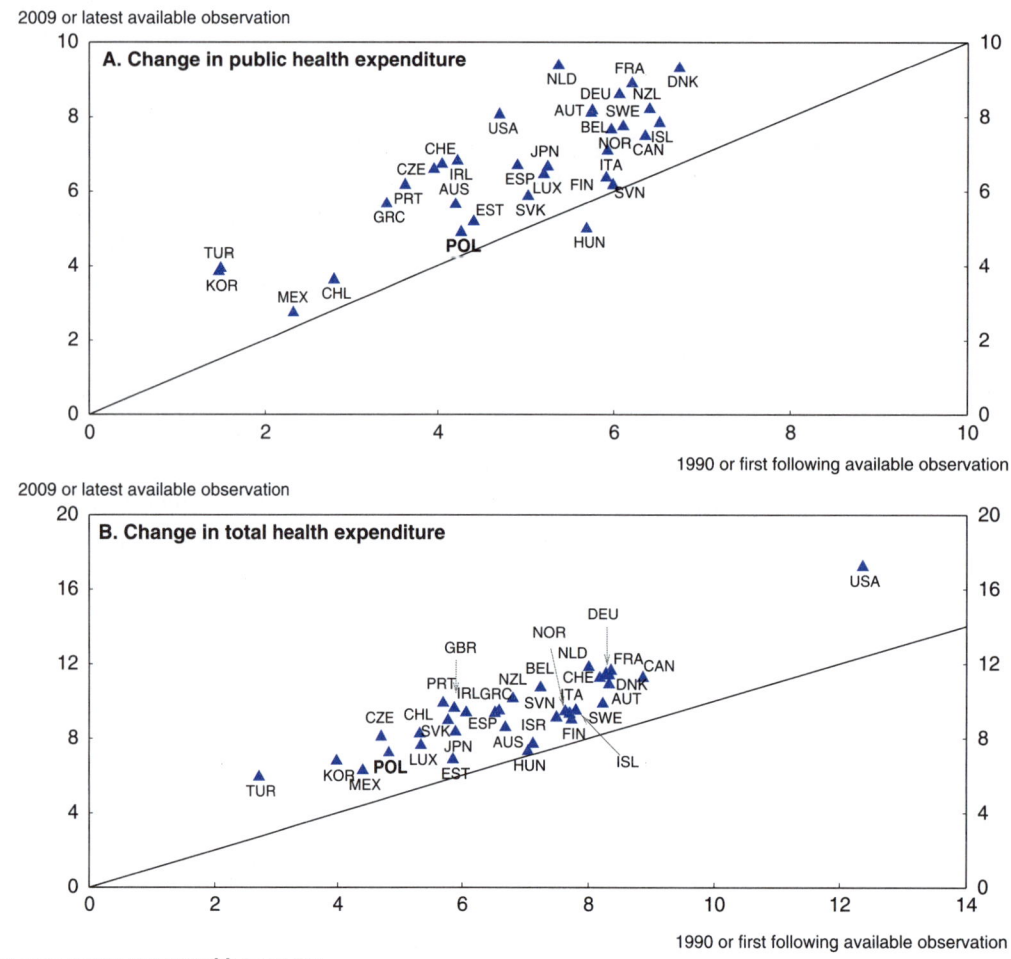

Source: OECD, *OECD Health Data 2011.*

StatLink ⬛⬛⬛ http://dx.doi.org/10.1787/888932584281

Figure 1.2. **Health expenditures are modest but consistent with Poland's economic development level**

2009 or latest year available

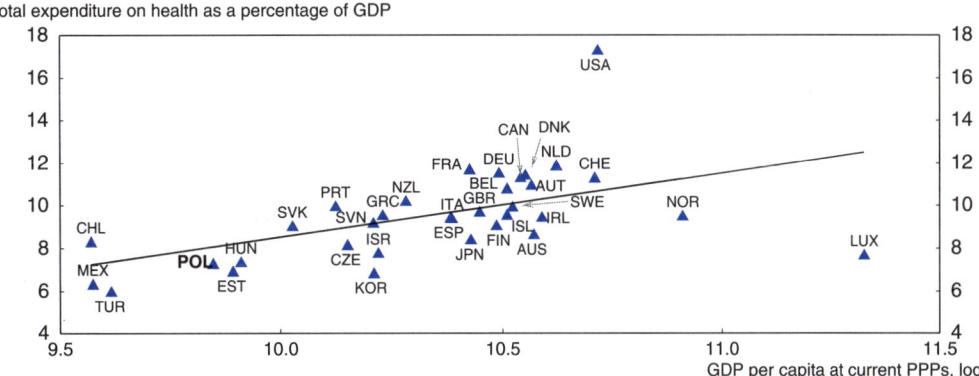

Total expenditure on health as a percentage of GDP

Source: OECD, *OECD Health Data 2011* and *National Accounts Database 2011.*

StatLink ᴴᴴᴴ *http://dx.doi.org/10.1787/888932584300*

Health care is an area where government involvement is inevitable (Box 1.1). Notwithstanding potential efficiency gains, public health-care spending is very likely to increase in Poland in the forthcoming decades. Indeed, rapid ageing, projected income growth and cost-increasing technology prospects are likely to generate mounting health-

---

Box 1.1. **Public intervention in health care**

Good health is a prerequisite for individual well-being, and health care is an integral component of social protection. Key objectives of health-care systems include the provision of both high-quality health-care services and insurance against major life risks. In addition, inequalities in health status are much less accepted than those in other areas. Fundamental moral reasons induce societies to devote substantial resources to providing health care as well as an equitable and efficient system of health insurance to their citizens, which makes government involvement inevitable (Cutler and Zeckhauser, 2000).

Health-care spending tends to grow faster than GDP in OECD countries as greater affluence enables nations to devote more resources to health care. Health seems to have superior-good characteristics, but the extent to which health spending grows faster than income is subject to debate. However, the causality also runs the other way: better health improves productivity and education performance, reduces absenteeism, extends working life and raises the incentive to acquire human capital. While the quantitative importance of health for economic growth is the subject of ongoing research (see Weil, 2011), Durlauf *et al.* (2005) show that life expectancy is one of the most robust determinants of economic growth.

Market failures in the health sector are rife. *First*, externalities arise from communicable diseases and immunisation. *Second*, health is also characterised by a high level of informational asymmetries among providers, payers and patients. The principal-agent relationship that results from this asymmetry is prone to induce paternalism, thus blurring the normative relevance of patients' willingness to pay (Hurley, 2000). *Third*, adverse selection and moral hazard in health-insurance markets prevent the competitive equilibrium from being efficient. *Fourth*, the health sector is highly R&D intensive, which intrinsically generates substantial fixed costs and increasing returns to scale, which in turn calls for heavy regulation of property rights and pricing. But formulating public policies

---

> **Box 1.1. Public intervention in health care** (*cont.*)
>
> to correct health-market imperfections is tricky, and badly designed health-related social policies and moral hazard might generate an overconsumption of health-care services, thus weighing on public finances.

and long-term care needs. As a result, health spending might exert significant but manageable strains on public finance in the forthcoming decades, provided that budgetary discipline prevails over this longer-term horizon. Needed extra resources should be financed by savings on other public expenditure items and possibly by additional revenues, which should be levied on tax bases that are least detrimental to economic performance, such as property and environmental taxes, and by cutting tax expenditures.

The most pressing issues to be addressed in the Polish health-care system concern: easing the substantial limitations in access to care; reducing persistent inequalities; better coordinating among major public actors; improving hospital management; strengthening the gate-keeping function played by generalists; carefully designing private health insurance; and developing a comprehensive long-term-care strategy.

Structure of the health-care system

The current health-care system was developed as a result of reforms that were conducted between 1989 and 2004. Highly centralised under Communist rule, it remained fully funded by general taxation until 1999, when the mandatory public health insurance was created, initially under the management of one occupational (for uniformed services) and 16 regional Sickness Funds. This decentralisation hindered patient mobility between regions because of complicated bureaucratic procedures and resulted in many cases of abuse and corruption due to an underdeveloped system of control (European Commission, 2010). The National Health Fund (NFZ) was created in 2003 through the merger of the Sickness Funds.

Tight budget constraint

The wide ranging cross-country dataset collected by the OECD in 2008 allows the identification of the main features of the Polish health care system.[1] Poland belongs to a group of countries with: a heavily regulated public system in which the budget constraint is particularly stringent; large provider choice for patients; restricted sub-national government autonomy; and limited "over-the-basic" insurance coverage, *i.e.* the share of both the population and spending covered by private insurers over and above the "basic" insurance package (OECD, 2010a). Hungary, Ireland, Italy, New Zealand, Norway and the United Kingdom tend to share similar characteristics (OECD, 2010a).

Overall, public spending accounts for 72% of health-care financing, which is similar to the OECD average. After having fallen from 90% at the beginning of the 1990s, that share has not changed substantially over the last decade. The level of public health-care spending is a joint decision of the Ministries of Health and Finance. Since its creation, the mandatory public health-insurance contribution, paid to the Sickness Funds and then to the NFZ, has become the main source of public funding, financing about 85% of the cost of public purchase of health-care services (Figure 1.3, Panel A). The health-care contribution is a fixed proportion of (uncapped) wages and thus does not reflect individual health risks. It has risen from 7.5% of gross wages (estimated separately for the employed, self-employed and

Figure 1.3. **Structure of the health-care system's revenues**

2009

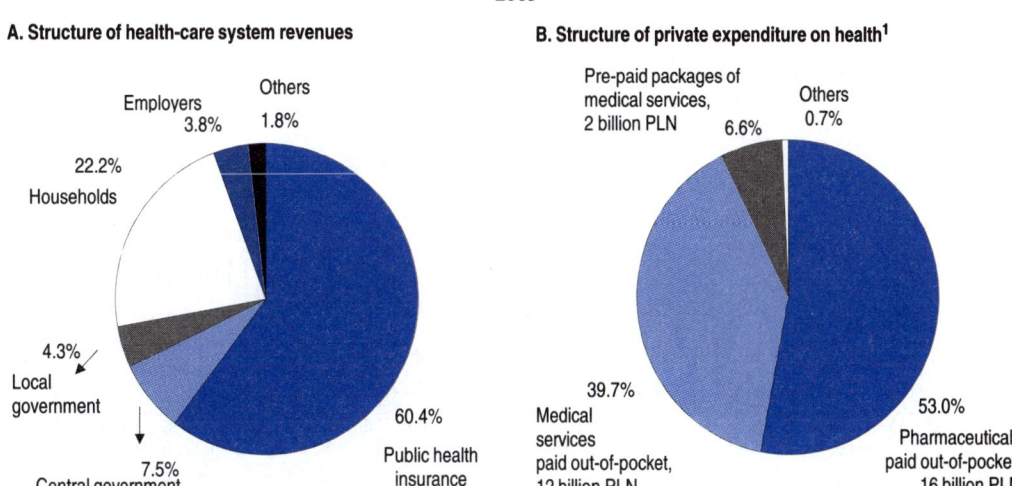

1. Percent of total private expenditure on health.

Source: OECD, *OECD Health Data 2011* (Panel A); Ministry of health 2011 (Panel B).

StatLink ⚏⚏⚏ http://dx.doi.org/10.1787/888932584319

farmers) after the 1999 reform to 9% since 2007. However, as 7.75 of these 9 percentage points represent a tax credit, making effective income tax rates much lower than their apparent levels, the central government still effectively finances a large part of health care. Moreover, non-working spouses are freely co-insured, which increases both the tax of taking up a job (even though this effect is limited by the tax credit), thus discouraging the employment of second earners, and the non-wage labour costs for those who pay (OECD, 2010b). Removing the free co-insurance would come at the cost of taxing marriage where only one of the couple works. Public health insurance covers employees, the self-employed, the unemployed receiving benefits, and the retired and disabled. The government also pays a health-insurance premium for farmers, the unemployed who do not receive benefits, people on leave to raise young children, and soldiers. As a result, almost everyone (about 98% of the population) is covered by public insurance. However, strangely, there is no system for controlling patients' public insurance status, such as a simple identity card.

Besides covering the health-insurance premium of selected groups of the population, central and local governments are responsible for reimbursing the costs of health services for certain groups of the uninsured, financing specific health programmes, emergency and lifesaving services and highly specialised medical procedures such as organ transplants and heart surgery. Also, while the NFZ covers the costs of medical services, local governments fund the every-day operational costs of hospital facilities (gas, electricity, water), the maintenance of buildings, repairs and renovations, and investments in medical equipment.

Large share of out-of-pocket payments

Overall, Poland is one of the OECD countries where out-of-pocket expenditure as a share of total health-care expenditure is the largest, although not in relation to household consumption (given the relatively low level of total health-care expenditure) (Figure 1.4). Given the importance of private resources to finance health care and the absence of a (formal) private insurance system, household expenditures are largely out of pocket (rather than private insurance premiums). Pharmaceuticals account for more than half of private

Figure 1.4. **Household out-of-pocket expenditure on health care**
2009 or closest year

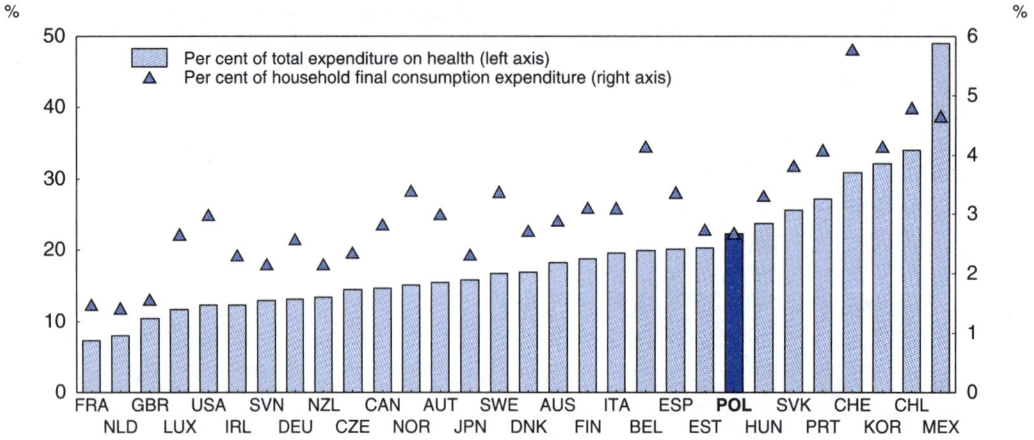

Source: OECD, OECD Health Data 2011.

StatLink ≡ http://dx.doi.org/10.1787/888932584338

expenditure (Figure 1.3, Panel B), and for those with long-term illness and retirees, that share rises to about 75% (Green Book, 2009). Specialist medical services paid out of pocket, typically consultations provided at private medical facilities, is the second largest component of private expenditure. Pre-paid packages of medical services are also purchased by employers from specific providers. These packages include occupational medicine as well as primary and secondary treatments and have been growing in importance in recent years. While a decade ago services were offered only to employers covering their employees, more recently packages of medical services covering primary and specialist care have been developed for private individuals (but they remain marginal). All these services are formally distinct from private insurance, in particular because they are not regulated by insurance laws.

National Health Fund (NFZ)

The NFZ has the primary not-for-profit task of providing access to publicly insured health-care services. Run under the principle of institutional separation between the provider and the payer functions, the NFZ cannot own entities engaged in the provision of health care, ensuring in principle equal treatment of providers. The NFZ is fully responsible for needs assessment, and medical services contracting and control. It operates 16 regional branches, which have some autonomy, as, for example, in the tendering process for health-care services.

In addition to contracting services, the NFZ also finances selected public-health programmes, prescription medicines in ambulatory care, experimental programmes, rehabilitation and spa treatments, as well as long-term care. Since 2008, the list has been broadened to include highly specialised procedures, which were previously financed directly from the general government budget. It was not until 2009 that legislation first mentioned the so-called guaranteed health-care services basket, which is a broad list of medical services covered by public health insurance, excluding such medical procedures as plastic surgery, vaccinations against influenza, sex-change operations and in vitro procedures.

Provider payment mechanism

Primary-care providers are paid by capitation (a flat fee per patient), while the payment scheme for outpatient specialist care is fee for service. Most primary care, independent of ownership status, is still covered by public health insurance. The share of privately owned ambulatory care units increased from 42% in 2000 to 82% in 2009, and the overall utilisation of ambulatory care has been increasing: for example, there were 6.8 doctor consultations per inhabitant in 2008, compared with 5.3 in 1999. Primary care also has a gate-keeping function aimed at limiting spending on specialist care by requiring patients to get a referral to see (most) specialists and receive non-emergency hospital care. Many individuals purchase services in the private market in order to overcome barriers in access to specialists. The main recent change in secondary- and tertiary-care financing was the introduction in hospitals (in 2008) and in parts of ambulatory care (in 2010) of the new system of Diagnostic Related Groups (DRGs) based on the British Health Care Resources Groups.

Aggregate health outcomes are broadly consistent with the country's level of development

Steady improvement in health outcomes following the transformation period

Since the mid-1990s gains in life expectancy have tended to match those in developed countries (Figure 1.5 and Table 1.1). Other measures of health outcomes, such as life expectancy at age 65, total mortality rates and premature mortality (the so-called potential years of life lost)[2] are tightly correlated across countries and have followed similar trends, while infant mortality displays a looser link to life expectancy overall. The total (age standardised) mortality rate of the Polish population decreased by 28% between 1990 and 2008 (from 1.07 to 0.77 percentage point of population), with a decrease in mortality due to cardiovascular system (CVS) diseases by 40%. CVS system diseases and cancers have been the focus of health policy through the National Programme of Prevention and Cure of Cardiovascular System Diseases (POLKARD) and the National Programme to Overcome Cancers, which were set up and legislated in 2003 (completed in 2008) and 2005, respectively. These programmes focused on prevention, early intervention and easier access to treatment innovations. The improvement in health status is also attributable to changes in lifestyle, such as decreasing alcohol consumption and smoking (especially among men), and increasing physical activity (Okolski, 2004; Golinowska and Sowa, 2006). Economic development has also triggered an improvement in the quality of food consumed, especially fresh fruits and vegetables, and has led to beneficial dietary changes, such as replacing the consumption of animal with vegetable proteins (Zato?ski and Willett, 2005). However, despite this improvement, Poland's health outcomes appear weak in cross-country comparison (Figures 1.6 and 1.7).

Outcomes close to average once level of development is controlled for

Once GDP per capita is controlled for, Poland's life expectancy is only slightly shorter than the average OECD country's (Figure 1.7). Other outcome variables as well as the efficiency indicator estimated by OECD (2010a)[3] and the European Health Consumer Index yield similar results (see Table 1.2, which shows seven indicators). Once GDP per capita is controlled for, the residuals are linearly scaled such that the mean across countries is equal to 0 and the standard deviation to 1 for each indicator. Overall, Poland seems to perform close to the average country. It does better (by about 1 standard deviation) in terms of infant mortality but worse as regards total and premature mortality. The best outcomes

Figure 1.5. **Trends in life expectancy at birth for the total population**

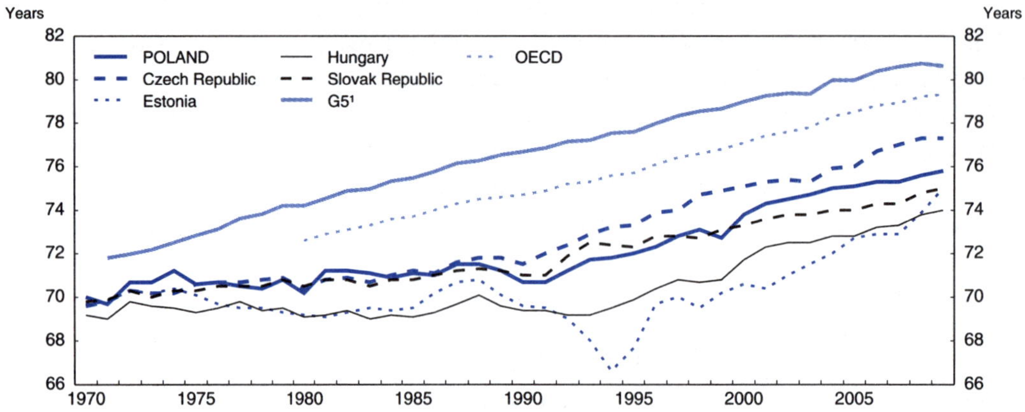

1. G7 less Canada and the United Kingdom, due to missing values in the period.
Source: OECD, OECD Health Data 2011.

StatLink http://dx.doi.org/10.1787/888932584357

Table 1.1. **Gains in life expectancy**

	Average 1985-89	Average 2005-09	% change		Average 1985-89	Average 2005-09	% change
Turkey	64.1	73.4	14.5	United Kingdom	75.1	79.7	6.2
Korea	69.9	79.4	13.7	Switzerland	77.4	81.9	5.9
Slovenia	72.5	78.4	8.2	**Poland**	**71.3**	**75.4**	**5.8**
Ireland	74.1	79.8	7.7	Belgium	75.2	79.6	5.8
New Zealand	74.5	80.3	7.7	Spain	76.8	81.1	5.6
Czech Republic	71.5	76.9	7.5	Norway	76.4	80.6	5.6
Luxembourg	74.5	79.9	7.3	Hungary	69.6	73.4	5.5
Portugal	73.7	79.0	7.2	Japan	78.3	82.5	5.4
Austria	74.8	80.1	7.1	Denmark	74.8	78.6	5.1
Israel	75.5	80.8	7.0	Sweden	77.1	81.0	5.0
Mexico	70.2	75.0	6.8	Iceland	77.6	81.3	4.8
Germany	74.9	79.9	6.8	Slovak Republic	71.1	74.5	4.8
Australia	76.1	81.3	6.8	Estonia	70.3	73.5	4.6
Italy[2]	76.2	81.4	6.7	Canada[1]	76.9	80.4	4.6
Finland	74.8	79.6	6.5	Netherlands	76.6	80.1	4.5
OECD	**74.2**	**78.9**	**6.4**	Greece	76.5	79.7	4.2
France	76.0	80.8	6.3	United States	74.8	77.8	4.0

1. Average 2005-07.
2. Average 2005-08.
Source: OECD, OECD Health Data 2011.

(conditional on the level of development) are achieved by Chile and Japan, while the United States, the Slovak Republic, Estonia, Hungary and Turkey are seen to perform badly (see Appendix 1.A1).

One of the strengths of the Polish health-care system lies in high vaccination rates of children, a feature shared by other Eastern European countries. In addition, the Polish (private) health-care system might have a comparative advantage in delivering health-care services as an internationally traded commodity, since Poland seems to be becoming a popular destination for "medical tourism". According to Zukowski (2010), about 300 000 foreigners (citizens of Germany, Ireland and the United Kingdom are the biggest

Figure 1.6. **Amenable mortality in OECD countries, 2007 or nearest year**

Nolte and McKee's list, age standardised rates per 100 000 population[1]

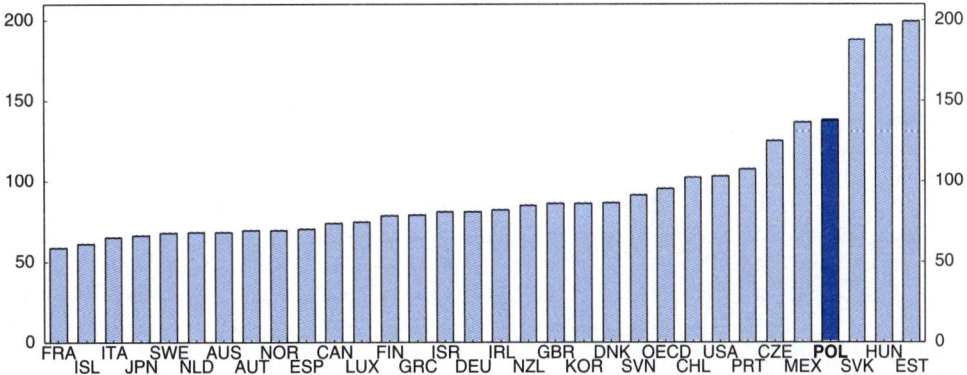

1. This graph presents a set of estimates for amenable mortality for OECD countries, based on the widely-used list developed by Nolte and McKee in 2008. Estimates based on the list developed by Tobias and Yeh in 2009 provide similar results.

Source: Gay, J.G. *et al.* (2011), "Mortality Amenable to Health Care in 31 OECD Countries: Estimates and Methodological Issues", *OECD Health Working Papers*, No. 55, OECD Publishing.

StatLink ⧉ *http://dx.doi.org/10.1787/888932584376*

Figure 1.7. **Health performance is related on the overall development level of the economy, 2008**

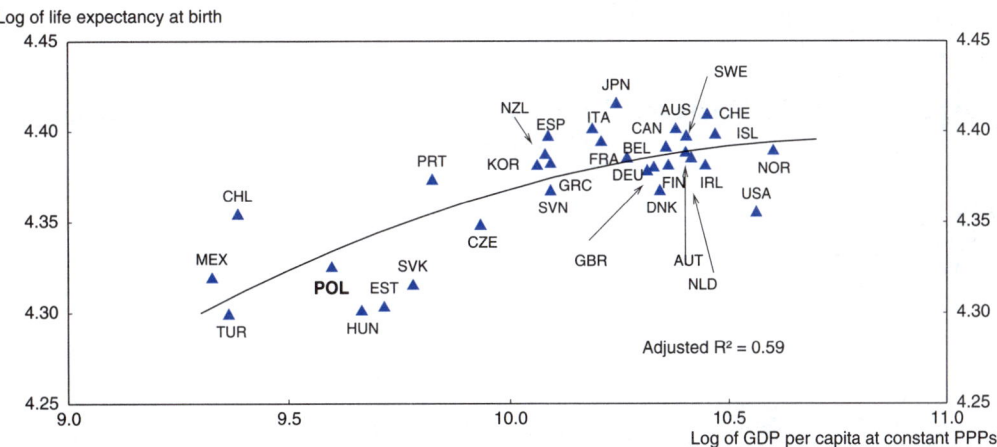

Source: OECD, *OECD Health Data 2011 and National Accounts Databases.*

StatLink ⧉ *http://dx.doi.org/10.1787/888932584395*

groups) made use of private Polish health-care institutions in 2009, mainly for dental care, plastic surgery, and orthopaedic and spa treatments.

Some indicators point to inefficiencies

However, other indicators point to various inefficiencies. Hospital admission rates for asthma, chronic obstructive pulmonary disease and diabetes, for which treatment approaches that avoid the need for costly admissions are available, are above the OECD average (Figure 1.8). Another example is cataract surgery, which can be performed on an outpatient basis at reduced cost. Available data reveal that the share of cataract surgeries carried out without hospital admission varies significantly across countries, from above 97% in Canada, Finland, the Netherlands and Sweden to below 35% in Hungary,

Table 1.2. **Health performance**[1]

	Life expectancy at birth, total population	Life expectancy at 65, total population	Mortality rate, all causes	Infant mortality rate	Premature mortality	Potential gains in life expectancy at birth[2]	Euro Health Consumer index[3]	Average
Czech Republic	−0.8	−1.2	−1.3	1.1	0.1	−0.3	0.2	−0.3
Estonia	−2.1	−1.3	−1.2	0.6	−1.3	–	0.7	−0.8
Hungary	−1.9	−1.6	−2.2	0.5	−1.4	−1.7	0.9	−1.1
Poland	**−0.4**	**0.1**	**−1.1**	**0.8**	**−1.0**	**0.5**	**−0.1**	**−0.2**
Slovak Republic	−1.8	−2.0	−2.2	−0.2	−1.1	−1.6	−1.1	−1.4
Slovenia	−0.4	−0.5	−0.1	1.1	0.4	–	−0.5	−0.0
OECD	**0.0**	**0.0**	**0.0**	**0.0**	**0.0**	**0.0**	**0.0**	**0.0**
Minimum	−2.1	−2.0	−2.2	−3.7	−3.1	−1.9	−1.9	−1.8
Maximum	2.1	2.3	2.2	1.1	2.7	1.5	2.1	2.1
Adjusted R[2]	0.6	0.6	0.4	0.5	0.6	−0.1	0.6	–

Note: For life expectancy at birth as an example, Polish performance is 0.4 standard deviation worse than the OECD average, once GDP per capita is controlled for.

1. A regression is first run for each indicator (in log; for mortality variables, *minus* log is used) with GDP per capita in PPP terms (in log) and a constant on the right hand side. The corresponding indicator is computed as the residual of that regression divided by the standard deviation of the residuals. By construction, the average of each indicator across OECD countries is equal to 0. The "Adjusted R[2]" row corresponds to the adjusted R[2] of that regression.
2. Underlying data are *Data Envelopment Analysis* (DEA) efficiency scores for 2007 obtained by using two inputs: health-care spending per capita and a composite indicator of the socio-economic environment and lifestyle factors.
3. The EHCI, published by the Health Consumer Powerhouse, measures and ranks the performance of health-care provision in 33 European countries from a consumer point of view.

Source: OECD calculations based on *OECD Health Data* and OECD (2010), *Health Care Systems: Efficiency And Policy Settings*, OECD Publishing.

Figure 1.8. **Avoidable hospital admission rates by main diagnostic category, 2009 or nearest year**

Standardised scores[1]

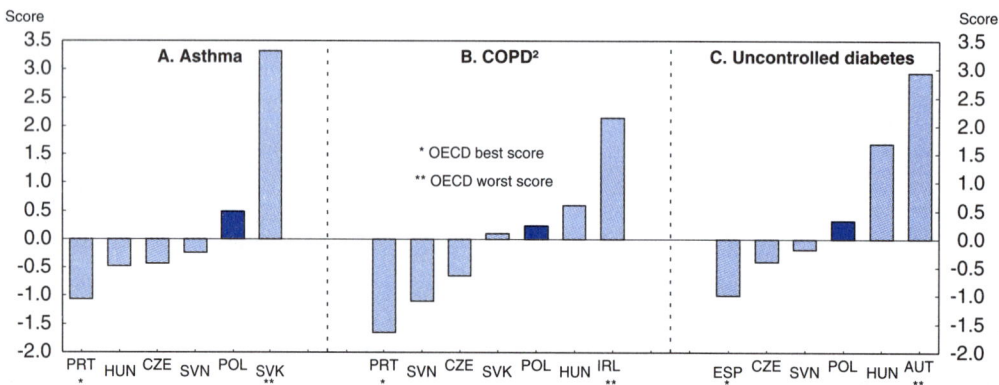

1. Data represent the difference from the OECD average and are expressed in number of standard deviations; original admission rates are age-sex standardised to 2005 OECD population aged 15 and over.
2. Chronic obstructive pulmonary disease.

Source: OECD, *OECD Health Data 2011*.

StatLink ⟨⟩ http://dx.doi.org/10.1787/888932584414

Luxembourg, Poland, Slovenia and the Slovak Republic (OECD, 2011a). Overall, the number of hospital discharges (relative to the population) is among the highest within the OECD and in-patient care is an especially large share of total health-care outlays by OECD standards, signalling a potential misallocation of resources and an overuse of hospital care (Figure 1.9). Also there is a lack of access by providers to information regarding whether

Figure 1.9. **Expenditure on in-patient hospital care, 2009 or closest year**

As a percentage of total health expenditure

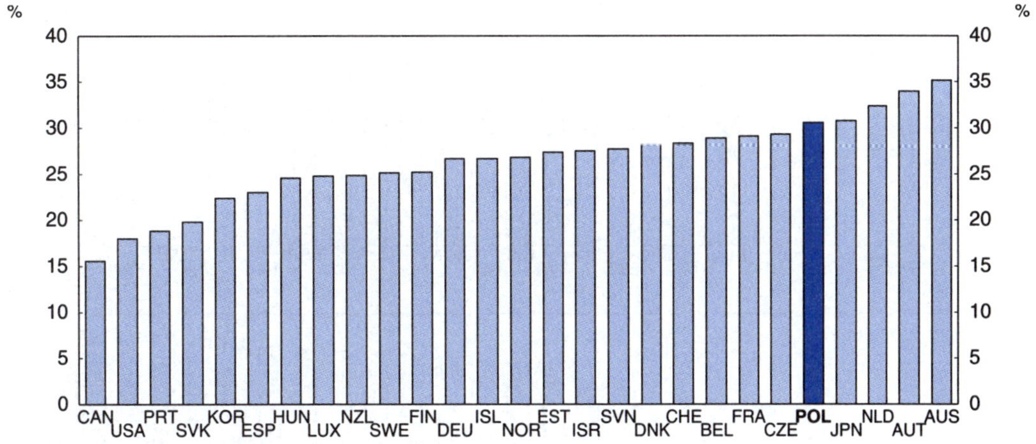

Source: OECD, OECD Health Data 2011.

StatLink ⟶ http://dx.doi.org/10.1787/888932584433

people are publicly insured. The recent government attempt to make doctors and pharmacists liable in case public care and prescription drugs have been provided to non-insured people met fierce opposition. Some people covered by a specific form of temporary contract (*umowa o dzieło*) related to the generation of some intellectual property right (typically freelancers) are not required to pay health-care contributions.

Addressing the substantial limitations in access to care

Poor self-assessed quality of care...

As discussed above, public health insurance covers almost the whole population, as in most OECD countries. However, coverage is an imperfect indicator of both accessibility, which depends on overall supply, the services included and the degree of cost-sharing applied to those services (OECD, 2009), and quality. There are basically no barriers to accessing primary care in Poland. While accessibility to hospital care seems to be relatively good, accessibility to specialist care is unsatisfactory (European Commission, 2007). Also, the self-assessed quality of care appears to be one of the poorest in Europe (Figure 1.10), most likely due to poor access to new technologies and long waiting times for highly specialised treatment. The insufficiency of diagnostic equipment (in the public system) is especially visible for cancer, for which an early diagnosis is crucial to successful treatment. For example, access to magnetic resonance imaging (MRI) services is only about a third of the average OECD country level. Furthermore, based on self-reported unmet care needs or health status, Polish health outcomes also appear weak in cross-country comparison (Figure 1.11).

... and large persistent inequalities

While issues related to waiting times seem to affect all income groups similarly, those related to financial costs induce inequalities in access to care, even though these inequalities seem to have diminished sharply over the recent past (Table 1.3). For dental care as an example, about two-thirds of expenditure is financed privately – only basic treatment is covered by the public insurance, and the NFZ has been limiting financing of dental care in recent years (Zukowski, 2010) – leading to highly unequal access. A similar situation may occur for other types of specialist care, for which private services are used to jump queues.

Figure 1.10. **Quality of care in the EU27, 2007**

Share of respondents reporting good or very good access to care

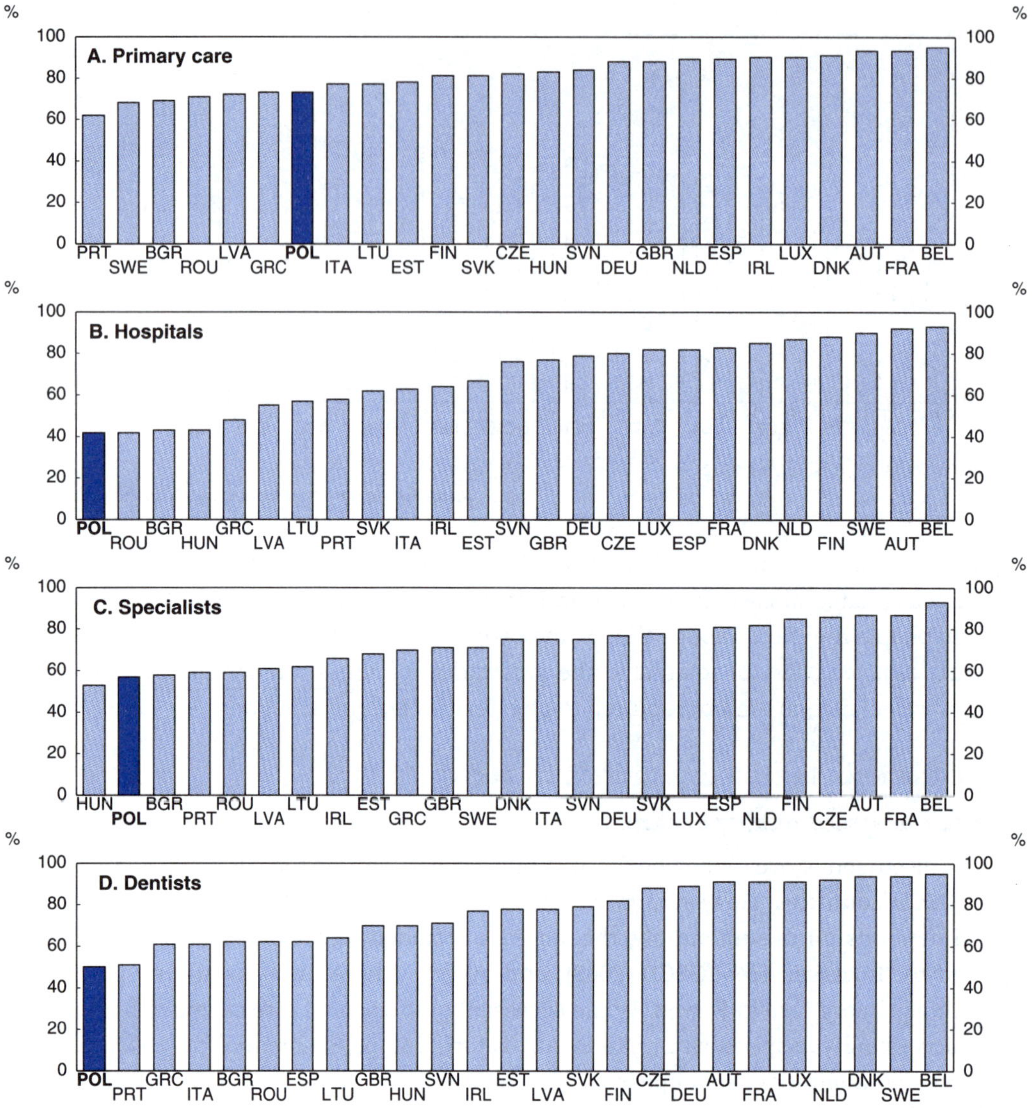

Source: European Commission (2007), "Health And Long-Term Care In The European Union Report", *Special Eurobarometer 283.*

StatLink ⫶⫶⫶ http://dx.doi.org/10.1787/888932584452

Inequalities with respect to mortality risks are high in Poland as shown by various different indicators. More than in many OECD countries, mortality is greatly influenced by education level, especially for men: life expectancy is 12 years more at age 30 for those with a high educational attainment than those with low attainment (Sowa, 2011; and Figure 1.12, Panel A). Based on another inequality indicator, the dispersion in the age of death among individuals (although imperfect, this indicator has the advantages of simplicity and availability; see Joumard *et al.*, 2010), Poland's health inequality would be the third highest in the OECD – after only the United States and Hungary (Figure 1.12, Panel B). Moreover, the difference in life expectancy at birth between women and men was 8.5 years in 2009, well above the OECD average of 5.6 years and the highest in the OECD except for Estonia. This might also signal risk factors related to lifestyle that could be more prevalent

Figure 1.11. **Self-reported unmet care needs, 2009**
Percentages of population aged 16 and over

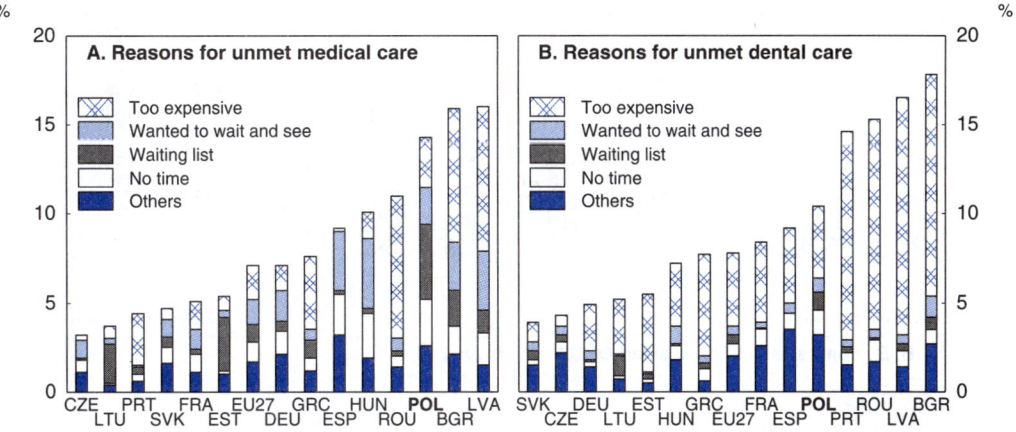

Source: Eurostat, *SILC Database.*

StatLink 🔗 http://dx.doi.org/10.1787/888932584471

Table 1.3. **Poland: unmet care needs by income quintile**
Per cent of population

	2004	2009
First quintile		
Too expensive	12.3	5.8
Waiting list	1.6	3.5
Too far to travel	0.3	1.5
Fifth quintile		
Too expensive	2.5	0.8
Waiting list	3.7	4.4
Too far to travel	0.1	0.2

Source: Eurostat, *SILC Database.*

for men: alcohol and tobacco consumption are each indeed high in OECD comparison, while fruit and vegetable consumption is low (OECD, 2011a). It is important to note, as shown by OECD (2010a), that there is no trade-off between improving health outcomes on average and reducing inequalities in health status, which reinforces the justification for aiming at reducing such dispersion. Grimm (2011) even provides evidence that, controlling for the overall level of life expectancy, health inequality negatively affects economic growth. One suggested channel for this result is that labour productivity rises with health outcomes but at a decreasing rate, such that a more unequal distribution of health outcomes might imply lower average productivity.

Long waiting times tend to reflect inefficiencies

Poland is the European country in which waiting times for medical care restrict access the most (Figure 1.13). Long waiting times are especially damaging for specialised procedures in cardiovascular system diseases, oncology, orthopaedics and ophthalmology, as well as diagnosis requiring the use of specialised medical equipment. They seem to result mainly from insufficient funding of health care and poor co-ordination of patients' treatment. As could be expected, waiting times differ regionally, depending on the number of specialists, medical facilities and equipment.

Figure 1.12. **Health inequalities**

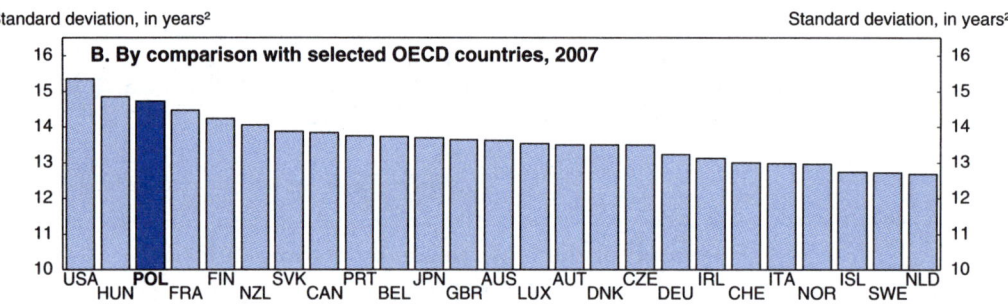

1. Gaps in life expectancy between persons with high and low educational attainment at age 30; data for Italy refer to 2007.
2. Standard deviation in mortality ages for population older than 10.

Source: OECD (2011), *How's Life? Measuring Well-Being*, OECD Publishing, for Panel A; Joumard, I., C. André and C. Nicq (2010), "Health Care Systems: Efficiency And Institutions", *OECD Economics Department Working Papers*, No. 769, OECD Publishing, for Panel B.

StatLink ⫘ *http://dx.doi.org/10.1787/888932584490*

Figure 1.13. **Waiting times restrict access to medical care in Poland**[1]

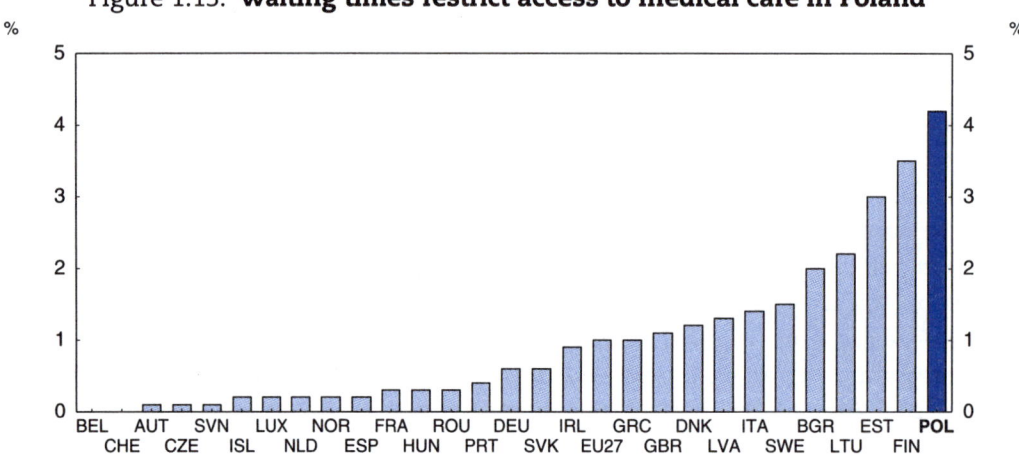

1. Unmet needs in medical care due to excess waiting, as a percentage of population aged 16 and over.
Source: Eurostat, *SILC Database.*

StatLink ⫘ *http://dx.doi.org/10.1787/888932584509*

Waiting lists for publicly funded health-care services might be a way to limit spending by non-price means. However, long waiting times are one aspect of poor quality, likely reflecting inefficiencies and generating inequality, as they might impose costs on patients that are not offset by gains to producers or payers. Indeed, waiting lists reduce the value of a treatment because of the extra discomfort, and, for some pathologies, a higher risk of permanent deterioration in health (Gravelle and Siciliani, 2008). While countries with short waiting times happen to spend more on both total and public health care on average and to have higher capacity, they tend also to have higher productivity in delivering health-care services (Siciliani and Hurst, 2004). Indeed, a lack of incentives for higher productivity in hospitals might generate queuing. A short queue is probably desirable, though, since if there were never any waiting list there would be costly periods of idle capacity (Hoel and Saether, 2003).[4] Overall, however, on both efficiency and equity grounds, the case for lengthy optimal waiting times is weak (Marchand and Schroyen, 2005; Gravelle and Siciliani, 2008).

In Poland, most efforts should focus on seeking efficiency gains and extending supply capacity targeted at reducing waiting lists. Siciliani and Hurst (2005) provide a survey of measures several OECD countries (Australia, the Netherlands, Spain, Sweden, the United Kingdom) have implemented to cut waiting times. On the supply side, they argue that the most efficient way to allocate extra resources to hospitals is to make them specifically conditional upon delivering extra activity and shortening waiting lists. Another would be to specifically link remuneration to extra activity and reductions in waiting times.

The computerisation of patient records through a new project ("e-health") is also likely to help to improve the administration of waiting lists. Poor use of information technology is often pointed to as a drawback of the Polish health-care system. There are no common standards of collection and use of data, some registers are not electronic, and information systems are not mutually compatible. The implementation of the new legislation on information systems and of the "e-health" programme, which is planned to be completed by 2015, should improve the situation. First, the *Law on Information Systems in Health Care*, in force since January 2012, sets rules for co-ordination and integration of information systems and medical registries as well as for on-line access to the integrated system supervised by the Ministry of Health. Moreover, it introduces a System of Medical Information covering individual treatment, providers, medical employees and prices of services provided by public sources. Second, "e-health" aims at integrating working databases, creating both a centralised source of information regarding the history of patients' treatment and a medical Internet portal available to all interested parties.

Long waiting times encourage informal payments and other queue-jumping mechanisms

Facing difficulties with access to hospital treatment, patients have developed a number of strategies to avoid queuing. Around the end of the 1970s, they began to make informal payments to physicians in order to obtain faster and more personalised service. By the end of the 1980s this practice had become widespread (OECD, 2000), and such payments were often perceived as a supplement to the low salaries of medical staff. Chawla *et al.* (1998) estimated that in the mid-1990s informal payments made by patients to physicians effectively doubled physicians' salaries. Informal payments can take many forms ranging from small "tokens of gratitude" (such as flowers or bottles of alcohol) to outright cash bribes. The extent to which they are akin to corruption is difficult to assess. In 2005, the government implemented an anti-corruption campaign, which decreased the frequency of informal payments. The Ministry of Health too has been taking steps to reduce corruption and fraud. In 2009, the European Healthcare Fraud and Corruption Network Excellence Award was granted to Mrs. Ewa Kopacz, then Minister of Health, for her anti-corruption and anti-fraud actions.

Nevertheless, Poland's health service usually ranks unfavourably in all bribery and corruption statistics, often a legacy of the "shadow" economies of Communist countries (Allin *et al.*, 2006). According to a survey conducted in May 2010 by the Public Opinion Research Center, 87% of respondents considered corruption in Poland as a major problem and 44% as a very important one. During the previous four years the latter percentage declined by 4 percentage points. The respondents believed that corruption is most common among politicians and in the health-care system.

Lately, patients needing hospital care have tended to jump the queue by ordering a private consultation (paid out of pocket) with a physician who also works in a public hospital and is responsible for decisions about specialised treatment and, in many cases, surgery. The doctor next arranges the hospital visit and operation without further delay. Queue jumping can also operate via pre-paid schemes, which enable patients to have an operation faster in a public facility based on the contract or arrangement that the pre-paying company has with this facility. Limiting the extent to which specialists are allowed to have dual practices (combining work in publicly and privately funded institutions) has been used by some OECD countries (Ireland, England) to reduce waiting times (Siciliani and Hurst, 2005). Legal rules are needed to better separate the activities in private practices from access to treatment in public facilities in order to ensure equal access. At a minimum, promoting the transparency of dual practices, which is currently insufficient (Golinowska, 2010), is necessary, especially given that specialists working for public hospitals have an incentive to maintain long waiting times for public patients to boost demand for their private practices (Siciliani and Hurst, 2005). Some countries go further by imposing restrictions in terms of either earnings, authorisations or other regulations. Spain, Sweden and the Netherlands forbid specialists from treating private patients in public hospitals (Siciliani and Hurst, 2005).

Limiting out-of-pocket payments and ensuring greater affordability of pharmaceuticals

Out-of-pocket payments also contribute to restricting access. As shown in Figure 1.4 above, their share in Polish health-care financing is one of the highest in the OECD. However, expenditures borne directly by patients raise equity concerns; they are correlated across countries with catastrophic health expenditures, commonly defined as payments for health services exceeding a threshold (generally 40%) of household disposable income after subsistence needs are met (OECD, 2009). Various studies have shown how private cost sharing, while limiting moral-hazard issues and reducing health-service utilisation, sometimes efficiently, fosters the privatisation of risk and increases inequality (Wendt, 2009).

In Poland, as in the majority of European countries, price controls for outpatient drugs are limited to pharmaceuticals with reimbursement eligibility, while for non-reimbursable pharmaceuticals, which are often over-the-counter (OTC) products, the manufacturer/importer sets the price freely (PPRI, 2011). In Poland since 2012, the regulated prices for reimbursable drugs are set by the Ministry of Health based on price negotiations between marketing authorisation holders (producers) and the Economic Committee (which is an advisory body of the Ministry). Only a limited number of drugs can be purchased outside pharmacies (52 active substances listed by the Ministry of Health), and pharmaceuticals are provided free of charge in hospitals.[5]

The *Act on Reimbursement of Medicines, Food for Particular Nutritional Uses and Medical Devices*, adopted in 2011, aims at controlling public spending through tighter drug-reimbursement regulation. It introduces a threshold on public spending on drugs set at 17% of NFZ spending on guaranteed medical services, which triggers a producer pay-back above this ceiling. Companies must now return 50% of the total amount of overspending per drug in a given group of reimbursed drugs. In addition, drug companies will no longer be allowed to offer discounts to pharmacists or patients. The size of the discounts was apparently previously underestimated by the NFZ, such that it actually reimbursed a higher-than-planned share of the final price including the discount. This new legislation seems to offer a poor alternative to more aggressive negotiation for lower prices, and letting market forces operate beyond this.

Although decreasing over the past decade from a peak of 30% reached in 2002, the share of pharmaceuticals in total health expenditure is high compared with other OECD countries (Figure 1.14). Less developed countries tend to have a larger share of drug expenditures for at least two reasons: i) pharmaceuticals are a necessity good, which implies a relatively income-inelastic demand; and ii) there is a relative-price effect, since in a catching-up country drugs (especially new drugs) tend to be imported at internationally traded prices, whereas other domestic service-type outlays are usually cheaper.

Figure 1.14. **Pharmaceuticals spending as a share of total health expenditures in OECD countries, 2009[1]**

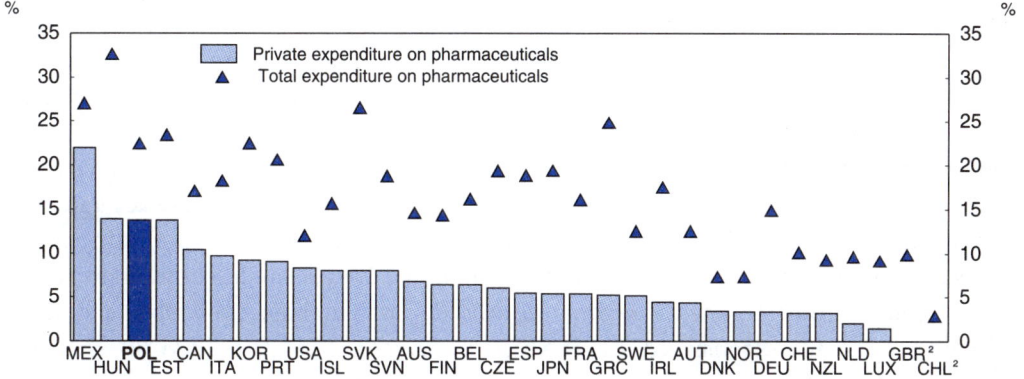

1. 2007 for Greece; 2008 for Australia, Korea, Mexico, Portugal and the United Kingdom.
2. Not available for private expenditure on pharmaceuticals.
Source: OECD, OECD Health Data 2011.

StatLink ⟶ http://dx.doi.org/10.1787/888932584528

However, high co-payments for prescribed drugs and the lack of coverage by private health insurance (PHI) result in the share of out-of-pocket payments for drugs being the highest in the OECD, (out-of-pocket data for Mexico are missing). It is often argued that Poles have a tendency to over-consume drugs through self-medication. It is true that both financial costs and long waiting times for specialists might induce such behaviour. However, per capita expenditure on drugs is one of the lowest (in PPP terms) across OECD countries (OECD, 2008a). Hence, the high share of out-of-pocket payments on drugs seems to primarily reflect the narrow range of reimbursed medicines.[6] Private expenditure on drugs in Poland, almost exclusively out of pocket, is 61% of total pharmaceutical spending (excluding hospital expenditure on pharmaceuticals). It clearly exceeds its public counterpart in only four other OECD countries (Canada, Estonia, Mexico and the United States). Also, spending on OTC products as a share of pharmaceutical expenditure is by far the greatest in Poland at above 40% of total pharmaceutical expenditure.

This structure of drug financing might seriously limit access to medicines especially for the poor, the chronically ill and the elderly. In 2009, only one third of households reported having no financial constraints in buying pharmaceuticals, and 13% of households spent more than 15% of their income on medications alone (Green Book, 2009). Moreover, since 2001, the share of reimbursement in total drugs sales has fallen continuously (Table 1.4). Luczak (2010) shows that between 2000 and 2009, catastrophic out-of-pocket drug expenditures have been increasingly concentrated on the poor, and argues that most of the increase might be related to the shortening of the reimbursement list in 2004. In December 2011, the reimbursement list was narrowed again as, according to the government, pharmaceutical companies did not reapply for reimbursement and price negotiations failed for some drugs that have cheaper generic substitutes.

Table 1.4. **Drug sales in Poland**

As a percentage of total drug sales

	2001	2007
Out-of-pocket drugs expenditure	49.2	57.6
Reimbursed drugs	39.1	32.9
Hospitals' use	11.7	9.5

Source: Ministry of Health, Health Care Financing In Poland: The Green Book 2008.

In order to limit affordability problems, Poland could adopt some kind of graduated cost-sharing mechanism, such as that implemented in Sweden, whereby co-payments diminish as out-of-pocket payments increase over the course of the year, with a cap on total yearly individual (or family) outlays. Many OECD countries make special coverage provision for those in need, including exemptions and caps on out-of-pocket spending. Accordingly, relatively few patients in OECD countries are unable to obtain needed medicines simply because they cannot afford them (OECD, 2008a). In contrast, in Poland, 50% of people from the lowest income quintile do not purchase prescribed medicines because they are too expensive, due to the high co-payment level (Luczak, 2010). The social assistance does provide benefits to cover part or total cost of health-care services, but for extreme cases only: income must not exceed a monthly threshold, which is currently set at about PLN 350/480 or EUR 85/115). Beyond pharmaceuticals, exemptions from co-payments based on either income thresholds or out-of-pocket payment caps exist in all OECD countries except Australia, Hungary, Mexico, Poland and Spain (Table 1.5).

The use of generics is an area where Poland achieves excellent outcomes. Eastern European countries have historically had a stronger focus on the production of generics than on innovative pharmaceuticals, and therefore in these countries local generic manufacturers play an important role. This is particularly the case in Poland, where 12 of 13 drug companies are generics producers (PPRI, 2011). Poland has by far the highest shares of generic drugs market penetration in the OECD (Figure 1.15), representing 75% in volume terms and 58% in value, which contributes to the comparatively low price of drugs (in Purchasing Power Parity terms) (OECD, 2008a).

Currently, pharmacists are obliged to inform patients of a cheaper equivalent drug with the same active substance (unless the doctor states on the prescription "do not substitute") and to have the drug in stock. They then provide the cheaper drug on patients' request. However, in practice, these obligations are rarely met. According to calculations by

Table 1.5. **Exemptions for co-payments**

	For those whose income is under designated thresholds	For those who have reached an upper limit for out-of-pocket payments
Australia		
Austria	X	X
Belgium	X	X
Canada	X	
Czech Republic	X	X
Denmark		X
Finland		X
France	X	
Germany	X	
Greece	X	
Hungary		
Iceland		X
Ireland	X	X
Italy	X	
Japan		X
Korea	X	X
Luxembourg		X
Mexico		
Netherlands		X
New Zealand	X	X
Norway		X
Poland		
Portugal	X	
Slovak Republic	X	
Spain		
Sweden		X
Switzerland	X	X
United Kingdom	X	X

Source: OECD, *Value For Money In Health Spending*, 2010.

Figure 1.15. **Generic market shares in Europe**
2008 or nearest year

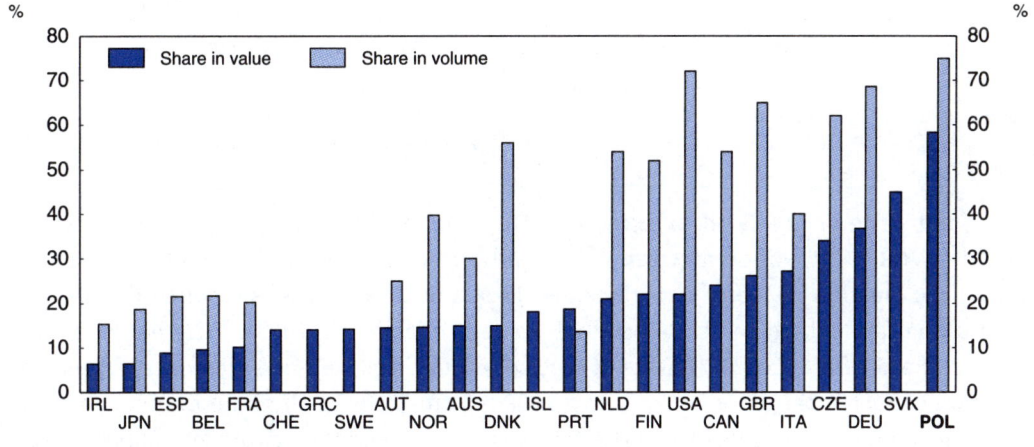

Source: OECD, *Value For Money In Health Spending*, 2010.

StatLink ᴹᴵᴸᴾ http://dx.doi.org/10.1787/888932584547

the Ministry of Health, patient co-payment levels (calculated for reimbursable drugs only) could be reduced from 32% at present to 18%, if patients were always dispensed the cheapest generic drug. With the 2011 *Act on reimbursement of drugs*, pharmacists no longer have any financial incentives to dispense the more expensive drugs, as the mark-ups are equal within the same substance group.

Carefully designing private health insurance

Another way to reduce the importance of out-of-pocket payments would be to extend insurance coverage through the development of PHI, which plays a very limited role. Figure 1.16 shows how heterogeneous the size of PHI markets is across countries. In general, countries with high PHI financing shares tend to have low levels of out-of-pocket expenditures (OECD, 2004). Poland has some pre-paid schemes designed to overcome barriers in access to specialists, but they amounted to only PLN 2 billion in 2010, compared to PLN 99 billion for total health-care expenditures, PLN 60 billion for public health insurance and PLN 22 billion for out-of-pocket payments. For at least a decade these services have been offered to employees by some employers. These pre-paid schemes cover rather low-risk populations: people active in the labour market and their families. The way they allow queues to be jumped is not entirely transparent.

Figure 1.16. **Size of private health insurance markets across OECD countries, 2009[1]**

As a percentage of total expenditure on health

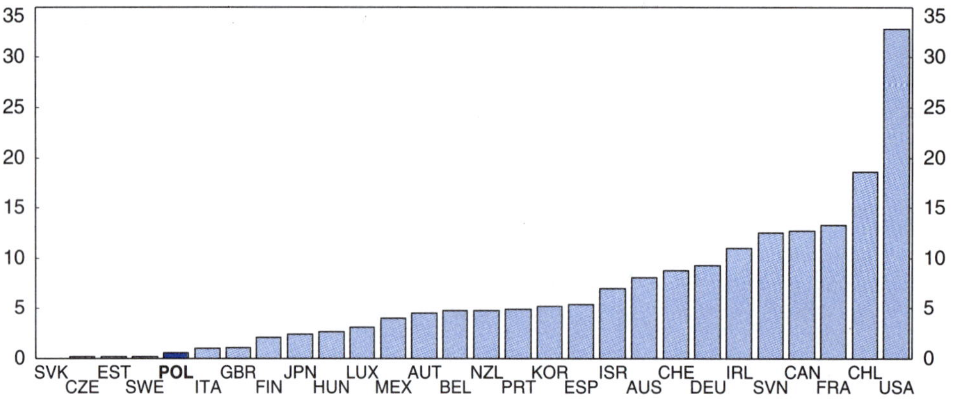

1. 2007 for Austria; 2008 for Australia, Japan and Portugal.
Source: OECD, *OECD Health Data 2011.*

StatLink ᵐˢ⁹ http://dx.doi.org/10.1787/888932584566

The debate on the need to introduce PHI in Poland has been going on for at least a decade. While competition between public and private payers was originally supposed to follow the creation of the regional Sickness Funds in 1999, it was postponed due to their operational difficulties, which led to their re-centralisation in 2003. After that, the main obstacle became the lack of a basket of precisely defined guaranteed medical services. The creation of such a basket resulted from a 2008 reform. The growing importance of private funding and the lack of rules about the cooperation between the private and public sectors led the government to formulate a draft law on the introduction of PHI in 2011, but it never made it through Parliament. The main objective was to provide a legal framework for the operation of an optional duplicative medical insurance (which means that the insured person would pay for both the public and private insurance, possibly covering the same type of services) ostensibly in order to: increase accessibility to medical services; develop an additional source of funding and as a result increase the overall level of health-care financing; develop methods to increase the utilisation of medical resources; and improve the quality of medical services. While new legislation might be inspired by this draft law, legislative work is expected to start basically from scratch.

It may be desirable, in order to improve risk-sharing, to shift part of out-of-pocket payments to PHI contributions, especially for drugs, dental and specialist care. This could be combined by better coverage of dental care and reduced coverage of specialist care by the public insurance package. PHI could also be introduced to attract more resources into the health-care system, provide quicker access and make the system more responsive. However, PHI markets generally raise two main challenges. First, as with public insurance, moral hazard due to imperfect agency relationships and adverse selection could lead to excessive expenditures if the price elasticity of demand is high and/or the incentives facing providers are totally disconnected from insurers' interests. Second, while when supply is constrained it may be efficient to ration services on the basis of willingness to pay through voluntary purchase of private insurance, this generates equity concerns (OECD, 2004). Indeed, insurance is not always affordable, and high-income groups are more likely to purchase it. Moreover, the advantages offered by PHI in terms of access to care create inherent disadvantages for those populations without it.

Overall, PHI would likely contribute to improving health-care performance in Poland, but policy makers need to be aware of its possible downsides. As full private coverage of the share not covered by the public package would encourage over-utilisation, some patient cost sharing should be retained in order to maintain individual cost awareness and contain public spending. The integration of insurance and provision of services may also be desirable to align producer and insurer incentives in the delivery of medical care (Cutler and Zeckhauser, 2000). Moreover, the degree of differential access across income groups varies depending on the specific design of PHI, especially with respect to avoiding cream-skimming, as unregulated PHI markets are poorly equipped to ensure access to coverage for people with chronic conditions and other high-risk individuals (OECD, 2004). Indeed, somewhat paradoxically, addressing the equity challenges induced by PHI might even result in increasing overall public health-care expenditure relative to a purely public system (OECD, 2004).

Health-related fiscal issues are important but manageable

In most OECD countries public spending on health and long-term care is likely to put pressure on government budgets in the future, mainly due to ageing, higher incomes, cost-increasing technological progress and reduced family-provided long-term care (Box 1.2). Indeed, an increase in public expenditure due to rising health needs will probably be difficult to avoid, even though ageing could help to reduce public spending on education and unemployment benefits; the real question – especially given uncertainties about technological progress – is that of its scale.

Like most Eastern European countries, Poland's population will age rapidly. The fertility rate is one of the lowest among the EU27 countries, and the effective old-age dependency ratio – defined as inactive population aged 65 and over as a percentage of employed population aged 15 to 64 – is projected to be the highest in 2060 (Figure 1.17). While for the

> ## Box 1.2. **Determinants of the increase in spending on health and long-term care**
>
> OECD (2006) suggests that the ageing and income effects may not contribute as much as sometimes thought to increased expenditure. Indeed, while an increase in the share of older age groups tends to boost health-care spending because health needs increase with age, longevity gains could translate into "healthy ageing". For long-term care, however, there may be less of an offset: extra longevity is unlikely to reduce dependency, and long-term care costs are concentrated on the very old age groups, whose numbers will increase the most. The reason why income gains on their own might not generate tremendous pressure is related to the size of the aggregate elasticity of health expenditure per capita to GDP per capita. The hypothesis that health care is a "superior" good is generally rejected based on micro-data analysis where health spending is found to be relatively inelastic to individual income (implying that health is a "necessity", even though estimates might be blurred by the extent of insurance coverage). Moreover, evidence that the aggregate elasticity is significantly greater than unity is not very robust (see Oliveira Martins and de la Maisonneuve, 2006, Annex 2B). As a result, long-term financial simulations generally assume an aggregate income elasticity within the range of 1.0-1.2.
>
> Technological progress is thus considered to have been the major driver of health-care expenditure growth in recent decades. The discoveries of new medical techniques and treatments will keep boosting both demand for and supply of health-care services. Despite some possible beneficial impacts in terms of lower prices, at least for specific treatments, technological progress is therefore likely to raise health-care spending, especially given the market failures highlighted in the text.
>
> In addition, in some countries, including Poland, female labour-force participation is likely to rise substantially, reducing the scope for informal care and boosting demand for public provision (OECD, 2006). Current public expenditures on long-term care in Eastern European countries are significantly lower than in their Western European counterparts. This is due (beyond the aggregate income effect) to a lower demand for these services, given the later population ageing in these countries, and to cultural norms implying greater family responsibility for elderly care. As a result, long-term-care institutions are underdeveloped.

EU27 as a whole, that ratio is projected to rise sharply from 37% in 2007 to 72% in 2060, it would surpass 100% in Poland: inactive old people would outnumber the employed population (European Commission, 2009). Overall, OECD (2006) and European Commission (2009) estimate that changes in demography alone will boost public health-care spending in Poland by 0.9% of GDP between 2005 and 2050 and by 1.3% between 2007 and 2060, respectively. The impact of demography on long-term care spending is estimated at 1.9 and 0.7% of GDP, respectively. As for the impact of income gains, an average annual increase of 1.5% in GDP per capita over 40 years would result in a rise in health-care spending of only 0.4% (0.9%) of GDP based on an income elasticity of 1.1 (1.2).

Table 1.6 summarises the projected increase in health- and long-term-care spending when all factors are taken into account based on OECD (2006) and European Commission (2009). The two estimates are significantly correlated across countries for health care but not for long-term care. According to OECD (2006), the total change in public spending will amount to 3.6% of GDP for Poland over 45 years (2.3% for health care and 1.3% for long-term care). This increase compares with a minimum of 1.5% estimated for Sweden and a

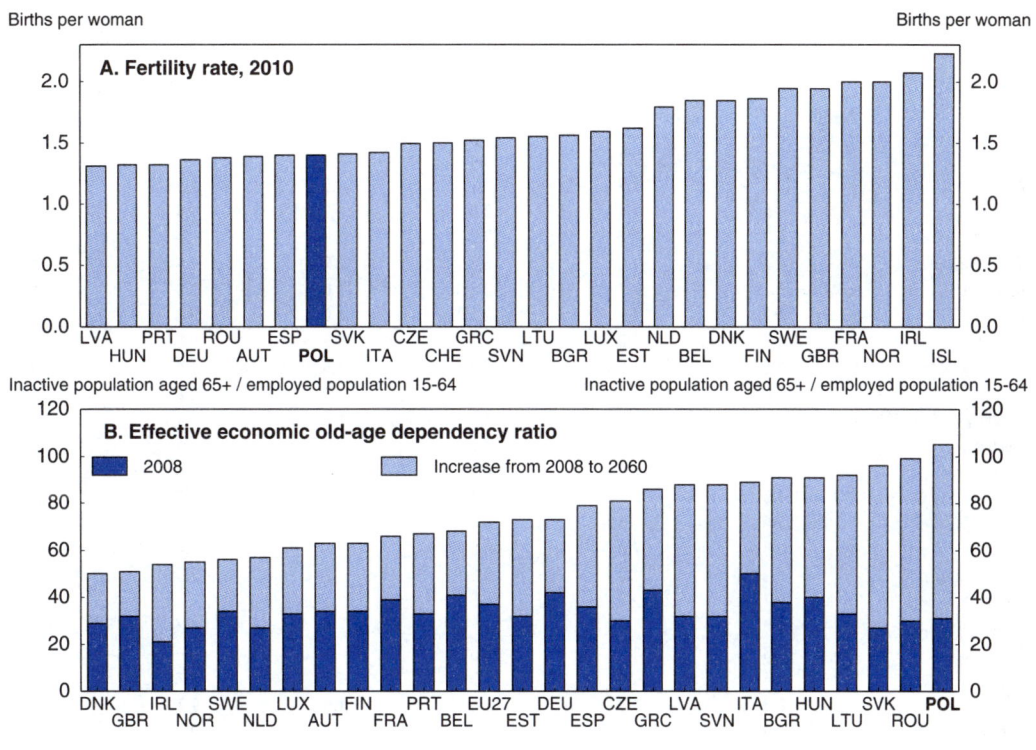

Figure 1.17. **Poland's population will age rapidly**

Source: Eurostat, EUROPOP 2010 Database.

StatLink ⟶ http://dx.doi.org/10.1787/888932584585

maximum of 5.8% for Korea, and is close to the OECD average of 3.4%. According to European Commission (2009), the estimated impact is smaller: public spending would increase by 1.7% of GDP for Poland over 2007-60 (1.0% due to health care and 0.7% to long-term care). This is lower than the total impact for EU15 countries (2.6% of GDP) and for the 10 "New EU Member States" (2.0%).[7]

The general implication of these projections is that for all countries, including Poland, there will be increasing pressure to conduct sound fiscal policies and improve the efficiency of the health-care system. In Poland's case, those challenges seem to be manageable, given the tight grip on the supply of health services and the currently low level of and controlled growth in health-related public spending relative to other OECD countries. Public health spending is also low relative to total general government outlays (Figure 1.18), which suggests that public finance consolidation efforts should, as needed, be directed towards other expenditure items. Moreover, realising available efficiency gains in the health-care sector, which are estimated by the OECD at about 1.5% of GDP for public spending in Poland (OECD, 2010c), would help the government to face these ageing challenges.

Nevertheless, there is no room for complacency, as other scenarios with stronger latent cost pressures are possible. Options to raise revenues may include an increase in the health-insurance contribution rate, the use of other tax bases that are less detrimental to growth, further development of co-payments and broadening of the health social contribution base (for example, by indexing farmers' health-insurance premiums more directly on their incomes). Golinowska *et al.* (2007) report that the central government paid PLN 1.6 billion, or about 30% of the total central-government health-care expenditure, to

Table 1.6. **Projected increases in public health and long-term care spending by main source, 2005-50**

Percentage points of GDP

	OECD (2005-50)			European Commission (2007-60)		
	Health care	Long-term care	Total	Health care	Long-term care	Total
Australia	2.3	1.1	3.4			
Austria	2.0	1.2	3.1	1.5	1.2	2.7
Belgium	1.5	1.1	2.6	1.2	1.4	2.6
Canada	2.2	1.3	3.5	–	–	–
Czech Republic	2.3	1.0	3.3	2.2	0.4	2.6
Denmark	1.7	0.7	2.4	1.0	1.5	2.5
Finland	1.8	1.3	3.1	1.0	2.6	3.6
France	1.7	1.0	2.7	1.2	0.8	2.0
Germany	1.8	1.2	3.0	1.8	1.4	3.2
Greece	2.0	1.8	3.9	1.4	2.2	3.6
Hungary	1.8	0.7	2.5	1.3	0.4	1.7
Iceland	2.1	0.6	2.7	–	–	–
Ireland	2.2	2.4	4.6	1.8	1.3	3.1
Italy	1.9	2.2	4.1	1.1	1.3	2.4
Japan	2.5	1.5	4.0	–	–	–
Korea	3.0	2.8	5.8	–	–	–
Luxembourg	1.9	1.9	3.8	1.2	2.0	3.2
Mexico	2.7	2.9	5.6	–	–	–
Netherlands	2.0	1.2	3.2	1.0	4.7	5.7
New Zealand	2.3	1.2	3.5	–	–	–
Norway	1.6	0.9	2.5	1.3	2.7	4.0
Poland	**2.3**	**1.3**	**3.6**	**1.0**	**0.7**	**1.7**
Portugal	2.4	1.1	3.5	1.9	0.1	2.0
Slovak Republic	2.8	1.2	4.0	2.3	0.4	2.7
Spain	2.3	1.7	4.0	1.6	0.9	2.5
Sweden	1.4	0.1	1.5	0.8	2.3	3.1
Switzerland	1.6	0.7	2.3	–	–	–
Turkey	2.3	0.7	2.9	–	–	–
United Kingdom	1.7	1.1	2.8	1.9	0.5	2.4
United States	1.6	0.9	2.5	–	–	–
OECD average[1]	**2.1**	**1.3**	**3.4**	–	–	–

1. Unweighted average.
Source: OECD (2006); European Commission (2009).

Figure 1.18. **Public expenditure on health care across OECD countries, 2009**[1]

As a percentage of general government expenditure

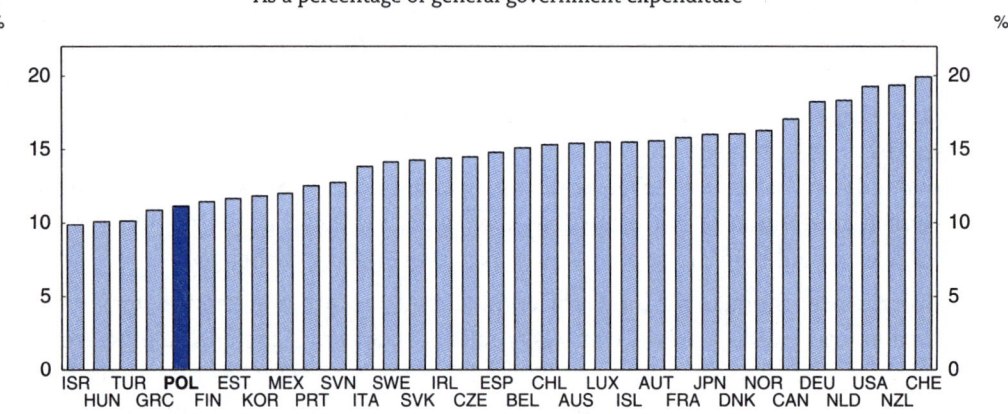

1. 2007 for Greece; 2008 for Australia, Japan, Portugal and Turkey.
Source: OECD, *OECD Health Data 2011.*

StatLink 🔗 http://dx.doi.org/10.1787/888932584604

insure farmers in 2005. This compares with health contributions of PLN 1.1 billion paid from KRUS to NFZ that same year (giving a total of PLN 2.7 billion to insure farmers). In early 2012, the government passed a (transition) law linking farmers' premia to the size of land holdings, but with a low premium (1 zloty per hectare per family member) and only for farmers holding more than 6 hectares, thereby covering only about half of farmers; the measure is supposed to yield only PLN 113 million in 2012. After 2012, the government intends to link farmers' premia to their incomes.

Improving hospital efficiency

In-patient care represented 31% of total health expenditure in 2009 compared with 27% in 2004 (Figure 1.9 above). While the total number of hospitals has been broadly stable over the last decade, the share of private hospitals has risen steadily from 5% in 2000 to 30% in 2009 (Table 1.7). Increased efficiency might be seen from the greater number of hospitalised people and the decrease in the average length of stay (up to a certain limit, the use of hospital beds tends to be more efficient when the number of days per capita spent in the hospital is low), which has been halved over the last 20 years, and Poland now has a shorter average length of stay than the OECD average. At the same time, the occupancy rate has diminished: there remains some overcapacity, as the number of beds per 100 000 inhabitants (441 in 2008) is well above the EU average (383), although it has decreased sharply since 1990 (632). Also, as mentioned above, the data point to excessive use of hospital care, probably resulting in serious inefficiencies and calling for rationalising the resources allocated to hospital care, especially using integrated delivery models.

Table 1.7. **Hospital resources**

	Public/Non-public	2000	2004	2009
Number of hospitals	Public	714	643	526
	Non-public	38	147	228
	Total	752	790	754
Number of beds	Public	189 707	175 631	165 012[1]
	Non-public	1 583	7 649	18 028[1]
	Total	191 290	183 280	183 040[1]
Beds per 10 000 population	Total	49.5	48.0	48.0[1]
Occupancy rate (in per cent)	Total	76.1	71.8	69.7[1]
Average stay (in days)	Total	8.5	6.9	5.8[1]
Hospitalised persons per year	Public	6 207 379	6 705 060	7 249 283
	Non-public	70 686	295 923	781 669
	Total	6 278 065	7 000 983	8 030 952

1. Compared to previous years, figures for 2009 differ slightly in their underlying definition due to a change in the methodology of counting beds in general hospitals. Beds and incubators for newborns are now included.
Source: CSIOZ (Centre for Health Information Systems).

Providing clear incentives to rationalise hospitals' use of financial resources

The financial liabilities of medical providers are one of the most persistent problems in the Polish health-care system. This is due to inefficient supply limitations combined with weak incentives facing hospitals to respect their financial commitments, management deficiencies and an unclear division of responsibilities among the different stakeholders. Tight financial constraints by the payer (NFZ) and owners (local governments, central government and universities) limit the supply of services causing excess demand. However, health-care units are given confusing incentives to manage their budgets efficiently, which generates moral hazard and indebtedness. Indeed, the central government has repeatedly had to take over the liabilities of medical providers (in 1994-95, 1997 and 1998). With the 1999 reform, the liabilities of health-care units were consolidated, and providers restarted with clear accounts. However, this did not stop the process of accumulating further debts, which may act as a safety valve, given budget constraints, such that another government intervention was needed in 2005. As a result, the overall level of public medical providers' net liabilities decreased before stabilising at about PLN 2.5 billion.

In practice, the NFZ has tended to reimburse service providers for excess provision of services. This in turn has created perverse incentives, as they have taken for granted that overproduction will be reimbursed, while debt forgiveness has not rewarded solvent and well managed institutions, potentially generating a misallocation of resources. Moreover, local governments, which are the main level of administration responsible for hospital care, are generally reluctant to close down inefficient and indebted units. Ultimately, it is difficult to gauge whether such a cost-containment policy is effective in setting the appropriate priorities to produce the most useful services.

Corporatisation might generate efficiency gains

The recent global economic crisis has heightened financial pressure on the public health-care system. Given the persistent problem of hospital indebtedness the legislation adopted in 2011 (*Law on Therapeutic Activity*) aims at improving hospitals' cost efficiency and limiting their liabilities through a change in operational framework and in ownership status via corporatisation (or "commercialisation" in Polish parlance). In contrast to privatisation, corporatisation refers to the transformation of the public entity into a state-owned company in order to introduce corporate management techniques. In such a case, the owner, typically a local government, remains the same, but its activity becomes regulated by the code of commercial companies. Any negative financial result that the public medical facility accumulates by the end of each year should be paid off by the owner in the following year; otherwise the medical facility would be closed or transformed. In order to encourage corporatisation, the government agreed to assume part of the debts of those hospitals willing to go through that process until the end of 2013.

Transformation had already been encouraged in 2009. The Ministry of Health gave hospital authorities an opportunity to transform indebted tertiary-care facilities from publicly owned institutions managed by local governments into companies owned by such governments with the further option to also involve a private investor. In the 2009-11 period, this form of transformation of public health-care units was supported by public resources from the general budget. Moreover, following a process implemented by local governments, 23 local governments had decided to privatise their hospitals by April 2010. Overall, around 117 or 16% of public hospitals have been transformed into commercial companies and seem to be in good financial condition, while providing high-quality health-care services. However, this is also likely to reflect a selection bias: only hospitals that viewed transformation as profitable seized the opportunity. Yet, corporatisation might lead to more effective management and improve quality. In any case, while some hospitals might need to be closed, the 2011 reform should be implemented across regions in such a way that it does not threaten equal access to care. From that standpoint, health-care capacity across the nation, which is in large part inherited from infrastructures developed long ago, might not correctly reflect current health needs. Hence, a broad assessment of the quality of this match is called for.

Improving managerial competencies and coordination

The separation of responsibilities and insufficient cooperation between the NFZ and health-care unit owners has important consequences. Ageing hospital infrastructure has become a serious systemic weakness, and the majority of public hospitals will soon require huge capital expenditures. For example, the average age of buildings used by university hospitals and institutes is 48 years, and only 12% of university hospitals are located in buildings constructed after 1990 (Golinowska *et al.*, 2007). Financing investments is especially thorny, as regional and local governments do not seem to have the resources to invest in medical facilities, and the NFZ has no mandate to do so. As a consequence, as hospitals buy equipment and renovate their wards, they continually fall into debt (Golinowska *et al.*, 2007). Moreover, there is no thorough planning of those investments that correspond to the most pressing needs of the population globally; on the contrary, renovations and investments seem to be conducted in a somewhat random manner. This calls for the adoption of clear responsibilities for financing investments that would better take into account the bigger picture.

The degree of consistency, a measure of the extent to which responsibilities are clearly defined and allocated consistently and with a minimal degree of overlap, is relatively weak in Poland (Figure 1.19). It declines when several levels of government are involved in key health-care decisions, as is the case, for example, for financing new hospital building and high-cost equipment in several countries, including Poland (OECD, 2010a). Golinowska *et al.* (2007) and Zukowski (2010) highlight the imprecise division of financing responsibilities, differences in financial capacity between entities (NFZ and governments), unstable regulations and the lack of coordination among institutions responsible for health care, especially concerning capital decisions. According to Zukowski, the NFZ should play such a co-ordinating role, including planning of long-term needs, prevention, and financial and quality supervision.

Figure 1.19. Consistency in responsibility assignment across levels of government, 2008-09[1]

Indicator scale of 0-6

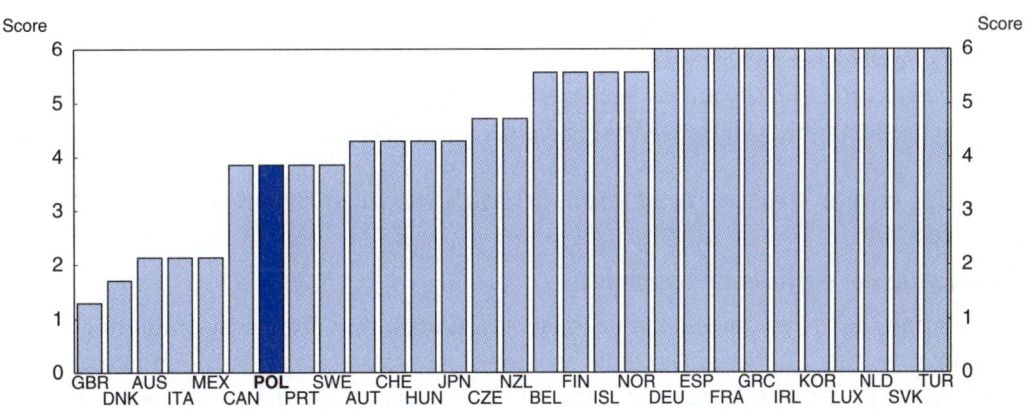

1. The lower the score, the lower the consistency in responsibility assignment across government levels.
Source: OECD (2010a), *Health Care Systems*, p. 112.

StatLink ⟪⟫ http://dx.doi.org/10.1787/888932584623

Moreover, the so-called "ward-head" system is often viewed as a barrier to rational restructuring efforts. It implies substantial power of physicians, heads of clinics and wards in the management of service provision. Complaints that their choices routinely neglect economic-efficiency criteria have been common (Golinowska *et al.*, 2007). Also, the capacity of universities as hospital owners to perform oversight of management functions is, in fact, limited. University rectors who supervise directors and have an impact on their decisions are typically active researchers and scientists, with few managerial qualifications for solving financial issues or developing strategies to rationalise hospital activity. It follows that hospital-management skills should be recognised and encouraged as such, including by linking remuneration to performance.

A study conducted by the European Commission (Green Book II, 2009) showed that big hospitals, among which are those run by universities, have greater problems paying off their liabilities. Indeed, the share of university hospitals in total unpaid liabilities, at about 25%, has more than doubled since 2004. The increasing level of indebtedness of hospitals owned by medical academies is related to their dealing with more severe cases, where expensive specialised treatment is needed, but also to the managerial difficulties induced by the traditionally high level of independence of the different clinical departments within these hospitals. This independence means diminished control, including in financial matters, presumably due to their high prestige. If medical universities take the most severe cases, adjusting the DRGs to better account for the severity of cases can be a way to compensate them.

Evaluating the DRG system to ensure a more effective implementation

The DRG system introduced in 2008 relies on a concept of payment according to defined procedures, the number of which exceeds 1 000 (Paris *et al.*, 2010). It was introduced in rehabilitation as well, and attempts have also been made to extend it to ambulatory care, but without success (even though the list of DRGs and other requirements have been settled). Overall, the DRG system effectively promotes transparency, as costs are identified and can be monitored for each DRG at hospital, regional and national levels. On the other hand, services may be classified up to a more profitable DRG, even if it is not medically justified. Efforts are underway to harmonise the method of calculating the costs of health-care services in order to enable their full comparability and increase the possibilities of evaluating the activities of individual service providers. As it is three years since its implementation, an evaluation would now be appropriate to assess the efficiency of the system and identify any weaknesses that need to be corrected. This is important as DRGs, if used properly, can be used to consolidate excess capacities in acute inpatient care.

Improving the career prospects of medical staff and reforming generalists' remuneration

Careers are not sufficiently attractive

Restraining the volume and price of labour inputs is one direct way of limiting health spending. Setting quotas for medical students (*numerus clausus*) is the most common method of controlling the overall number of doctors over time; these constraints exist in Poland as in all but three OECD countries (OECD, 2010c). Clearly, the number of practising nurses and physicians relative to the population is substantially lower in Poland than the OECD average and even than in other CEEC OECD Members (Figure 1.20). Addressing these potential shortages might generate some trade-off between the supply and the quality of labour inputs. Whereas initially the education requirements of medical professionals were extended as nurses became obliged to complete higher education and doctors to pass the national medical exam (LEP), shortages in personnel have recently stimulated some

Figure 1.20. **Health professionals are lacking**

Per 1 000 population, 2009 or closest year

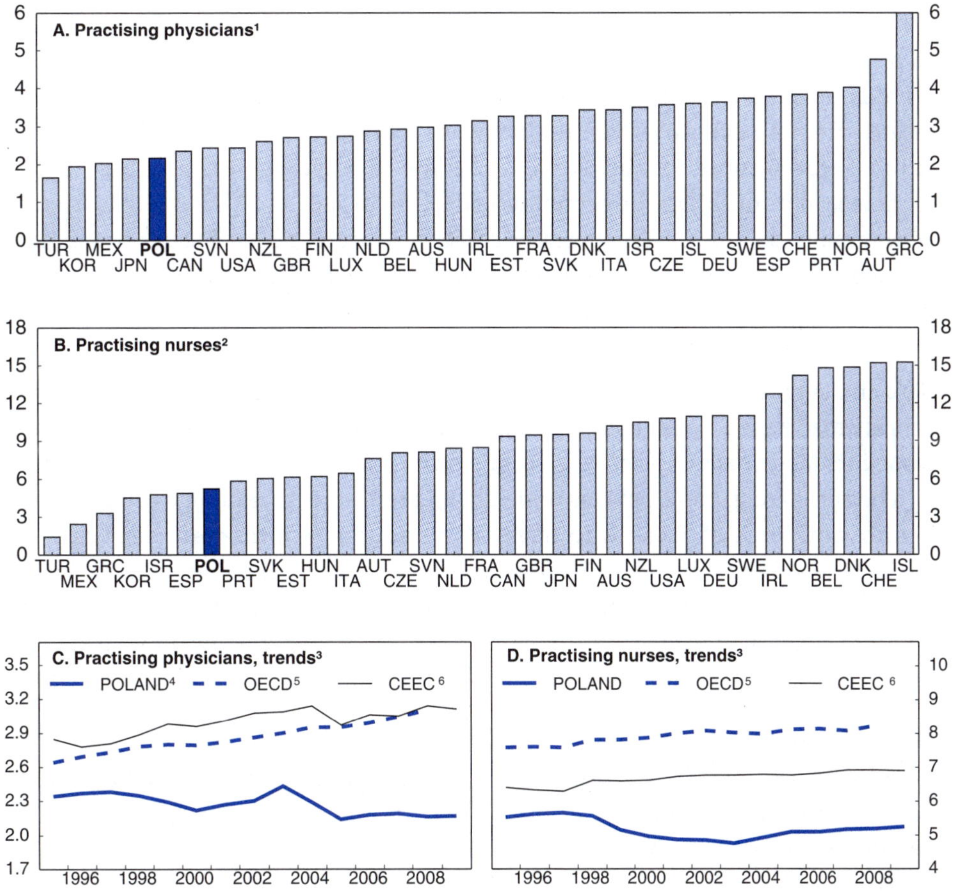

1. Professionally active physicians for Canada, France, Ireland, Mexico, Netherlands, Slovak Republic, Sweden and Turkey. Physicians licensed to practice for Portugal.
2. Professionally active nurses for France, Greece, Portugal, Slovak Republic, Sweden and Turkey. Nurses licensed to practice for Belgium and Italy.
3. For missing values in the series practising physicians and nurses the series professionally active physicians and nurses has been used.
4. Break in series in 2003.
5. Unweighted averages, computed on 26 and 16 OECD countries for practising physicians and practising nurses, respectively.
6. Excluding Poland, unweighted averages computed on the Czech Republic, Estonia, Hungary, the Slovak Republic and Slovenia.

Source: OECD, *OECD Health Data 2011.*

StatLink ᵃˢᵖ *http://dx.doi.org/10.1787/888932584642*

changes in medical education through legislation, approved in March 2011, which shortens the period of medical studies and training.

Insufficient staff might also result from insufficient incentives to attract students. While medical professions enjoyed high prestige in the past, higher wages and a less stressful work environment are now available in other sectors. Moreover, richer OECD countries have tended to attract foreign doctors and nurses, while less developed countries have more severe problems with satisfying their need for health professionals (OECD, 2008b). The scale of the brain drain after Poland's accession to the EU in 2004 was not massive. However, the outflow of the highly skilled may have serious consequences locally and in some sectors. The monitoring of migration of medical professionals is based on the registers of certificates confirming qualifications issued by the National Chamber of Physicians for the purpose of taking up employment abroad. Cumulatively 8 200 doctors, 13 500 nurses and 850 dentists had received such certificates by 2011. In addition, other nurses took up employment abroad in the social or long-term care sectors, where similar certificates are not necessary. Even though wage increases in the health-care sector have started to outpace those for the overall economy (the average wage in the health-care sector increased from 78% of the economy-wide level in 2004 to 93% in 2008), current levels probably remain too low to offer attractive career prospects. Young doctors still undergoing professional medical training were the main beneficiaries of that increase, the goal of the up-rating having been to limit their emigration. On the other hand, the increase in the remuneration of nurses did not substantially improve their relative position.

The challenge in responding to the demand for health-sector workers over the next 20 years is broad based across countries (OECD, 2008b). Policy recommendations to address this issue include a mix of measures: training more staff; improving retention, particularly through better management policies and delaying retirement; enhancing re-integration in the health workforce of those who have left it; adopting a more efficient skill mix by enhancing the role of advanced practice nurses and physicians' assistants; improving productivity, in particular by linking pay to performance; and developing targeted immigration policies. In most cases, these solutions are costly, thereby making the problem closely related to the overall constraint on the level of funding of the health-care system.

Improving the gate-keeping function

Another weakness of the system is that the gate-keeping role played by generalists seems to be ineffective. Indeed, the number of generalists per specialist is low, a characteristic shared by other CEECs (Figure 1.21). Although the cost effectiveness of generalist-provided primary care is broadly recognised, specialists greatly outnumber generalists in these countries. It is therefore essential to strengthen primary-care services

Figure 1.21. **Ratio of general practitioners to specialists**[1]
2009 or closest year

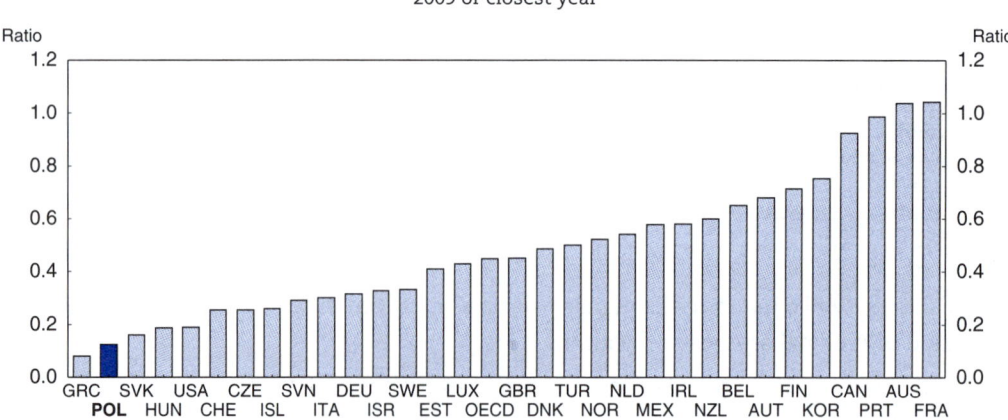

1. Doctors are classified in either of three categories: General Practitioners (GPs), Specialists and Other Physicians. For Poland, most of the "Other physicians" might actually be GPs. If these two categories are merged into "GPs" then the ratio of GPs to specialists increases from 0.12 to 0.30 for Poland. Specialists include paediatricians, obstetricians/gynaecologists, psychiatrists, medical specialists and surgical specialists.

Source: OECD, OECD Health Data 2011.

StatLink http://dx.doi.org/10.1787/888932584661

through a strong enforcement of the gatekeeping role of primary-care doctors, which might require more training efforts.

One important factor that contributes to health-sector inefficiency is the incentive structure created by provider-payment mechanisms. In primary care, capitation alone is applied, whereby payments per patient are fixed regardless of the quality of services provided, and rates have been set at low levels. Under these circumstances, primary-care physicians tend to refer even minimally justified cases to more expensive outpatient specialist services or to hospitals (Golinowska *et al.*, 2007). Thus, instead of the treatment being concentrated at the least expensive level, the costs are being pushed into more expensive segments. Moreover, no referral is required to access a long list of specialists.[8] OECD (2010a) recommends that, in countries relying solely on capitation (Ireland, Poland and the Slovak Republic), reforming provider-payment schemes should be investigated in both the in-patient and out-patient sectors with a view to introducing an activity-based component into physicians' remuneration. This would lead to a mixed payment system, which is becoming the norm for OECD countries.

Designing a comprehensive long-term care system

Long-term care (LTC) helps those needing support in many facets of living over a prolonged period of time (OECD, 2011b). It includes both health-care and other services and is often provided by family members, friends and low-skill caregivers or nurses. Expenditure on formal health-related LTC represents 0.4% of GDP in Poland and is fully publicly funded. This level, although potentially underreported, is relatively low within the OECD but similar to other less affluent Member countries (Figure 1.22). In 2008, approximately 0.9% of the over-65 Polish population received long-term care in an institutional setting, well below the OECD average of 4.2% (OECD, 2011b), reflecting a lack of supply.

Figure 1.22. **Public expenditure on long-term care, 2009 or nearest year**

As a percentage of GDP

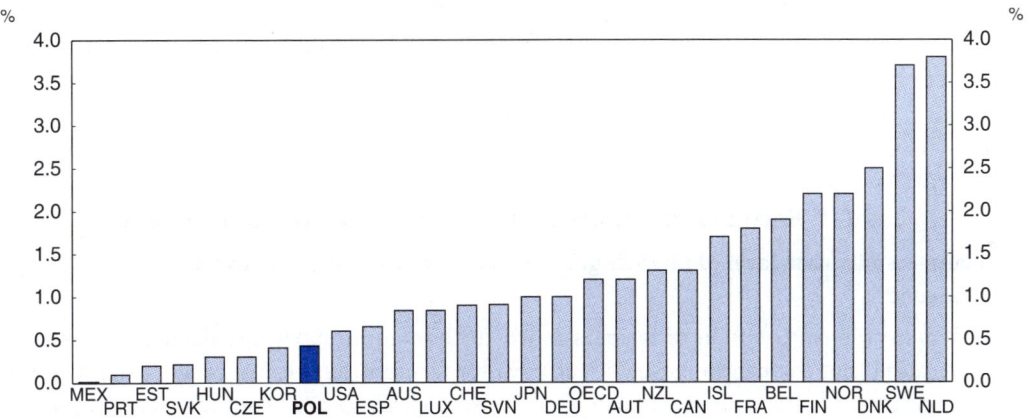

Source: OECD, *OECD Health Data 2011.*

StatLink ᵫˢ┛ http://dx.doi.org/10.1787/888932584680

Formal residential LTC services are provided either by local governments in residential-care homes within the social-assistance scheme or by "local nurses" (*pielegniarka srodowiskowa*) in care and nursing homes within the health sector. In the social-assistance sector, the provision of home services is tightly constrained by stringent, income-based eligibility criteria[9] and the financial capacities of local governments, while in the health sector residential LTC is provided to individuals who have a high level of health limitations as measured by the Barthel index.[10] The health-care sector represents about 20% of all LTC beds, thanks to a more than doubling of LTC beds within that sector over the past decade, while residential social-welfare homes provide about 80% (Golinowska, 2009). In the latter facilities, medical or rehabilitation services are not provided except for nursing, although the elderly living in these facilities often face similar health problems as those living in the facilities managed by health-care authorities. However, due in part to culturally strong family ties, the main responsibility for providing care has traditionally fallen on the family, which is estimated to supply approximately 80% of the care to the fragile elderly (Golinowska, 2009). The provision of care is typically the obligation of spouses and children (mainly daughters), inducing a high level of co-residence and contributing to keeping women out of the labour market (Golinowska and Sowa, 2010).

The LTC system is highly fragmented and lacks a comprehensive policy, which would help to satisfy growing needs. Given the projected rapid ageing of the Polish population and without policy changes in the provision of LTC, a growing gap may occur between the number of elderly who are in need of care and the actual supply of formal care services (European Commission, 2009). The increasing participation of women in the labour market may constrain the supply of informal-care provision even further.

The family's role could be supported by the development of home-based social services targeted at people in need of LTC; it could include benefits in cash and in kind targeted on people with a high level of dependency. A similar policy was introduced in the Czech Republic in 2006. Additionally, the access to institutional care and the quality of offered treatment should be improved. Specifically, this requires better adjusting the number of available beds and services to the demand for care, but also monitoring standards of institutional care. So far no national standards for monitoring the quality of institutional care have been introduced, even though they have been defined by appropriate legislation. More generally, the creation of a comprehensive LTC system should aim to: integrate activities of the social-assistance and health-care systems; make eligibility for the social services offered to the elderly dependent on the level of their limitations; and introduce alternative methods of funding through co-payments for home-based social services or some form of long-term care insurance, such as has been introduced in a number of other OECD countries.

Box 1.3. **Recommendations to improve the health-care system**

Secure an adequate level of financing, better allocate resources and expand them as needed

- Increase the contribution of farmers much further, and remove the health insurance premium that the central government pays for farmers' health insurance. Extend the social insurance contribution base to uncovered earnings. To avoid discouraging the labour force participation of second earners, remove the free co-insurance of spouses.

- Improve spending efficiency by: reallocating resources from hospitals to primary and long-term care, potentially by integrated health-care delivery models; strengthening the gate-keeping role played by generalists; promoting primary medicine; and boosting training efforts to avoid unnecessary specialist consultations. Introduce an activity-based element into generalists' remuneration through a hybrid system of capitation and fee-for-service payments.

Box 1.3. **Recommendations to improve the health-care system** (cont.)

- Avoid labour shortages in the health-care sector by: training more staff; improving retention, particularly through better management policies and delaying retirement; enhancing re-integration in the health workforce of those who have left it; adopting a more efficient skill mix by enhancing the role of advanced practice nurses and physicians' assistants; improving productivity, in particular by linking pay to performance; and developing targeted immigration policies.

- To expand financial resources and make the system more responsive, carefully design a system of complementary and supplementary private insurance (i.e. covering cost-sharing and items not included in the basic public package, respectively) in a way that does not exclude low-income households.

Ensure broader access and reduce inequality

- Make some hospital resources conditional on the specific delivery of extra activity that reduces waiting times, including by linking pay to this objective.

- Extend dental services covered by public insurance, introduce co-payments on medical services and limit out-of-pocket expenditures by introducing a ceiling for such payments in terms of annual income.

- Assess the relevance of introducing a separate public financing scheme to cover long-term care risks. Integrate long-term-care-related activities of the social and health-care systems. Make the social services offered to the elderly dependent on their incapacities rather than their incomes, and consider introducing alternative methods of funding through co-payments for home-based social services. Promote the development of physician specialisation in geriatric care.

Improve efficiency and transparency

- At a minimum, promote the transparency of dual employment in the public and private sectors. Define standards and conditions for the use of public resources by private providers, and monitor their application. Consider whether more stringent restrictions are justified, including outright prohibition of dual practices.

- Improve hospital efficiency by providing clear incentives to rationalise the use of financial resources. In particular, enhance incentives by rewarding (punishing) providers who respect (fail to respect) their financial commitments. Assess the efficiency of the DRG system in overcoming potential weaknesses. Regularly adjust the reimbursement rate to the level of the most efficient hospitals while ensuring adequate quality.

- Promote the development of hospital management skills, including through linking remuneration to performance, with a special emphasis on university hospitals by strengthening financial controls. Adjust the DRG system to better account for the severity of cases dealt with by university hospitals so as to compensate them. Implement the planned corporatisation (or "commercialisation") of hospitals carefully in a way that does not threaten equal access to care, especially across regions.

- Improve consistency by streamlining responsibilities between the NFZ and central and local governments and promoting coordination. Carry out a thorough study of those investments that would correspond to the most pressing needs of the population across the country to ensure that ageing hospital infrastructure is modernised. Extend the coordination role of the regional NFZ branches, in particular concerning investment decisions.

- Develop a simple information system to ensure that providers can clearly identify who is covered by public insurance. Enhance computerisation to generate efficiency gains and shorten waiting lists.

Notes

1. This dataset contains detailed information on health policies and institutions governing health insurance and coverage, health-care delivery, and the allocation and management of public health-care spending. It comprises 269 mainly qualitative variables covering 29 OECD countries.

2. Potential years of life lost is a summary measure of premature mortality providing an explicit way of weighting deaths occurring at younger ages (see OECD, 2009).

3. The OECD (2010a) efficiency indicator is based on an envelope analysis using life expectancy as an outcome variable and total health-care expenditure as a control. Other efficiency indicators have been computed by OECD (2010a) and yield broadly similar results.

4. There are several justifications for permanent queues (Hoel and Saether, 2003). The queue could by itself deter the least needy patients from queuing for treatment. Another possibility is that the illness resolves itself while waiting for treatment. A more subtle argument arises from the existence of a private-sector alternative. In that case, the waiting time might be an equilibrating mechanism making the demand for public treatment equal the supply.

5. There are four co-payment levels (30%, 50%, a flat rate of PLN 3.20 per drug package and free of charge) applying to the amount paid within the reimbursement limit. In addition, when the price of a drug exceeds the reimbursement limit, the surcharge over the limit applies and is paid in full by the patient (the so-called "internal reference pricing"). The co-payment level is then based on the treatment duration and the ratio of the standard treatment cost relative to the minimum wage. For example, the flat rate of co-payment applies if the standard treatment duration is over 30 days and its cost exceeds 5% of the minimum wage. Exemptions from co-payments apply to drugs administered in the treatment of cancers, psychotic disorders, mental impairment, developmental disorders and some infectious diseases. Listed drugs are free or with no co-payment up to the reimbursement limit for some population groups (for example soldiers, military invalids and blood and transplant donors).

6. The relatively low price of drugs in Poland implies, however, that spending in volume terms is higher than in value terms compared with other OECD countries.

7. Based on the ILO social budget methodology, Golinowska and Kocot (2010) estimate not only changes in public health expenditures, but also in public health insurance revenues from changes in labour force participation and productivity. Overall, a good part of their estimated increase of 1.3% of GDP in public health-care spending over 2010-50 would be offset by revenue increases, thus raising the government's net borrowing requirement by only about 0.5% of GDP. That the growth in social contributions outpaces GDP gains results from the increase in the labour share in total value added, which is consistent with the European Commission convergence scenario, even though the underlying forces justifying this feature are unclear.

8. This list includes gynaecologists and obstetricians; dentists; dermatologists; oncologists; ophthalmologists; and psychiatrists. Moreover, some groups do not need a referral including: people living with HIV; war and military invalids and veterans; and people addicted to alcohol, narcotics and psychotropic substances.

9. The level of maximum eligible income for the cash benefit in the social assistance system is PLN 477 (about EUR 110) per household and PLN 351 (about EUR 80) per person living in a larger household. These levels were set by the Ministry of Labour and Social Affairs in 2006 and have been stable since then.

10. The Barthel test is a standardised assessment of an individual's level of independence in basic everyday life activities.

Bibliography

Allin, S., K. Davaki and E. Mossialos (2006), "Paying For 'Free' Health Care: The Conundrum Of Informal Payments In Post-Communist Europe", in "Transparency International", *Global Corruption Report 2006 – Special Focus: Corruption And Health*, Pluto Press, London.

Chawla, M., P. Berman and D. Kawiorska (1998), "Financing Health Services In Poland: New Evidence On Private Expenditures", *Health Economics*, Vol. 7.

Cutler, D.M. and R.J. Zeckhauser (2000), "The Anatomy Of Health Insurance", in A.J. Culyer and J.P. Newhouse (eds.), *Handbook Of Health Economics*, Vol. 1, Chapter 11.

Durlauf, S.N., P.A. Johnson and J.R.W. Temple (2005), "Growth Econometrics", in P. Aghion and S.N. Durlauf (eds.), *Handbook Of Economic Growth*, Vol. 1A, Chapter 8.

European Commission (2007), "Health And Long-Term Care In The European Union", *Special Eurobarometer*, No. 283.

European Commission (2009), *Ageing Report*, European Economy.

European Commission (2010), "Joint Report On Health Systems", *Occasional Papers*, No. 74.

Golinowska, S. (2009), "Long-Term Care In Poland Country Report", *mimeo*.

Golinowska, S. (2010), "Opłaty nieformalne w ochronie zdrowia. Perspektywa i doświadczenia polskie", in *Zeszyty Naukowe Ochrony Zdrowia Zdrowie Publiczne i Zarządzanie*, No. 1, Kraków.

Golinowska, S. and E. Kocot (2010), "Żeby zdrowia nie było zbyt drogie", *Obserwator Finansowy*.

Golinowska, S. and A. Sowa (2006), "Health And Morbidity In The Accession Countries. Country Report – Poland", *ENEPRI Research Report*, No. 29, AHEAD project WP2, CEPS, Brussels, December.

Golinowska, S. and A. Sowa (2010), "Development Of The Long-Term Care In Post-Socialist Countries, International Conference Of Evidence Based Policy In Long-Term Care", London School of Economics, 8-11 September, London.

Golinowska, S., C. Sowada and M. Wozniak (2007), "Sources Of Inefficiency And Financial Deficits In Poland's Health Care System", *Report commissioned by the World Health Organization Regional Office for Europe*.

Gravelle, H. and L. Siciliani (2008), "Optimal Quality, Waits And Changes In Health Insurance", *Journal Of Health Economics*, Vol. 27.

Green Book (2009), Commission on the preparation of the report: *Health Care Funding In Poland* – the Green Book, S. Golinowska (ed.), Vesalius, Kraków.

Green Book II (2009), Commission on the preparation of the report: *Health Care Funding In Poland* – the Green Book II, S. Golinowska (ed.), Vesalius, Kraków.

Grimm, M. (2011), "Does Inequality In Health Impede Economic Growth?", *Oxford Economic Papers*, Vol. 63.

Hoel, M. and E.M. Saether (2003), "Public Health Care With Waiting Time: The Role Of Supplementary Private Health Care", *Journal Of Health Economics*, Vol. 22.

Hurley, J. (2000), "An Overview Of The Normative Economics Of The Health Sector", in A.J. Culyer and J.P. Newhouse (eds.), *Handbook Of Health Economics*, Vol. 1, Chapter 2.

Joumard, I., C. André and C. Nicq (2010), "Health Care Systems: Efficiency And Institutions", *OECD Economics Department Working Papers*, No. 769.

Luczak, J. (2010), "Financial Burden Of Drug Expenditures In Poland", *Erasmus University Rotterdam*, School of Economics thesis, June.

Marchand, M. and F. Schroyen (2005), "Can A Mixed Health Care System Be Desirable On Equity Grounds", *Scandinavian Journal Of Economics*, No. 107, Vol. 1.

OECD (2000), *OECD Economic Surveys: Poland*, OECD Publishing, Paris.

OECD (2004), *Private Health Insurance In OECD Countries*, OECD Publishing, Paris.

OECD (2006), "Future Budget Pressures Arising From Spending On Health And Long-Term Care", *Economic Outlook*, No. 79, Chapter III, OECD Publishing, Paris.

OECD (2008a), "Pharmaceutical Pricing Policies In A Global Market", *OECD Health Policy Studies*, OECD Publishing, Paris.

OECD (2008b), "The Looming Crisis In The Health Workforce", *OECD Health Policy Studies*, OECD Publishing, Paris.

OECD (2009), *Health at a Glance*, OECD Publishing, Paris.

OECD (2010a), *Health Care Systems, Efficiency And Policy Settings*, OECD Publishing, Paris.

OECD (2010b), *OECD Economic Surveys: Germany*, OECD Publishing, Paris.

OECD (2010c), "Value For Money In Health Spending", *OECD Health Policy Studies*, OECD Publishing, Paris.

OECD (2011a), *Health at a Glance*, OECD Publishing, Paris.

OECD (2011b), *Help Wanted? Providing And Paying For Long-Term Care*, OECD Publishing, Paris.

Okólski, M. (2004), *Demografia zmiany społecznej*, Wydawnictwo Naukowe "Scholar", Warszawa.

Oliveira Martins, J., and C. de la Maisonneuve (2006), "The Drivers Of Public Expenditure On Health And Long-Term Care: An Integrated Approach", OECD *Economic Studies*, No. 43.

Paris, V., M. Devaux and L. Wei (2010), "Health Systems Institutional Characteristics: A Survey Of 29 OECD Countires", *OECD Health Working* Papers, No. 50.

PPRI (2011), *Pharmaceutical Pricing and Reimbursement Information*, 2011 Report.

Siciliani, L. and J. Hurst (2004), "Explaining Waiting-Time Variations For Elective Surgery Across OECD Countries", *OECD Economic Studies*, No. 38, No. 1.

Siciliani, L. and J. Hurst (2005), "Tackling Excessive Waiting Times For Elective Surgery: A Comparative Analysis Of Policies In 12 OECD Countries", *Health Policy*, Vol. 72.

Sowa, A. (2011), "Who's Left Behind? Social Dimensions Of Health And Medical Services Utilization", *unpublished PhD. Thesis*, Boekenplan, Maastricht.

Weil, D.N. (2011), "Accounting For the Effect Of Health On Economic Growth", *Quarterly Journal Of Economics*, Vol. 122, No. 3.

Wendt, C. (2009), "Mapping European Healthcare Systems: A Comparative Analysis Of Financing, Service Provision And Access To Healthcare", *Journal Of European Social Policy*, Vol. 19, No. 5.

Zato?ski, W.A. and W. Willett (2005), "Changes In Dietary Fat And Declining Coronary Heart Diseases In Poland: A Population-Based Study", *British Medical Journal*, No. 331.

Zukowski, M. (2010), *Pensions, Health And Long-Term Care*, ASISP, Annual National Report 2010.

APPENDIX 1.A1

Health performance[1]

	Life expectancy at birth, total population	Life expectancy at 65, total population	Mortality rate, all causes	Infant mortality rate	Premature mortality	Potential gains in life expectancy at birth[1]	Euro Health Consumer index[2]	Average
Australia	0.6	0.7	0.8	−0.4	0.3	1.5	–	0.6
Austria	−0.1	−0.0	−0.0	−0.2	−0.1	−0.2	0.8	0.0
Belgium	−0.4	−0.2	−0.8	0.1	−0.7	−0.4	−0.2	−0.4
Canada	0.2	0.4	−0.0	−0.9	−0.5	0.3	–	−0.1
Chile	2.1	–	2.2	1.1	2.7	–	–	2.1
Czech Republic	−0.8	−1.2	−1.3	1.1	0.1	−0.3	0.2	−0.3
Denmark	−1.0	−1.3	−1.5	−0.3	−0.6	−1.6	1.5	−0.7
Estonia	−2.1	−1.3	−1.2	0.6	−1.3	–	0.7	−0.8
Finland	−0.4	0.1	−0.1	0.5	−0.6	−1.0	−0.5	−0.3
France	0.7	1.1	0.7	−0.0	−0.2	0.7	1.1	0.6
Germany	0.0	−0.0	−0.2	0.1	0.1	−0.3	1.1	0.1
Greece	0.4	0.1	0.3	0.8	0.4	−1.1	−1.9	−0.2
Hungary	−1.9	−1.6	−2.2	0.5	−1.4	−1.7	0.9	−1.1
Iceland	0.4	−0.2	0.5	0.5	1.1	1.3	0.9	0.6
Ireland	−0.5	−0.7	−0.5	0.1	−0.4	−0.7	−1.2	−0.5
Israel	0.9	0.7	0.6	−0.3	0.7	–	–	0.5
Italy	1.1	0.9	0.8	0.1	0.8	0.6	−0.8	0.5
Japan	1.7	2.0	1.8	0.6	1.1	1.3	–	1.4
Korea	0.4	0.2	0.6	0.1	0.4	1.4	–	0.5
Luxembourg	−0.1	−0.1	−0.1	0.8	0.5	−0.8	−0.5	−0.0
Mexico	0.8	2.3	1.1	−2.3	−0.8	0.9	–	0.3
Netherlands	−0.3	−0.7	−0.1	0.4	0.5	−0.2	2.1	0.3
New Zealand	0.7	0.9	0.4	−0.4	−0.3	0.1	–	0.2
Norway	−0.2	−0.5	0.0	0.3	0.1	0.3	−0.8	−0.1
Poland	**−0.4**	**0.1**	**−1.1**	**0.8**	**−1.0**	**0.5**	**−0.1**	**−0.2**
Portugal	0.9	0.8	0.6	1.1	0.9	0.6	0.0	0.7
Slovak Republic	−1.8	−2.0	−2.2	−0.2	−1.1	−1.6	−1.1	−1.4
Slovenia	−0.4	−0.5	−0.1	1.1	0.4	–	−0.5	−0.0
Spain	1.2	1.3	0.9	0.3	0.8	0.5	−1.3	0.5
Sweden	0.4	−0.1	0.3	0.5	0.7	0.5	0.1	0.4
Switzerland	1.0	1.1	0.7	−0.4	0.5	1.4	0.5	0.7
Turkey	−0.5	−0.7	–	−3.7	–	0.6	–	−1.1
United Kingdom	−0.4	−0.4	0.1	−0.6	−0.2	−0.9	−1.1	−0.5
United States	−1.9	−1.2	−1.2	−1.9	−3.1	−1.9	–	−1.8
Adjusted R[2]	0.6	0.6	0.4	0.5	0.6	−0.1	0.6	–

Note: For life expectancy at birth, Polish performance is 0.4 standard deviation worse than the OECD average, once GDP per capita is controlled for.

1. A regression is first run for each indicator (in log; for mortality variables, minus log is used) with GDP per capita in PPP terms (in log) and a constant on the right hand side. The corresponding indicator is computed as the residual of that regression divided by the standard deviation of the residuals. By construction, the average of each indicator across OECD countries is equal to 0. The "Adjusted R^2" row corresponds to the adjusted R^2 of that regression.

2. Underlying data are *Data Envelopment Analysis* (DEA) efficiency scores for 2007 obtained by using two inputs: health-care spending per capita and a composite indicator of the socio-economic environment and lifestyle factors.

3. The EHCI, published by the Health Consumer Powerhouse, measures and ranks the performance of health-care provision in 33 European countries from a consumer point of view.

Source: OECD calculations based on *OECD Health Data* and OECD (2010), *Health Care Systems: Efficiency and Policy Settings*, OECD Publishing.

Chapter 2

Climate change policies in Poland – minimising abatement costs

Poland is on track to meet its international greenhouse-gas emissions commitments. However, it will need to cut emissions significantly in the future, if the European Commission's proposal on the Low Carbon Roadmap is adopted. Policies should ensure that the country's substantial reduction potential, mainly linked to the energy sector's high emissions intensity, and implying overall abatement costs above the EU-average, is realised in a least-cost fashion by imposing an economy-wide single carbon price. This stands in contrast with current explicit and implicit carbon prices, which vary widely across different sectors of the economy. Crucial to least-cost abatement is also a high responsiveness to the EU-ETS carbon price signal. While Poland has made good progress in complying with EU regulations related to the energy sector, the large share of public ownership and the lack of effective separation between electricity producers and distributors may blur the price signal for investment decisions in generation capacity. The isolation of the Polish electricity market implies a need for more investment in low-emission technologies in Poland to achieve a given emissions-reduction target, whereas a deeper integration with neighbouring electricity markets would spread the burden more efficiently across countries. The cost-efficiency advantage of uniform support to renewables via green certificates should be retained to minimise abatement costs. Government policies aimed at a higher share of nuclear power and natural gas from shale formations need to take fully into account tail risks and the short- and long-term environmental costs of the use of the former and fully consider environmental risks related to extraction of the latter. Energy efficiency policies can help to address market failure but should not be allowed to distort relative carbon prices.

A large GHG-emissions reduction due to economic transformation followed by relative stability

Poland has reduced its greenhouse-gas (GHG) emissions substantially since its economic transformation started in 1990 and is on track to meet its international and European commitments. As elsewhere in Central and Eastern Europe, the economic collapse of the former Soviet bloc resulted in a considerable drop in domestic and foreign demand for the country's very energy- and carbon-intensive products. As a result of the structural shift towards less energy-intensive sectors, the country's overall GHG emissions fell by around 20% between 1988, the Kyoto base year, and 1994. Despite the economic catch-up that has subsequently taken place, a further decrease of more than 10% had occurred by 1999, reflecting mainly investment in more energy-efficient technologies. Since the early 2000s, annual GHG emissions have remained broadly stable, abstracting from cyclical movements. To date, in managing to cut its total GHG emissions by more than 30% between 1988 and 2009, Poland looks set to go well beyond its Kyoto commitment of a 6% reduction between 1988 and the average of 2008-12 (Figure 2.1). It is also on track to meet the EU 2020 target for the sectors not included in the European Union's Emissions Trading System (EU-ETS), primarily the residential, transport and agriculture sectors. The EU-wide goal of cutting emissions by 20% from 1990 levels by 2020 translates into a national target for Poland's non-EU-ETS sectors of a 14% increase by 2020 compared to 2005, whereas emissions actually declined slightly between 2005 and 2009 (Figure 2.2). Given the country's 8% share in total EU27 GHG emissions, Poland's compliance with the 2020 non-ETS target is an important factor of the EU's ability to meet that objective.

Figure 2.1. **Changes in GHG emissions, 1990-2009**

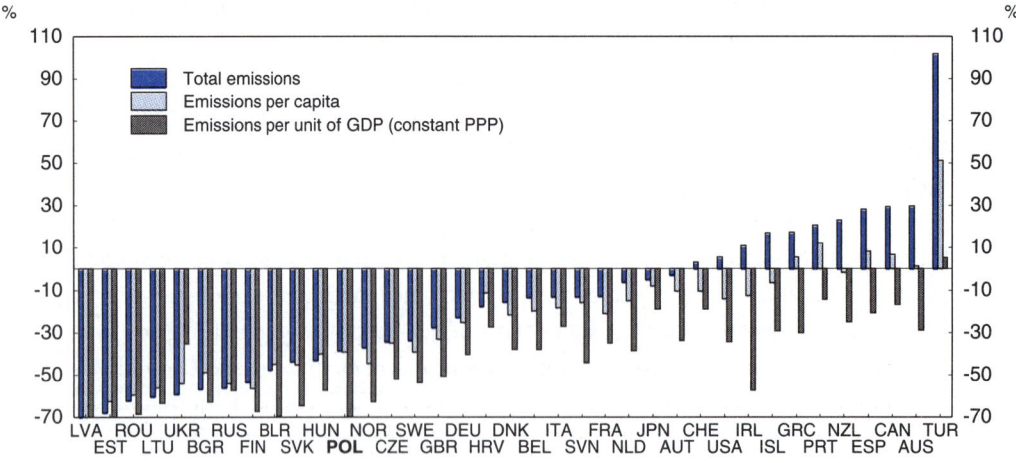

Source: OECD calculations based on data from UNFCCC.

StatLink ⭑⭑⭑ http://dx.doi.org/10.1787/888932584699

Figure 2.2. **Percentage change in non-EU-ETS GHG emissions relative to the 2020 country-specific target**

Outcome minus target, between 2005 and 2009

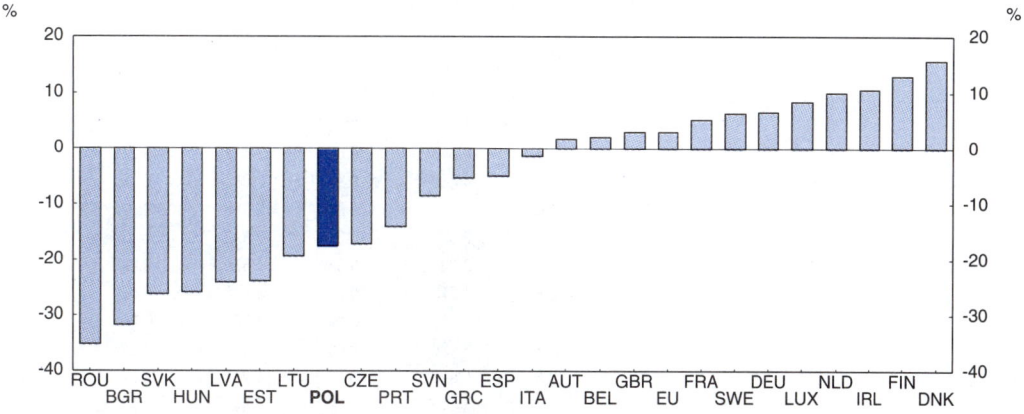

Source: OECD calculations based on data from the European Commission (http://ec.europa.eu/europe2020/pdf/overview_of_member_states_national_targets.pdf).

StatLink 🔗 http://dx.doi.org/10.1787/888932584718

Poland does not have any direct climate-change policy. The country's energy policy strategy, outlined in *Energy Policy Of Poland Until 2030* (Ministry of Economy, 2009), is mostly focused on improving energy security, efficiency and competitiveness, and implies a small reduction in overall GHG emissions by 2020 and then a 4% increase between 2020 and 2030. Poland will have to develop an explicit climate-change policy to contribute more substantially to the overall long-term EU effort. Indeed, the government is in the process of formulating a national plan for reducing GHG emissions, the National Programme for a Low-Emission Economy, which it expects to finalise and adopt in 2013. The European Council, that is EU member countries, decided in early 2011 on a 80-95% GHG emissions reduction objective by 2050 (European Council, 2011). The European Commission's proposal on the *Low Carbon Roadmap 2050* is currently being discussed by EU Member States (European Commission, 2011a). The EU-wide GHG emissions reduction of 80-95% by 2050 would facilitate the worldwide 50% GHG reduction that would help keep global warming below 2 degrees Celsius. Evidently, the EU's ambitious target only makes sense if other large emitters join the world-wide effort, given the global nature of the negative externalities of GHG emissions.

Poland's large emissions-reduction potential should be realised at least cost via a single carbon price

The usual justification for allowing developing countries to cut GHG emissions less than their mature industrialised counterparts is based on equity considerations: they tend to emit less GHGs on a per capita basis and, as real convergence progresses, they should be allowed to move towards the per capita emissions levels of their more affluent counterparts. Within the EU, however, this argument does not seem to hold for Poland, as its per capita emissions are higher than in 11 other EU member countries with higher per capita income. Per capita energy-related emissions can be decomposed into: i) the carbon intensity of energy production; ii) the energy intensity of a unit of GDP; and iii) per capita GDP (Table 2.1):

$$GHG^{EN}/CAP = GHG^{EN}/EN * EN/GDP * GDP/CAP$$

Table 2.1. **Per capita GHG emissions and their decomposition, 2009**

	GHG (tCO$_2$-eq) per capita for specific sectors				Energy sector		Electricity and heat prod (E&H)		GDP
	Total	Non-energy	Energy	E&H	GHG/Energy production	Energy prod/ GDP	GHG/E&H production	E&H prod/ GDP	Per capita GDP (1 000 EUR)
Sweden	6.4	1.7	4.8	0.9	1 545	0.10	509	0.05	32
Hungary	6.7	1.7	5.0	1.5	4 646	0.06	3 412	0.03	17
Slovakia	8.0	2.7	5.3	1.2	4 880	0.06	1 886	0.03	19
Italy	8.2	1.4	6.8	1.6	15 759	0.02	3 395	0.02	27
France	8.3	2.5	5.8	0.7	2 831	0.07	893	0.03	30
United Kingdom	9.2	1.4	7.8	2.5	3 037	0.08	4 579	0.02	32
Japan	9.5	0.9	8.6	2.8	11 776	0.02	3 970	0.02	30
Poland	**9.9**	**1.8**	**8.1**	**4.2**	**4 600**	**0.10**	**7 842**	**0.03**	**17**
Germany	11.2	1.9	9.3	3.8	5 926	0.05	4 957	0.02	32
Germany	11.2	1.9	9.3	3.8	5 926	0.05	4 957	0.02	32
Estonia	12.6	1.8	10.7	7.7	3 412	0.20	6 829	0.07	16
Czech Rep.	12.7	2.2	10.5	5.5	3 487	0.14	5 763	0.04	22
Canada	20.5	3.7	16.8	2.9	1 478	0.33	1 802	0.05	35
United States	21.5	2.8	18.7	7.1	3 405	0.13	5 843	0.03	42

1. The energy production-to-GDP ratio is multiplied by 1 000 to fit in the table. E&H denotes Electricity and Heating. See Appendix 2.A1 for a more extensive country coverage.
Source: OECD calculations based on data obtained from UNFCCC.

Poland's high per capita emissions are due to the predominance of fossil fuel combustion, in particular in electricity and heat production. In 2009, only Finland, Greece, the Czech Republic and Estonia recorded higher per capita emissions in heat production.

It is also interesting to compare Poland with its Central and Eastern European peers with similar GHG emissions levels (the Czech Republic and Estonia) and with lower emissions (Hungary and Latvia) and with one of the more developed countries at the cutting edge (Sweden). Poland's per capita emissions are especially high in the residential sector, three to four times higher than in Estonia and Latvia and nine times higher than in Sweden (Table 2.2). The reason for these differences is a radical shift in Sweden from heating oil to district heating based on biomass, triggered by an increase in energy and CO$_2$ taxes (OECD, 2011a) and the heavy reliance on biomass in Estonia and Latvia. Per capita fugitive emissions from fuels and industrial processes in Poland are also above the levels observed in most other countries. This is mostly related to coal mining and the transportation and handling of oil and natural gas. By contrast, per capita emissions due to the commercial sector and agriculture are comparable in Poland to levels seen elsewhere. Emissions from waste and transportation are particularly low. Offsets from land use, land use change and forestry (LULUCF) are important, one tonne per habitant, even though well below levels recorded in the Baltic countries and Sweden.

Calculations carried out by McKinsey (2009) and the World Bank (2011) show that an emissions reduction of 40% by 2030 compared to the 1990 level can be achieved in Poland. Such a cut would be consistent with the path of the European Commission's *Low Carbon Roadmap 2050* (Figure 2.3). The average unitary abatement cost consistent with a 40% GHG emissions reduction is roughly EUR 10 (in 2005 prices) for each tonne of CO$_2$ avoided and the marginal abatements costs to go beyond a cut of 50% is estimated at about EUR 70 per tonne. Historical CO$_2$ prices of about EUR 10 to 20 in the EU-ETS would need to rise above EUR 70 (in constant prices) if Poland wanted to further cut emissions efficiently in the non-

Table 2.2. **GHG emissions – sectoral indicators, 1990-2009**

	Shares, 2009						Per cent changes, 1990-2009						GHG (tCO$_2$-eq) per capita, 2009					
	POL	HUN	CZE	EST	LAT	SWE	**POL**	HUN	CZE	EST	LAT	SWE	**POL**	HUN	CZE	EST	LAT	SWE
1. Energy eq.	**82**	75	83	86	67	74	**–17**	–28	–30	–60	–62	–16	**8.1**	5.0	10.5	10.7	3.2	4.8
Energy	**44**	24	44	64	18	17	**–27**	–26	2	–62	–70	5	**4.4**	1.6	5.6	8.0	0.8	1.1
Manufacturing	**8**	8	12	4	8	15	**–30**	–62	–66	–73	–76	–29	**0.8**	0.5	1.5	0.5	0.4	0.9
Transport sector	**12**	19	14	13	26	34	**76**	55	140	–13	–7	7	**1.2**	1.3	1.8	1.6	1.2	2.2
Commercial sector	**2**	6	2	0.5	5	1	**–29**	–6	–67	69	–82	–74	**0.2**	0.4	0.3	0.1	0.2	0.1
Residential sector	**9**	13	6	1	6	2	**–2**	–45	–66	–84	–51	–80	**0.9**	0.9	0.7	0.2	0.3	0.1
Agriculture sector	**2**	2	0.2	1	3	3	**37**	–67	–91	–61	–78	10	**0.2**	0.1	0.0	0.2	0.2	0.2
Fugitive emissions from fuels	**3**	3	4	2	1	2	**–27**	–8	–45	–58	–62	186	**0.3**	0.2	0.4	0.3	0.0	0.1
2. Industrial processes	**6**	6	8	3	3	8	**4**	–53	–43	–57	–40	–20	**0.6**	0.4	1.1	0.3	0.2	0.5
3. Solvents	**0.2**	1	0.4	0.1	0.3	0.5	**18**	50	–34	–17	–46	–11	**0.0**	0.0	0.0	0.0	0.0	0.0
4. Agriculture	**9**	12	6	8	21	14	**–29**	–43	–51	–57	–62	–11	**0.9**	0.8	0.8	1.0	1.0	0.9
5. LULUCF	**–10**	–5	–5	–42	–191	–69	**85**	55	89	–32	35	–7	**–1.0**	–0.3	–0.7	–5.2	–9.1	–4.5
6. Waste	**2**	6	3	4	8	3	**–8**	13	31	–16	0	–43	**0.2**	0.4	0.3	0.5	0.4	0.2

Source: OECD calculations based on data obtained from UNFCCC.

ETS sectors. At the same time, according to World Bank (2011) estimates, the overall abatement costs of an emissions reduction of about 40% by 2030 would peak in 2020, when the level of real GDP would be 1.8 to 3.1 percentage points below that of the baseline scenario. But the cost would decrease to about 0.7 percentage point by 2030. Overall abatement costs are found to be about two to three times higher for Poland than for the EU average. The World Bank report also shows that off-shoring GHG emissions reduction outside the EU, based on a very flexible clean development mechanism (CDM), would cut costs by a factor of four both for Poland and the EU as a whole.

Figure 2.3. **Changes in Poland's emissions implied by the European Commission's proposal on the *Low Carbon Roadmap 2050* and by government projections**[1]

Percentage changes compared to 1990

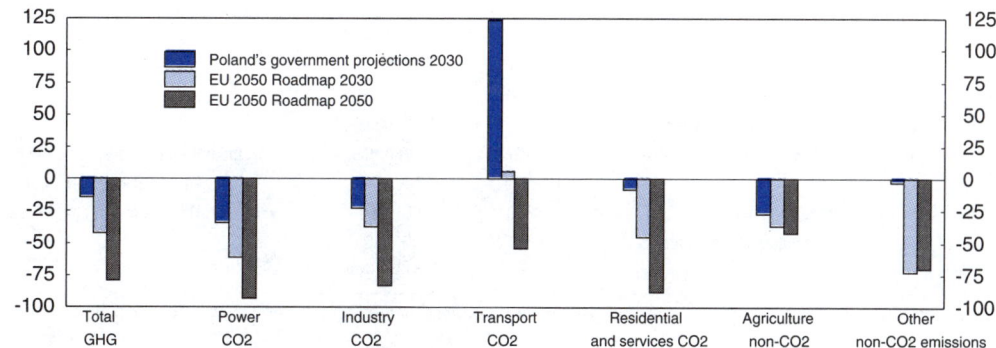

1. Government projections show outcomes based on current and new policies.

Source: Polish Government (2011), "Projections Of Greenhouse Gas Emissions And Removals Up To 2030"; European Commission (2011), *A Roadmap For Moving To A Competitive Low Carbon Economy In 2050*, Brussels, 8.3.2011, COM(2011) 112 final; UNFCCC.

StatLink ᴹᴸᴶᴾ http://dx.doi.org/10.1787/888932584737

Governments can impose a single carbon price to fully internalise the external costs of GHG emissions either by imposing a tax or setting up a permit trading system. Ideally, to minimise the total abatement cost, a single carbon price should be applied across all countries and sectors to reduce GHG emissions where it is the cheapest to do so, especially if marginal abatement costs are different in some countries or sectors (OECD, 2006). If the carbon price were to differ across sectors, the same amount of emissions reduction would be achieved only at a higher cost, because some high-cost abatement measures will substitute for minimum-cost options.

But explicit and implicit carbon prices vary widely in Poland

A carbon price is already imposed in Poland via multiple channels. First, the Polish power and heavy energy-using industries are covered by the EU-ETS. Second, Poland is one of the few countries to have an explicit carbon tax, even though it is only symbolic at EUR 0.065/tonne of CO_2 for industrial sectors outside the EU-ETS (Table 2.3). Finally, a range of excise taxes are levied on fossil energy products. However, natural gas used as a heating fuel, liquefied natural gas (LNG), heavy industrial oil for agricultural use and for electricity and heat generation are not taxed. In 2012, Poland introduced a tax on coal used outside the EU-ETS. Yet it is very limited in both size and coverage, because it applies only to companies' own heat production but not to household heating. The exemption for electricity and heat generation is justified by the inclusion of this sector in the EU-ETS. Table 2.4 shows the carbon prices implied by the excise tax, which vary significantly across different fossil-energy products. For example, the implicit carbon price derived from the excise tax in 2010 amounted to EUR 187 for petrol and to EUR 120 for automotive diesel, but the distortions are even larger between automotive fuel and other fossil energy products. Imposing a single carbon price may eventually increase the price of many fossil fuels. A well targeted direct lump-sum (cash) compensation, financed by a higher effective carbon price, would be needed to offset the adverse effects of higher energy prices on poor households.

Table 2.3. **Countries with a direct carbon tax in 2011**

	Name	Year of introduction/ year of last revision	EUR/tonne CO_2	Coverage
Canada (British Columbia)	Carbon tax	2008/2009	CAD 15 ($\approx$ EUR 11)	Exemptions are: bio-fuels, ethanol and fuel for civil aviation
Denmark	Duty on CO_2	1998/2010	$\approx$ EUR 30	
Finland	CO_2 tax	1990	EUR 10-35	
Finland	Charge on exceeding GHG emission limits	2004	EUR 100 000	
Poland	**Tax on air pollutants, tax base for CO_2**	**1990/2001**	**EUR 0.065**	**Industries not covered by the EU-ETS**
Slovenia	CO_2 tax	1997/2011	EUR 10-20	Automobile fuels exempted
Sweden	Energy and CO_2 tax on petrol	2010	EUR 250	This is a straight excise tax
Switzerland	CO_2 levy on heating and process fuel	2008/2010	CHF 36 ($\approx$ EUR 30)	

Source: OECD/European Environment Agency, Economic Instruments Database, www2.oecd.org/ecoinst/queries/index.htm.

The carbon prices for automobile fuels shown in Table 2.4 are biased upward, since part of the taxes can be ascribed to negative local externalities, which are not taken into account in the calculations.[1] When considering the costs of local negative externalities, the implied carbon price for automotive fuels decreases significantly, and the relative distortion in favour of diesel increases as the local external costs of burning diesel are higher than for petrol.[2] Accounting for differences in local input prices and the valuation of human life, which are important parts of the costs of local pollution, results in a higher implicit carbon price for diesel in Poland than in other more developed OECD countries, although still much lower than that for petrol (Figure 2.4).

Table 2.4. **Implicit carbon prices based on excise taxes**
EUR/tonne, 2010Q4

	Petrol	Diesel	Diesel/ petrol	LPG	Natural gas		Electricity		Light fuel oil		Coal
					HH	IND	HH	IND	HH	IND	
United Kingdom	302	251	0.83		0	2	0	6	48	48	2
Germany	292	174	0.60	54	–	–	133	–	23	23	0
France	271	159	0.59	35	6	8	156	100	21	21	0
Sweden	267	174	0.65		130	39	1 937	36	153	25	–
Italy	252	157	0.62	74	–	–	72	98	149	149	0
Czech Republic	231	164	0.71	51	0	7	2	2	10	10	2
Slovak Republic	230	136	0.59	0	0	7	0	0	–	0	–
Japan	223	113	0.51	51	–	0	8	8	7	7	2
Hungary	200	135	0.68	55	0	5	0	3	–	–	0
Estonia	189	146	0.77	41	12	9	14	13	41	41	–
Poland	**187**	**120**	**0.64**	**68**	**0**	**0**	**6**	**6**	**22**	**22**	**0**
Canada	106	55	0.52	–	0	0	–	–	13	8	–
United States	40	37	0.92		–	–	–	–	–	–	0
Mexico	0	0	–		0	0	0	0	0	0	0

Note: The implied carbon price is computed as the amount of the tax levied per litre times the amount (litres) of fuel that needs to be burnt to reach a CO_2 emission of one tonne of CO_2 eq. One litre of diesel (light fuel oil for households and industry), petrol and LPG (liquefied petroleum gas) is assumed to produce respectively 2.7, 2.24 and 1.7 kg of CO_2. It is assumed that 4 535 269 kcal of natural gas generates 1 tonne of CO_2 and that burning 1 kg of coal generates 2.93 kg of CO_2. HH and IND refer to households and industry, respectively. See Appendix 2.A1 for a more extensive country coverage.

Source: OECD calculations based on data obtained from International Energy Agency (2011), *Energy Prices And Taxes*, Paris.

Figure 2.4. **The implied carbon price in automotive excise taxes accounting for local negative externalities**[1]
2010Q4

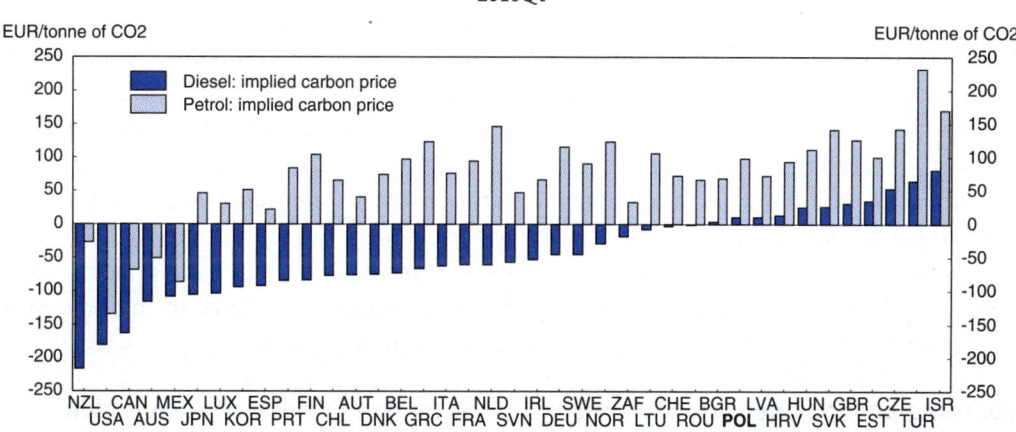

1. The implicit carbon tax is obtained by using the same methodology as in Table 2.4; the basis of the calculation is the excise tax from which two sets of the external costs of negative local externalities are subtracted.

Source: OECD calculations.

StatLink ⬛ᶤˢᵖ *http://dx.doi.org/10.1787/888932584756*

Overall, Poland, as with most OECD countries, is a far cry from having a unique carbon price. Low carbon prices for any fossil energy products are tantamount to direct subsidies that result in overconsumption of those sources of energy (Metcalf, 2009). The differences in implied carbon prices should be gradually decreased by eliminating existing tax exemptions, by increasing the implied carbon price on underpriced products and the near-zero carbon tax to the carbon price prevailing in the EU-ETS, which is exogenous for Poland, and by correcting the distorted relative price of diesel *versus* petrol. When adjusting relative carbon prices policymakers should of course consider the external costs of local pollution. A uniform carbon tax levied on top of existing taxes would not satisfy this goal as tax adjustments should explicitly account for local negative externalities. A simulation exercise (details of which are available upon request), using a very simple model calibrated to reflect the features of the Polish economy, shows that, abstracting from investment decisions and labour-market outcomes, a single carbon price would achieve GHG-emissions reduction of between 10 and 20% at a cost that is 0.2 to 0.7 percentage points of GDP lower than various alternative scenarios involving heterogeneous carbon prices. With a more ambitious reduction objective the savings might even be more than proportionally larger.

Raising the responsiveness to the EU-ETS carbon price signal in order to minimise abatement costs

The EU-ETS is the backbone of the European GHG emissions–reduction programme. The Europe-wide 20% decrease by 2020 requires a cut of 21% between 2005 and 2020 and the European Commission's proposal on the *Low Carbon Roadmap 2050*, which aims at a 80 to 95% reduction by 2050, implies almost zero emissions in the industries currently covered by the European cap-and-trade system. Such a system makes it possible to target directly (multi-annual) GHG emissions, the total amount of which corresponds to the desired quantitative emissions target at the relevant horizon. Firms can then buy or sell permits depending on whether their actual GHG emissions are higher or lower than the emissions limit given by their permits. This ensures that companies that can cut emissions at a lower cost than the permit price will sell their emissions permits to companies facing marginal abatement costs that exceed the price.

While the EU-ETS would ideally take care of changes in the electricity mix to generate required cuts in GHG emissions, in practice a number of practical barriers exist preventing the electricity mix from being endogenously determined in an optimal fashion, thereby increasing abatement costs. They include preponderant state ownership and the lack of competition in electricity generation, an underdeveloped organised wholesale electricity market (power exchange) and the vertical integration of electricity producers and distributors. In Poland, it is all the more important to increase responsiveness of investment decisions in generation capacity to the carbon price signal, since nearly half of base-load coal-fired generation capacity will have to be retired by 2030 by tranches of about 10% every five years, and another 10% of installed capacity will have to undergo deep modernisation between 2011 and 2015 (Ministry of Economy, 2009).

Reducing public ownership while ensuring competition in electricity generation

State-owned firms dominate electricity generation in many countries. In such cases investment decisions as to generation capacity are probably especially heavily influenced by political considerations. In Poland, the Treasury has a controlling stake in three major electricity producers covering roughly 50% of Poland's electricity production and a minority stake in a fourth company accounting for another 15%. The State's political role in investment decisions should be minimised and special care taken to ensure a high degree of competition, which is crucial for the long-term efficiency and stability of the system. The market for generation capacity and electricity production is among the least concentrated in Europe, measured by the Herfindahl-Hirschmann index (HHI), with only Great Britain, Norway and the Netherlands having lower HHIs in 2009 (European Commission, 2011). However, concentration relative to other competitive industries is nonetheless high (Energy Regulatory Office, 2011a). Increasing competition would render the sector more responsive to the carbon price signal.

Ownership of electricity generation should be unbundled from distribution

Poland has gone a long way in legally unbundling vertically integrated companies in the energy sector, as required by the EU (Table 2.5). But legal separation is not sufficient, the bulk of the bilateral contracts having been concluded within holding companies. In 2010, bilateral contracts between electricity producers and distributors belonging to the same holding company absorbed more than 70% of electricity, and another 20% was sold on the OTC market between groups (Energy Regulatory Office, 2011a). Even if investment decisions in generation capacity are private, they are limited by the size of the distribution grid (for small-scale plants). With electricity generation and distribution belonging to the same owner, distributors may tend to favour their own electricity production over that of independent producers. Separating the ownership of electricity production from distribution is a straightforward way to cut short not only any such potential bias but also incentives for within-company bilateral contracts and to shift sales to the spot market.

Table 2.5. **The power sector, 2008**

	Power exchange	Unbundling					
		Distribution system operators			Transmission system operators		
	Spot traded volume[1]	Total number	Ownership unbundled	Legally unbundled	Total number	Ownership unbundled	% of public ownership
Austria	7.8	129	0	11	3	0	76.5
Belgium	12.1	26	11	26	1	0	35.6
Czech Republic	3.8	3	0	3	1	1	100.0
Denmark	91.1	84	0	84	1	1	100.0
Estonia	n.a.	38	n.a.	1	1	0	100.0
Finland	54.3	88	1	50	1	1	12.0
France	10.8	148	0	5	1	0	84.8
Germany	25.2	866	0	171	4	2	0.0
Great Britain	3.3	19	10	9	1	1	0.0
Greece	106.9	1	0	0	1	0	51.0
Hungary	n.a.	6	0	6	1	0	0.0
Ireland	128.9	1	0	1	1	1	100.0
Italy	66.5	144	121	11	9	1	30.0
Netherlands	24.8	8	6	8	1	1	100.0
Norway	230.6	152	7	38	1	1	100.0
Poland[2]	**15.0**	**22**	**0**	**7**	**1**	**1**	**100.0**
Portugal	81.3	13	10	11	3	1	51.0
Slovakia	5.1	3	0	3	1	1	100.0
Slovenia	n.a.	1	0	1	1	1	100.0
Spain	88.7	351	0	351	1	1	20.0
Sweden	80.0	170	0	170	1	1	100.0

1. As a share of electricity consumption.
2. 2011, preliminary rough estimate for spot traded volume.
Source: European Commission (2011b); Energy Regulatory Office (2011a).

But ownership separation becomes somewhat artificial if both the producer and distributor companies remain under the supervision of the state. Consequently, ownership separation for electricity generation and distribution also requires the privatisation of at least one of the companies. But the privatisation of both companies is necessary if a similar approach is applied to the ownership separation of the transmission network from generation and distribution. In Poland, the Treasury is a 100% owner of the transmission system operator.

The role of the organised wholesale electricity market (power exchange) should be enhanced

Well designed privatisation and effective vertical separation of electricity producers will result in an increased role of the power exchange. In fact, the volume of electricity traded on the power exchange as a share of domestic electricity consumption is small. In 2010, only about 5% of electricity production transited through the power exchange (Energy Regulatory Office, 2011a). As a result of the Energy Law of 2010, which imposed the obligation on electricity producers to sell at least 15% of their production on the power exchange, the spot traded volume started to increase in 2011. Preliminary estimates suggest that spot traded volumes as a percentage of production reached about 15% in 2011. In many European countries including Denmark, Greece, Ireland, Portugal, Spain and Sweden, spot traded volumes were close to 100% of domestic electricity consumption (Table 2.5).

The Polish electricity market should be better integrated with neighbouring markets

If European energy markets were to be fully liberalised and integrated, in the short run the spot wholesale price of electricity (excluding transmission and distribution costs) would correspond to the cost of the marginal unit, the highest price in the market, i.e. close to today's price of electricity produced in Poland. In such a case, all over Europe the high profit rates would incentivise the deployment of generation capacities that would produce electricity at lower costs because of their lower carbon content. These new technologies would in turn crowd out old and carbon-intensive coal-fired power plants and eventually decrease the market price.

Nevertheless, the Polish market is rather isolated and electricity trade with its neighbours is asymmetric due to interconnection bottlenecks (Figure 2.5). For instance, in 2009, Poland imported 4% and 1% of its electricity production from Germany and Sweden, respectively, while electricity exports to these countries were close to zero. At the same time,

Figure 2.5. **Electricity openness as an indicator of electricity market integration and interconnections**[1]

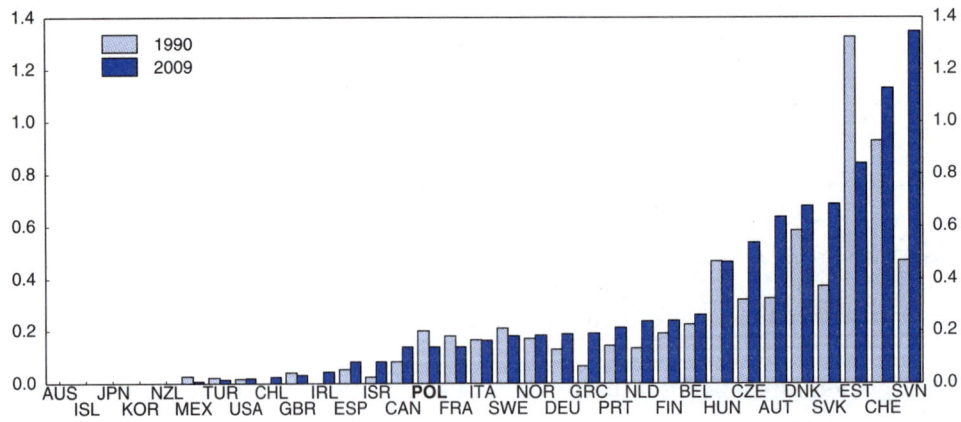

1. Electricity openness is calculated as the ratio of electricity imports plus exports over electricity consumption.
Source: OECD calculations based on IEA data.

StatLink ⌸⌸ http://dx.doi.org/10.1787/888932584775

exports to the Slovak and Czech Republics amounted to 2% and 5% of output, respectively, with no reverse flows. But even if the country's electricity openness were greater, the impact on the wholesale market would be modest because of the limited role of the Polish power exchange, as mentioned above. Consequently, auctioning emissions permits to Polish energy producers will increase electricity prices only in Poland, and the price signal will allow low-cost abatement only in Poland and not in Europe more broadly. From a general cost-effectiveness point of view, this is a good approach because emissions will be reduced where it is the cheapest to do so, that is in Poland (with its highly emissions-intensive generation). But the overall implications of a closed Polish electricity market are that initial EU-wide GHG reductions will occur in Poland and that this will cost Poland more in investment as a share of GDP than other countries. At the same time, changes in energy prices may penalise the Polish economy compared to its European competitors (Box 2.1).

Energy Policy of Poland until 2030 sets the objective of extending cross-border connections to increase electricity trade to 15%, 20% and 25% of electricity consumption, respectively, by 2015, 2020 and 2030. For instance, there are plans to construct a cross-border transmission line interconnecting the Polish and Lithuanian transmission grids by 2018. This line, supported financially by the EU Cohesion Fund, will be part of the Baltic Ring, which, if completed, will connect the Baltic and Nordic countries, Poland and Russia, creating a huge integrated electricity market (Ministry of Economy, 2009 and 2010). Further plans include interconnections with the Ukraine and Belarus and the construction of a third interconnector to Germany (Ministry of Economy, 2010). While this is a step forward, even greater electricity openness would certainly lower the burden of abatement on the Polish economy.

Box 2.1. **The impact of the EU-ETS on Poland's competitiveness**

The Polish government fears that the third phase of the EU-ETS, which will last from 2013 to 2020 and during which the number of permits will be decreased by 1.75% per year, will penalise Poland's competitiveness via higher energy and electricity prices. The main change in the third phase is that 50% of emissions permits will no longer be given away for free but will be sold at auction to the power and heating sectors and other participating industries. The European Commission proposed the establishment of emissions benchmarks: permits will be allocated for free corresponding to the emissions of the benchmark technology, and permits to cover emissions in excess of the benchmark will have to be purchased. The fact that natural gas is being proposed as the technological benchmark for power generation implies that Poland will pay for the largest share of the permits, since electricity produced in Poland is the most carbon-intensive in the EU27. This would be translated into a greater rise in Polish energy prices than elsewhere. A carbon price of 40 euros/tonne is estimated to generate a price increase of 35-50% (3 to 4 euro cents/kWh) for coal-fired plants (Mott MacDonald, 2010; Polish News Bulletin, 2011g). But these concerns may be exaggerated: Figure 2.6 below shows that the final price of electricity for industrial users is 10% to 25% higher in Poland's main CEE competitors (Czech and Slovak Republics, Hungary). Holding transmission and distribution costs

Box 2.1. **The impact of the EU-ETS on Poland's competitiveness** *(cont.)*

constant, the estimated increase in the price of electricity will not increase electricity prices above those countries' price levels, as coal plays an equally important role in their electricity mix.

Figure 2.6. **Pre-tax electricity prices for industrial users in the EU**

EUR/MWh, 2010

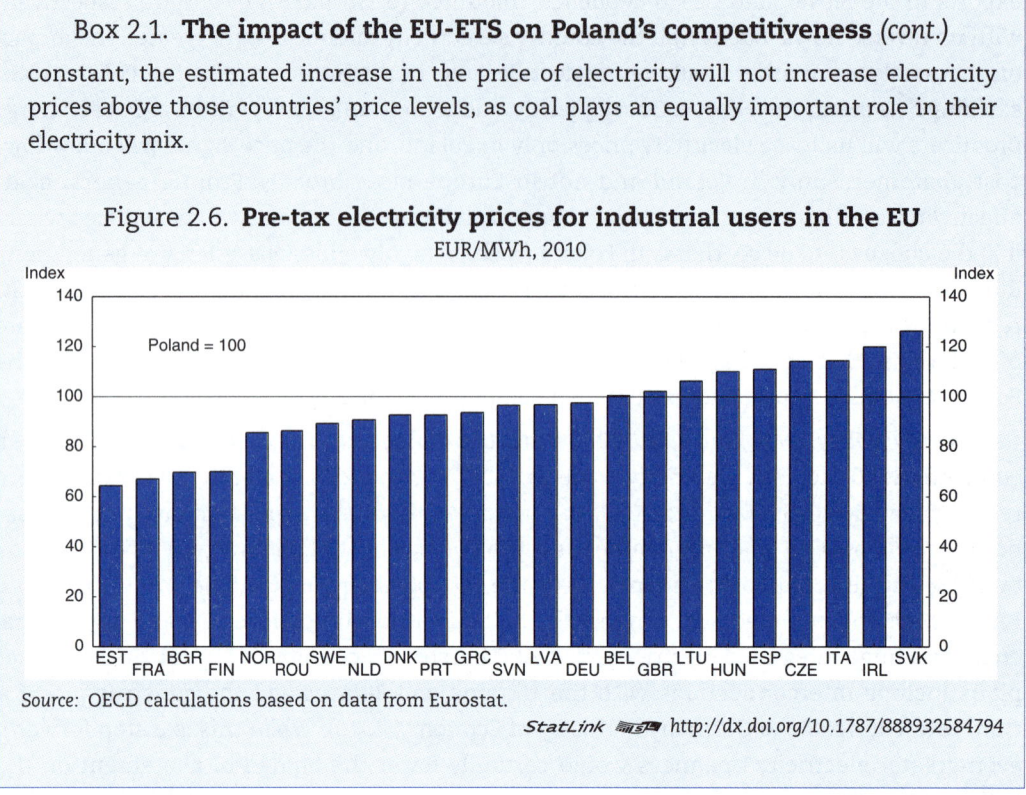

Source: OECD calculations based on data from Eurostat.

StatLink ⌱⌱ http://dx.doi.org/10.1787/888932584794

A cost-efficient support scheme for renewables in electricity generation is desirable in the long run

Maintaining equal abatement costs for different technologies is crucial to minimise total abatement costs

Renewables accounted for only a small proportion of Poland's gross electricity production in 2009 (Figure 2.7). While support schemes targeted at renewables overlap with price signals provided by the EU-ETS, and are therefore costly, actively supporting renewable in electricity generation is required if Poland wishes to comply with renewables targets determined at the EU level. Supporting renewables could be also justified on the grounds of positive externalities including learning by doing and scale effects or on the basis of infant-industry arguments. But in any event, if the government wishes to maintain support for renewables, it should do so in a cost-efficient and technology-neutral way: that is each technology should be awarded the same amount of support per tonne of CO_2 avoided. Since 2004, the Polish government's main instrument to promote renewable energy in electricity generation has been a quota system combined with tradable green certificates. At the heart of the system is the obligation for electricity distributors to prove that the electricity mix they sell to end users contains the amount of renewable sources required by the regulator. This quota is set to 10.4% in 2011 and 2012 and will increase by 0.5 percentage point each year to reach 14.4% in 2020. This seems to be out of line with the objective of 19.12% in gross final electricity consumption specified in the National Renewable Energy Action Plan (Ministry of Economy, 2010; RE-Shaping, 2011). To meet their quota obligations, the distributors can either buy the green certificates, initially issued for the producers of renewable energies and traded on the commodities exchange, or they can

Figure 2.7. **The share of renewables in gross electricity production, 2009**

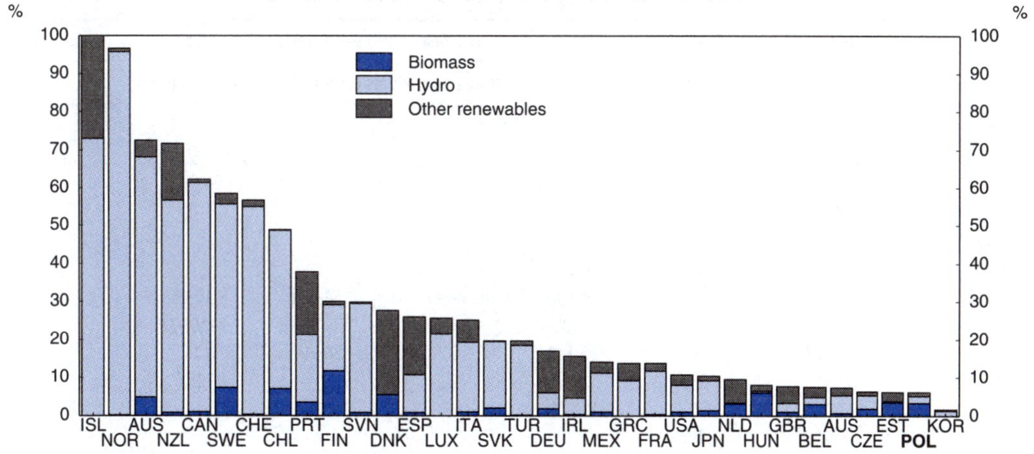

Source: OECD calculations based on IEA data.

StatLink ᘝᑫᔼ http://dx.doi.org/10.1787/888932584813

pay a substitution fee to the regulator (Energy Regulatory Office, 2011b; RE-Shaping, 2011). That fee represents a *de facto* price ceiling, because if the market price were to exceed the fee, all producers would choose to pay the fee, rather than buying the certificates in the market. Given that the quotas fixed for 2010 and 2011 were higher than the observed amount of electricity produced from renewables, the market price of the certificates has equalled the substitution fee.

The subsidy implied by the certificates is technology-neutral, as it is the same for all forms of renewable energy. This, in principle, ensures that those with the lowest abatement costs are chosen. Using the most carbon-intensive technology, namely coal-fired power plants and the country's actual electricity mix as carbon-intensity benchmarks yields implied abatement costs of EUR 67 to EUR 71 per tonne of CO_2 (Table 2.6). By contrast, in other European countries (except the Netherlands) indirect subsidies, mostly in the form of feed-in tariffs, are differentiated across technologies to reflect the actual costs of investment in renewable energies, leading to utilisation of a wide range of technologies, but also a wide range of abatement costs for various abatement options. The Polish government's plan to modify the existing quota system by introducing support that accounts for technology-specific investment costs will lead to an outcome that is more diversified across alternative green technologies at the expense of considerably higher total abatement costs.

The timeframe of the support scheme should be expanded

The current system encouraged the development of co-firing, a practice consisting of adding biomass to coal in existing power plants, a way to lower CO_2 emissions without much investment. In 2009, more than half of gross electricity produced on the basis of renewable sources was related to biomass, accounting for a little more than 3% of total gross electricity production. The government's renewable energy strategy projects a further threefold increase in absolute terms by 2020 (Ministry of Economy, 2010).

But the current system has some flaws. Co-firing crowded out new investments in power generation using renewable energies because the green certificates represented windfall revenues for energy producers, and no new investment could compete in terms of

Table 2.6. **GHG abatement costs implied by indirect support schemes (feed-in tariffs, green certificates), 2011**

	Solar	Wind	Biogas	Biomass	Geothermal	Hydro	Tidal wave
Abatement cost, benchmark = coal-fired power plants (EUR/tonne of CO_2 equivalent)							
Austria	(−50)-280	47	135		25		
Belgium	150-250	50	50	50		50	50
China	90-456	16-28	44				
Czech Republic	254	41	−50	136		72	
Denmark	21	0					
Finland		30	24-74				
France	70-410	(−20)-80	(−30)-40	30-90	150-230	10-35	100
Germany	45-240	42-80	26-133	26-123	55-146	(−16)-77	
Greece	328-479	179	129-149	9-129	28-79	17	
Ireland		15-635	25	25		25	
Italy	177-335	153	113-213	153	133		273
Japan	332	138					
Netherlands	47	47		47		47	
Poland	**65**	**65**	**65**	**65**	**65**	**65**	
Portugal	208-421	25	66	70	121-221	46	211
Slovakia	332	31	76	63		11	
Spain	81-232	231	21-92	79-123	25	34	24.6
Switzerland	303-673	158-194	164-292	(−7)-213	227-439	42-268	
Turkey	29	−40	29	29	8	−16	
United Kingdom	37-436	(−6)-355	3	(−31)-43		(−6)-179	
Abatement cost, benchmark = country-specific electricity mix (EUR/tonne of CO_2 equivalent)							
Austria	(−180)-1 007	169	485		90		
Belgium	530-883	177	177	177		177	177
China	112 570	20 35	55				
Czech Republic	383	62	−75	205		108	
Denmark	29	115					
Finland		64	51-159				
France	803-4 701	(−229)-917	(−344)-459	344-1 032	1 720-2 637	115-401	1 147
Germany	75-402	70-134	44-223	44-206	92-244	(−26)-128	
Greece	420-614	229	165-191	12-165	36-101	22	
Ireland		25-1 050	41	41		41	
Italy	319-603	275	203-384	275	239		492
Japan	610	253					
Netherlands	74	74		74		74	
Poland	**67**	**67**	**67**	**67**	**67**	**67**	
Portugal	393-795	47	125	132	229-418	87	399
Slovakia	1 310	122	300	249		43	
Spain	176-506	503	46-200	172-268	54	75	54
Switzerland	7 488-16 632	3 905-4 794	4 053-7 216	(−173)-5 264	5 610-10 849	1 038-6 623	
Turkey	52	−72	52	52	14	−29	
United Kingdom	63-741	(−10)-603	5	−53-73		(−10)-304	

Note: Abatement costs are computed using the lower- and upper-bound feed-in tariffs in excess of wholesale electricity prices and the amount of avoided CO_2-equivalent emissions.
Source: OECD calculations.

profitability. Poland will achieve its 15% renewables target (in gross final consumption of energy) by 2020 thanks to co-firing. But this achievement will be very short-lived, as old coal plants, which provide the bulk of co-firing, will have to retire after 2020 as a result of EU regulation. The sudden drop could be taken up either by other renewables generation capacity, nuclear power or new fossil fuel-fired plants, but this will be difficult to achieve, given the long lead times of plant construction. Second, the certificate system does not ensure that investment in renewables capacity will break even, as the system is currently slated to last only until 2017, and, even if it will probably be extended until 2020, this period is clearly too short for new investment with a lifetime of 20 years and more. In this respect the system also favours existing power plants and incumbents over new investments and independent producers. Changes currently planned by the government aim to expand the time horizon of the system and to encourage new investment in renewable technologies.

Measures on top of the quota system should be kept consistent with least-cost abatement

On top of the quota system, the government supports renewable energies via: i) a 50% reduction of the costs of the grid access for small renewable plants (less than 5 MW) and for small co-generation plants (smaller than 1MW); ii) an exemption from the stamp duty for issuing green certificates and for the issuance of the operating licence and the annual licence for energy production from renewable sources; and iii) an exemption from the excise tax of PLN 20/MWh applying to electricity generated from renewable sources. Furthermore, investment subsidies and preferential loans are provided by the National Fund for Environmental Protection and Water Management, EU funds and the Norwegian government. In compliance with the EU's Renewable Energy Directive, administrative measures comprise preferential treatment of wind energy for commercial balancing and a priority transfer of electricity produced from renewable sources by the transmission and distribution network operators (Ministry of Finance, 2010; RE-Shaping, 2011) (Table 2.7). The government should make sure that those measures are consistent with the objective of least-cost abatement.

The sustainability criteria for biomass firing needs to be strengthened

The production of biomass may increase overall GHG emissions via direct and indirect land-use change (NL Agency, 2010). The European Commission (2010) suggests member states apply sustainability criteria when using biomass for electricity and heat production (in line with the sustainability criteria for bio-fuels): i) the use of biomass from land converted from forest and from areas with high carbon storage and high biodiversity should be banned; ii) the use of biomass should reduce GHG emissions by at least 35% (and by 50% in 2017 and 60% in 2018 for new plants) relative to the EU's existing fossil energy mix; iii) combined heat and power (CHP) plants with high energy efficiency should be promoted; and iv) the origin of biomass should be monitored. Therefore, Poland's heavy reliance on an ever increasing use of biomass in order to meet the government's medium-term objectives needs to go hand in hand with a careful monitoring according to the sustainability criteria proposed by the European Commission.

Administrative barriers for wind energy should be reduced

Wind energy harbours an important potential for electricity production, given the excellent wind conditions in most of the country and on its shores (Kolvits, 2008). Nevertheless, wind contributed to only 1% of electricity production in 2010, and the government expects it will provide only 3% of power generation by 2020 and afterwards. The wind industry is more optimistic: the European Wind Energy Association (EWEA) and the Polish Wind Energy Association predict that the share of wind will reach 14% of total electricity production by 2020 (PNB, 2011b). According to the Institute for Renewable Energy, 35 GW of gross electricity production capacity could be potentially installed in offshore wind farms (PNB, 2011c), which could satisfy over 40% of electricity consumption by 2030.

Table 2.7. **Overview of measures used to promote renewable energy**

	POL	AUT	BEL	BLG	CZE	DEU	DNK	EST	ESP	FIN	FRA	GRC	HUN	IRL	ITA	LIT	LVA	NLD	PRT	ROM	SWE	SVN	SVK	GBR
Electricity																								
Feed-in-tariffs		X	X	X	X	X		X	X		X	X	X	X	X	X	X		X			X	X	X
Premium					X	X	X	X	X									X				X	X	
Quotas	X		X												X					X	X			X
Investment grants			X		X					X		X	X			X	X							
Tax exemptions	X	X							X	X		X					X	X			X		X	
Fiscal incentives	X			X		X		X										X				X		
Heating																								
Investment grants	X	X	X	X	X	X		X		X	X	X	X	X	X	X	X	X	X		X	X	X	X
Tax exemptions		X	X				X				X	X				X		X			X		X	
Fiscal incentives				X		X		X			X								X					
Bio-fuels																								
Quotas	X	X	X	X	X	X	X		X	X	X	X	X	X	X	X	X	X	X	X	X	X	X	X
Tax exemptions		X	X		X	X	X		X		X		X	X	X	X	X		X	X	X	X	X	X

Source: European Commission (2011), "Renewable Energy: Progressing Towards The 2020 Target", Communication from the Commission to the European Parliament and the Council, COM(2011) 31 Final, Brussels, 31 January.

The under-use of wind energy in Poland is a result of administrative and grid-access barriers. One major obstacle is the long time needed to obtain a building permit: for onshore wind farms it was 43 months in 2008, more than the double the European average, with only Portugal, Spain and Greece having longer administrative lead times (Figure 2.8). The absence of clear requirements with regard to the scope of the environmental impact analysis is a major cause. In addition, developers have to deal with eight authorities to get the necessary paperwork done (EWEA, 2010). Another major obstacle relates to connecting new wind farms to the grid. While average grid-access lead time is low in a European comparison, 60% of respondents to a recent survey mentioned insufficient grid capacity as the second most important reason for postponing projects. In fact, the grid infrastructure is underdeveloped in Northern and Western Poland, precisely where wind conditions are best (Kolvits, 2008). Not only does building high-voltage lines take a long time (five years for permissions and two for construction), but the unpredictability of the regulated tariffs that network operators can charge for the use of the grid is also not conducive for long-term investment in the grid. This is related to the lack of a national master strategy for grid improvement and extension (EWEA, 2010). Also, long queues for grid connection hamper new wind projects. A recent change in the Energy Law aims to shorten delays by filtering out "virtual" projects: since March 2010 only projects with a development plan approved by local governments can apply for connection. The introduction in the same year of a high deposit fee for reserving wind-farm grid access goes in the same direction (RE-Shaping, 2011).

Figure 2.8. **Administrative and grid-access lead times for wind energy in Europe, 2008**

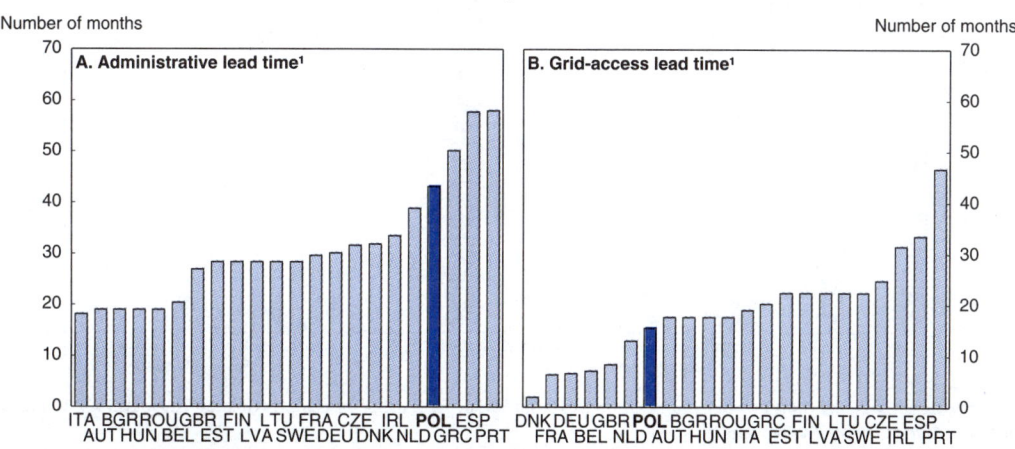

1. Administrative lead time refers to the period needed to obtain official permits and authorisations to start construction. Grid-access lead time indicates the time period needed to connect a new plant to the grid.
Source: European Wind Energy Association (2010).

StatLink ⌐⌐⌐ http://dx.doi.org/10.1787/888932584832

The survey conducted by EWEA (2010) shows that, notwithstanding long administrative lead times, administrative costs as a share of total investment costs are in line with the European average, and that connection costs are comparatively low. This latter finding is somewhat in contrast with the experience of the Polish Wind Energy Association, according to which high connection costs are a barrier, given the lack of nationwide cost standards for grid connection. The vertical integration of the big utility companies, which own electricity production capacity and the distribution system, may imply that new wind projects by independent producers may potentially be disadvantaged.

Electricity mix within the EU-ETS and the scope for direct government intervention

Coal accounts for about 90% of fuel used for Polish electricity production (Figure 2.9). Poland seeks to use coal as long as possible (Ministry of Economy, 2009) because the country's important coal reserves can guarantee energy security and the coal-mining industry employs over 100 000 workers (Suwala, 2010). But coal production has been on a rapid decline, with exports shrinking sharply: in 2010, domestic coal consumption was barely covered by domestic coal production, and the country's coal reserves will last only 43 years at current production levels (BP, 2011). With a single carbon price, which should rise significantly in the future to meet the ambitious GHG emissions-reduction objectives (and if local externalities related to burning coal were internalised properly), the economic appeal of coal-fired power generation would decline. While the transition to a low-coal economy will raise energy imports in the immediate future, the depletion of the country's coal reserves will increase coal imports in any case and thus lower the country's energy independence in the longer run. If the government sticks to its current energy strategy of keeping coal as a primary energy source as long as possible, the burden on the economy of achieving any given overall GHG emissions reduction target will be considerably higher, chiefly because of the reliance on more expensive abatement options.

Figure 2.9. **Primary energy demand and net electricity generation in 2006 and 2030, by type of energy**

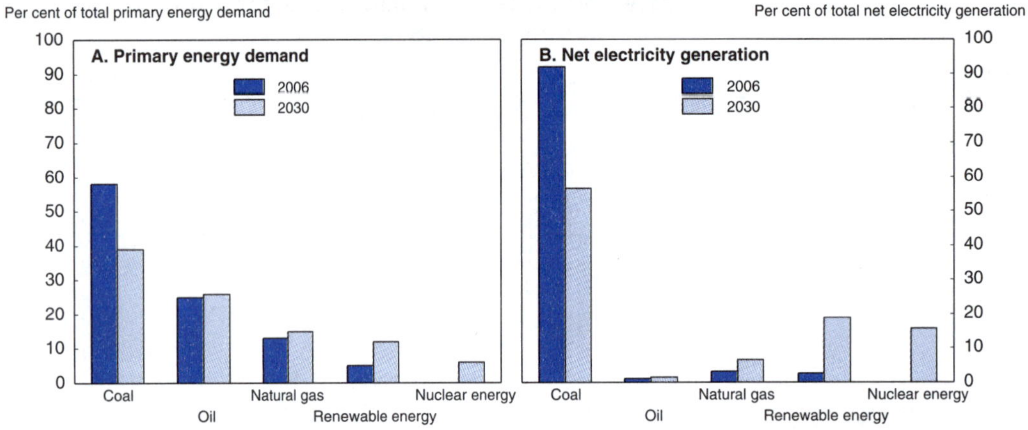

Source: Ministry of Economy (2009), "Projection Of Demand For Fuels And Energy Until 2030", Appendix 2 to *Energy Policy Of Poland Until 2030*, November.

StatLink http://dx.doi.org/10.1787/888932584851

Abatement scenarios

The electricity mix will depend on government policies and the responsiveness to the carbon price signal. The government's energy strategy implies a drop in the carbon-intensity of electricity production from 0.95 tonne of CO_2/MWh in 2008 to slightly above 0.6 tonne/MWh by 2030. This figure is still well above the current OECD and European averages of 0.5 and 0.4 tonne, respectively (Figure 2.10). Substituting natural gas for all coal and oil while keeping the share of renewables and nuclear power at levels predicted by the government's strategy would lower carbon intensity to 0.33 tonne of CO_2 per MWh. Increasing the shares of nuclear and renewable energy to 25% each in the electricity mix by replacing natural gas would result in a further drop to 0.25 tonne of CO_2 per MWh.

Figure 2.10. **Carbon intensity of electricity production, 2008[1]**

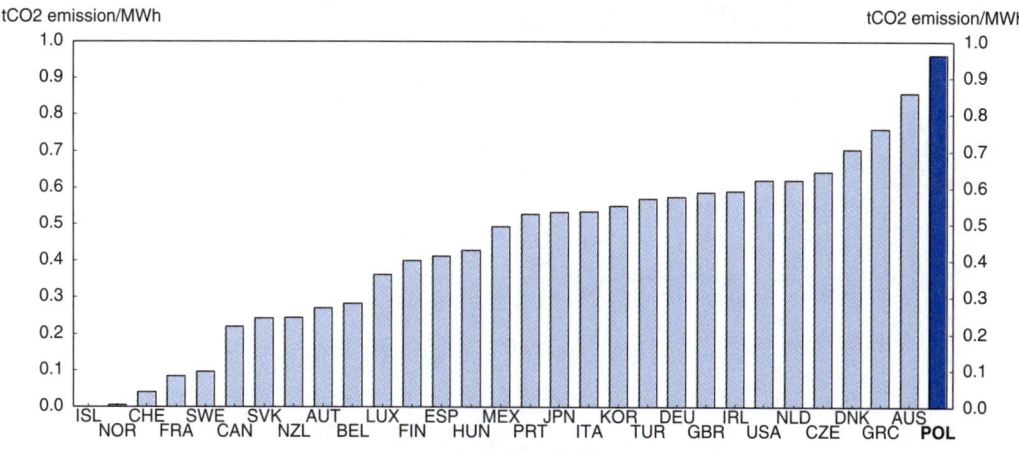

1. The share of various energy sources in total gross electricity production of each country is multiplied by the per MWh CO_2 equivalent emissions. For nuclear, hydroelectric, geothermal, solar, tidal and wind, the values of 0 tCO_2 equivalent/MWh, for natural gas 0.5 tCO_2 equivalent/MWh and for non-gas combustibles 1 tCO_2 equivalent/MWh are used.

Source: OECD calculations.

StatLink ⬛🔗 *http://dx.doi.org/10.1787/888932584870*

Alternatively, retrofitting old and equipping new coal and gas-fired plants with carbon capture and storage (CCS) facilities, a technology not yet proven on an industrial scale, but which could eventually become economically and technically feasible, could reduce carbon content to 0.17 tonne of CO_2/MWh, through sticking to government objectives. Even a virtually full decarbonisation is possible: a combination of the two scenarios, that is nuclear power and renewable energy together accounting for 50% of the electricity mix, coupled with the other 50% from gas-fired plants with CCS, would result in a carbon content of 0.07 tonne of CO_2/MWh.

The question to be answered in this context is how high the abatement costs are of moving from a carbon content of 0.95 to 0.07 tonne of CO_2/MWh. To put it differently, how does the electricity price implied by low-carbon generation technologies compare to the price given by investment, operations and maintenance and fuel costs related to coal- and gas-fired power generation? The estimated costs of electricity production indicate that nuclear power and, to a lesser extent, wind, hydroelectricity, biogas, biomass and geothermal energy are very cost competitive with coal- and natural gas-fired power plants. Photovoltaic stands out as currently the least cost-competitive technology (Table 2.8). The results are sensitive to: i) the discount rate used as (a higher rate penalises capital-intensive, low-carbon technologies and reduces the appeal of nuclear energy and wind power; ii) the evolution of fossil fuel prices, as lower future prices reduce the production costs of coal and natural gas-based plants relative to nuclear and renewable technologies; and iii) the relative costs of different technologies, which hinges crucially on national or even regional factors, including geographical endowments, meteorological conditions, the costs of local inputs and the regulatory environment. For instance, nuclear power is estimated to be cheaper than coal in Slovakia, Germany and France but more expensive in Hungary. However, the cost estimates for nuclear power do not reflect the need for higher security standards in the aftermath of the 2011 Fukushima accident. Electricity produced in onshore wind-power installations costs almost the same in the United States as electricity generated in coal-based power plants. Finally, a unit of electricity from photovoltaics is much more expensive in the

Table 2.8. **Country-specific abatement costs**

Power generation with a carbon price of EUR 40/tonne of CO_2

Abatement cost	Nuclear	Gas	Gas with CCS	Coal with CCS	Wind onshore	Wind offshore	Solar	Hydro	Biogas	Biomass	Geo-thermal
Austria		−40						−47			
Belgium	−38	−15			−12	56					
Czech Rep.	−33	−7	−9	−11	24		207	31			38
France	−41	−25			−16	24	130		−24		
Germany	−46	−15		−15	−4	19	142				
Hungary	−24										
Italy		−13			25		221				
Netherlands	−31	−12			−14	18	270			19	
Slovakia	−62										
Switzerland	−40	−1			38			0			
Industry-low	−28	−3		−17	−18	26	37				−34
Industry-high	−33	−3		−17	7	24	104				
EC1 low	−60	−40	−18	−26	−50	−40	165	−50	−50	−20	
EC1 high	−45	−60	−29	−11	−35	−10	335	35	75	75	
EC2 low	−65	10	16	−19	−65	−55	150	−65	−70	−30	
EC2 high	−60	−30	−7	−19	−60	−35	310	10	50	65	
Canada					−1	27	93				
Japan	−50	4									
Korea	−51	15									
Mexico		−9									
United States	−39	−18	−4	−21	−39	0	84		−39	−35	−50
Brazil	−39	−10			−50						
China	−40	−31			−16		29				
Russia	−44	−28		−1							

Note: Abatement costs are calculated on the basis of country-specific costs of specific technologies and compared to the cost of coal-fired plants (converted from USD to EUR at 1.35 USD/EUR). A negative abatement cost implies that the abatement option is cost-effective, considering the carbon price, and its implementation would be less costly than the savings it would produce. For Austria, Canada, France, Italy and Switzerland, data on the cost of coal-fired plants are unavailable. For these countries, German data are used. For Hungary, Czech data are used. Abatement cost estimates assume the following CO_2 emissions reductions: 100% for nuclear energy and renewable energies, 50% for gas-fired plants, 90% for gas-fired plants with CCS, and 70% for coal-fired plants with carbon capture and storage (CCS). Empty cells imply the lack of country-specific data. Industry-low and industry-high indicate general cost estimates by the electricity industry. EC1 and EC2 refer to data obtained from EC (2008) using a low and high-fuel price scenarios, respectively. EC low and EC high indicate lower- and upper-bound costs estimates.

Source: OECD calculations based on data obtained from IEA (2010) and EC (2008).

Netherlands than in China (Table 2.8). According to the US Energy Information Administration (2011), the discounted production costs of the same technology vary significantly across US states, implying strong regional differences in the relative cost-competitiveness position of a given electricity production technology.

The absolute difference in production costs can be translated into abatement costs (the costs of reducing one tonne of CO_2, using technology-specific CO_2 emissions per unit of electricity produced). Keeping in mind the sensitivity of the cost estimates to some of the underlying parameters, if a carbon price of EUR 40 per tonne were added to the production costs, abatement costs (relative to coal) would tend to be negative, except for photovoltaic. A negative abatement cost implies that the abatement option is cost-effective, considering the carbon price, and its implementation would be less costly than the savings it would produce, making it a worthwhile undertaking.

Poland's promising shale gas potential needs to be carefully developed to avoid local pollution

The recent discovery of potentially large reserves of natural gas from shale formations raises the possibility of significantly reducing Poland's natural gas supply dependence on Russia and opens up new possibilities for the use of gas in the country's electricity mix. Preliminary estimates quantify Poland's shale gas deposits, the biggest of their kind in Europe, at up to one fifth of proven shale gas reserves of the United States: 1.4 trillion to 5.3 trillion cubic metres, which would cover the current level of gas consumption for more than 200 years (IEA, 2011a; US EIA, 2011). The state-owned Polish Oil and Gas Company (PGNiG) estimates that small-scale (test production) shale-gas extraction could start within two years in 2014 (PNB, 2011d), whereas IEA (2011a) suggests that shale-gas production at an industrial scale could not begin earlier than 2020.

Natural gas from shale formations has been extracted at an industrial scale in the United States for many years, and such production is being considered in parts of Europe and elsewhere. However, there is increasing public scepticism with regard to the environmental impact of shale-gas mining, which relies on hydraulic fracturing or "fracking" (creating fractures in rock formations deep under the earth using pressurised water) in order to set free gas trapped in shale reservoirs. A serious concern relates to pollution of the underground water supply. Water pollution can occur directly through chemicals pumped into the rocks as part of the pressurised water to liberate shale gas, or indirectly, as injected water gets contaminated by radioactive materials and heavy metals from the rock (IEA, 2011b). Fracking also requires large amounts of water: 7 500 to 20 000 cubic metres of water injected per well, and can potentially cause seismic effects. Concerns relating to pollution of underground water supply have prompted a ban on shale gas mining in France. The potential seismic effects that drilling can trigger led to the suspension of drilling operations in the United Kingdom (The Guardian, 2011). In late 2010 and 2011, a temporary moratorium was placed on hydraulic fracturing in Québec and the US states of New York and Maryland, and the South African government also ordered a permanent ban in parts of the country (IEA, 2011b). The US Environment Protection Agency has recently launched an in-depth environmental impact analysis of shale-gas extraction in five US states, with first results to be published in 2012 (Reuters, 2011).

There are concerns regarding the over-the-lifecycle GHG balance of shale gas but also of conventional natural gas. Methane, which has a global greenhouse gas impact much greater than that of CO_2 and which escapes during the extraction phase, may wipe out the benefits of the decreased emissions when shale gas is used to replace coal. Based on data from the United States, Howarth *et al.* (2011) estimated that 4 to 8% of the methane from shale-gas production is released into the atmosphere via leaking and venting. As a result, the over-the-lifecycle GHG emissions from shale gas are estimated to be at least 30% higher than those for conventional gas or oil, and 20% greater than coal. But Cathles *et al.* (2012) argue that Howarth *et al.* (2011) substantially over-estimate life-cycle emissions because of some of their assumptions that are difficult to justify. Using more plausible assumptions results in life-cycle emissions, which are 30% lower for shale gas than for coal. In a similar vein, a special report by the International Energy Agency (2011b) finds that extra GHG emissions from shale-gas extraction are only 12% higher than for conventional natural gas and merely 4% if venting is avoided.

The existing legal system in Poland poses certain limits to shale-gas exploitation, including environmental protection, geology and water use, and property law. For instance, mining is prohibited in some areas, while other areas are protected by the EU Natura 2000 Programme (PNB, 2011e). Environmental barriers should be changed only if the changes would pass an independent environmental impact analysis. More generally, before entering the stage of full-scale exploitation, the government should commission an independent environmental impact analysis of Polish shale-gas mining. Potential sources of environmental pollution should be tackled by appropriate regulation enforced by a politically arms-length watchdog. Short- and long-term environmental risks (including excessive water use and underground water pollution) should be monitored continuously, and if potential damage is large and irreversible, a ban should be placed on the extraction technologies used.

Special attention is warranted for nuclear waste management

The Polish government's energy plan includes the construction of four to six third-generation nuclear reactors (depending on the technology chosen and investment plans). The first reactor is planned to start operations in 2020. By 2030, all reactors are expected to be fully operational. Nuclear power is an appealing alternative to carbon-intensive technologies, given the large amount of carbon-free base-load. But constructing nuclear power plants may be cumbersome because of the significant upfront investment costs and the many years needed for commissioning and construction. Also, the 40-to-60-year-long lifespan of the plants implies a very long lock-in to a specific technology. A permanent disposal of very long lived radioactive waste remains a largely unresolved issue. Whereas the idea of permanent deep geological disposal has been mooted for some time, no country has yet implemented this solution, because of the difficulty of finding suitable storage sites. Cost estimates for permanent storage are extremely uncertain, given the very long periods involved. As a result, the Swedish Radiation Safety Authority recently increased the nuclear waste fee paid by the industry to the Nuclear Waste Fund by 300% (Kokkvoll Tveit, 2011).

For the Polish nuclear programme to cover long-term costs, the final price of electricity should cover the full costs of long-term waste management and decommissioning. Strict safety and environmental standards should be set and implemented to minimise tail risks. An independent body composed of domestic and international experts should approve cost estimates, and money should be set aside in dedicated special reserve funds, untouchable by the nuclear industry and also by any future government tempted to use them to fix short-term budgetary problems. The legal framework, which entered into force in 2011, is well in line with those requirements. Nuclear energy producers are required to provision for the estimated future costs of decommissioning and long-term waste disposal. Based on expert assessment, the president of the nuclear energy agency proposes the amount of provisions to be set aside per unit of electricity production. The government (Council of Ministers) then evaluates and decides on the final amount for a multi-year period.

The current framework could be improved in two aspects. First, to ensure full transparency, the government's approval should be a purely administrative step that formal requirements of the cost estimation procedure were respected, rather than involving any judgement. Second, the independence of the regulator should be strengthened. The president of the nuclear energy agency is nominated by the prime minister for an indeterminate period of time and can be dismissed by the prime minister. Such an arrangement makes his/her removal relatively easy. Instead, he or she should be appointed for a period, extending beyond political cycles, for instance six or eight years, during which he or she cannot be fired. In principle, the price of nuclear energy should incorporate an insurance premium covering tail risks. But no private insurer would be ready to provide coverage at a reasonable price, as risks cannot be diversified sufficiently within Poland (for the small number of planned reactors). Such tail risks could, however, be meaningfully diversified at the global level. In any case, the low probability of an accident means that an explicit government insurance scheme would collect funds, which are very small compared to the total costs of a nuclear disaster. Nevertheless, in the absence of such an insurance scheme, nuclear energy would be under-priced, thus leading to its over-production. Therefore, imposing an insurance premium or a tax relating to tail risk is desirable in principle, even though estimating the probability and the costs of an extreme event is a very complicated task.

Smoothing peak electricity demand

Smoothing daily, weekly and annual peak demand is generally very helpful in lowering GHG emissions related to electricity production and consumption. Semi-base and peak electricity production usually relies on fast-reaction power plants using gas, coal or oil. If base-load electricity production relies on low-carbon technologies like nuclear or hydroelectric power, smoothing peak load will decrease the demand for high-carbon electricity produced by fossil-fuel-fired plants. Currently, smoothing peak demand in Poland would have a different benefit, given that both base and peak-load depend heavily on coal and other carbon-intensive fossil fuels. While flattening peak demand would do little to reduce GHG emissions, it would instead lower the costs of electricity production by increasing the utilisation rate of power plants and thus lowering the need to build new capacity used only to meet peak demand. The climate impacts of flattening peak demand could be partly offset by some increase in demand in response to the lower electricity prices that would ensue.

But in the longer run, a significant decarbonisation of base-load is expected to occur as a result of *Energy Policy of Poland Until 2030* and, if adopted, the European Commission's *Low Carbon Roadmap 2050*. Once in place, smoothing peak demand served by high-carbon power stations will decrease overall GHG emissions. An effective way of doing so is to introduce time-varying tariffs. At present, Polish households can choose between a flat rate and day/night tariffs (Barth, 2008). While day/night tariffs can smooth peak demand moderately, truly time-varying prices are more effective in encouraging people to modulate their electricity consumption in line with the price. A pre-condition of time-varying tariffs is a well functioning wholesale electricity market, which Poland still does not have. A second condition is that time-varying wholesale prices are passed through to end-user prices. Intelligent meters providing real-time information on electricity prices and the precise shape of users' load curves could encourage a proactive application of energy-efficiency measures (IEA, 2010). A recent study estimated that peak demand could be cut by 7% in Europe if 50% of households and small businesses were equipped with smart meters (Ollagnier, 2010).

In addition, smart or intelligent grids open new perspectives to network operators to modulate electricity demand during peak periods via demand withdrawal. The roll-out of smart meters can take as long as seven years from initial tender to operation and the deployment of a smart grid 20 years (Shargal, 2010). Poland's action plan relating to its energy strategy included a gradual roll-out of electronic meters, starting in 2011. Yet, little progress has been made thus far. Hence, Poland should start thinking about the development and implementation of a strategy aimed at deploying smart meters and a comprehensive smart grid. As part of the EU effort to improve energy efficiency by 20% by 2020, many member countries have developed strategies to deploy smart meters and roll out a smart grid. Italy and Sweden are front runners, but Denmark, Finland, France and the Netherlands are also making efforts to increase the penetration rate of smart meters. In those countries, the regulatory environment was conducive to their roll-out (Shargal, 2010). Yet, the Polish energy regulator has not set smart metering requirements nor any roll-out date. A recent position paper by the energy regulator, which sets minimum technical requirements for grid operators wishing to deploy smart meters and distribution tariffs incorporating investment costs, is an encouraging, but still insufficient step forward (Energy Regulatory Office, 2011c).

The role of renewable sources outside electricity production

The EU target set by the Directive on renewable energy to increase the share of renewable sources to 20% in gross final consumption of energy by 2020 and to 10% in the transport sector is translated into binding national targets of 15% for Poland, which is among the least ambitious: only the Benelux countries and a number of other new EU members have smaller targeted shares. The National Renewable Energy Action Plan (NREAP) foresees a modest increase to 16% by 2030 (Ministry of Economy, 2010). The overall objective of 15% is broken down into three sector-specific targets for electricity, heating and transport (bio-fuels). In 2010, almost 72% of all renewable fuel sources was used in heating, and only 28% went to electricity production and transport (Table 2.9).

Table 2.9. **Poland's renewable energy targets by sectors**

	Share of sector-specific renewable use in gross final energy use (%)			Share of sector-specific renewable use in total renewable use (%)		
	2010	2020	2030	2010	2020	2030
Electricity	1.3	3.9	4.2	14	26	26
Heating	6.8	9.0	9.5	72	60	59
Transport (bio-fuels)	1.3	2.1	2.3	14	14	15

Source: Ministry of Economy (2010), updated for 2010.

Releasing the potential of renewables in heat production and individual heating

The use of renewable energy is concentrated in individual heating, for which solid biomass dominates other renewable energy sources by a wide margin and accounts for almost all renewables in this sector (Ministry of Economy, 2010). About half of solid biomass, mostly woodchip, is currently used in the residential sector for heating purposes. This raises a number of concerns. First, individual heating devices, especially old ones, have low energy conversion rates and are an important source of local atmospheric pollution via fine-particulate-matter emissions. Therefore, the traditional use of solid biomass is not considered by IEA (2011a) as a sustainable renewable energy use. Second, as in the case of biomass used for electricity production, the sustainability criteria suggested by the European Commission for the use of biomass should be respected.

Promoting district heating via an economy-wide single carbon price

Poland has one of the most extensive district heating (DH) systems in Europe. In 2009, DH served half of the country's citizens, had a 40% penetration rate in total heating demand, and the length of the heating grid was just a little shorter than those in Germany

Figure 2.11. **Comparison of district heating (DH) systems in Europe, 2009**

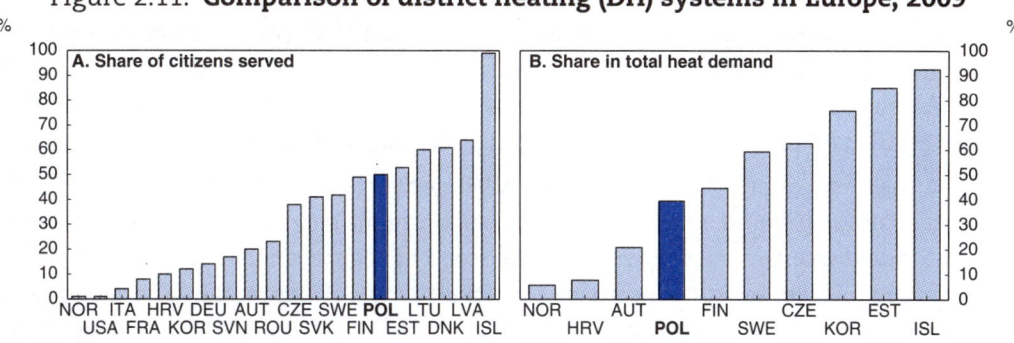

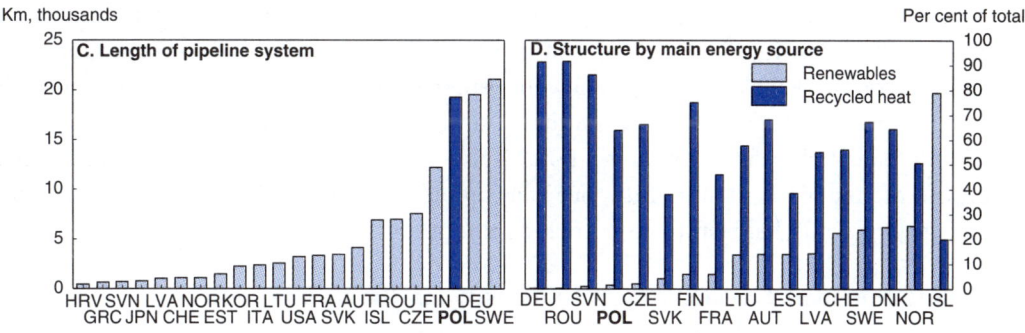

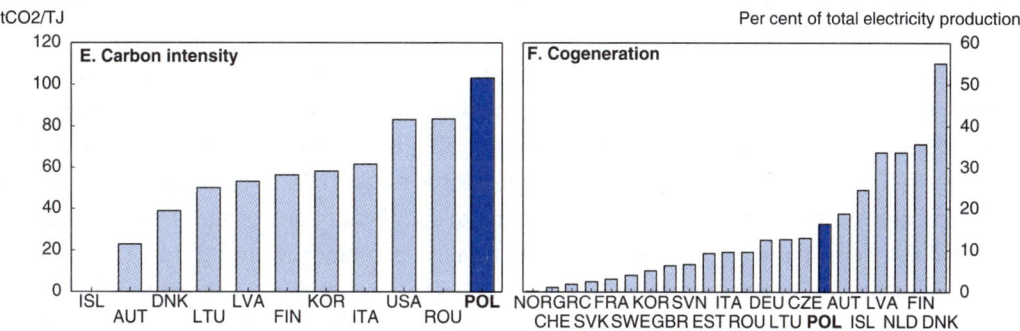

Source: Euroheat & Power, www.euroheat.org/Statistics-69.aspx.

StatLink ⟶ http://dx.doi.org/10.1787/888932584889

and Sweden (Figure 2.11). Indeed, DH systems have a number of advantages over individual heating applications. First, the energy conversion factor is higher, especially if heat is obtained from cogeneration (CHP plants). Modern cogeneration plants can reach fuel efficiency levels above 90%. Cogeneration can meet peak demand both for electricity and heat, given that low-grade heat generated during peak electricity production can be stored easily for up to two days. Second, DH systems can accommodate a variety of energy sources and production types such as CHP, geothermal heat, surplus heat from industry and a vast range of renewable sources, which are difficult to use in individual heating systems (unrefined biomass, wood waste, municipal solid waste and sewage sludge), as well as coal and gas (Euroheat & Power, 2011). High energy efficiency coupled with an extensive use of renewable fuels make cogeneration-based district heating a very powerful tool in the fight against GHG emissions. Finally, and importantly, compared to individual heating devices, DH systems have a limited number of emission points, which can be fitted more easily with modern filters to radically reduce air pollution and global warming: one tonne of black-carbon/soot particulate matter has a global warming potential 600 times higher than CO_2 over 100 years (Grieshop *et al.*, 2009). For instance, in 2008, 40% of Poland's total particulates emissions came from individual residential heating devices, whereas public electricity and heat production, including DH, was responsible for only 6%.

Yet, the average carbon intensity of one MWh produced in the Polish DH system is the highest in Europe (Figure 2.11). In addition to increasing the share of renewables in the fuel mix of the DH system (and cogeneration), the share of cogeneration, currently 60%, could be increased to cover most DH needs by the construction of new small- and micro-scale CHP plants or the modernisation and replacement of old turbines. COGENchallenge (2007) estimates that Poland's cogeneration capacity could be doubled to reach 40% of gross electricity production. Clearly, an economy-wide carbon price (applied also to individual heating and including the EU-ETS) would help investment in the construction and modernisation of CHP plants using renewable energies. Given that more DH coupled with CHP would mean a move away from individual heating, the government could consider providing loans for credit-constrained households to join the DH grid. At the same time, given the monopolistic nature of district heating pipelines, incentive regulation based on benchmarking could help simulate market competition and improve efficiency.

Achieving transport bio-fuel targets by focusing on the carbon content

The government's ambitions with regard to the development of bio-fuels have been in line with EU targets, but the measures taken to achieve them are not cost-efficient. Bio-fuels' share in the total energy consumption (in calorific values) in road transport was set to reach 5.75% in 2010 in accordance with the European objective and the 10% binding minimum European target for 2020. In 2009, bio-fuels accounted for just 4.6% of total fuel consumption (Ministry of Economy, 2010). The underlying justification for the use of bio-fuels is that related GHG emissions are lower than for conventional fuels. The life-cycle GHG outcomes of first- and second-generation bio-fuels are subject to significant controversy, however, mainly because the intermediate stages of the production cycle, including crop production and the transformation of crops into bio-fuels, can be very energy intensive (Steenblik, 2007; International Transport Forum, 2008), and direct and indirect land-use change can reduce, or even negate, overall GHG savings. Bio-fuels can directly increase life-cycle GHG emissions if crops are grown in areas that previously absorbed more CO_2 from the atmosphere such as forest cover. An indirect effect causing unfavourable GHG balances occurs if diverting crops in one country and making up for them elsewhere causes deforestation, for instance. In both cases, the reliance on bio-fuels may have a negative impact on biodiversity, and the indirect effect can trigger food shortages for the poor.

Realising the problem with the life-cycle GHG balances, the European Union's Renewable Energy Directive set new sustainability criteria for bio-fuels, which are similar to those proposed for biomass, and which have to be considered for the fulfilment of the 10% target. By 2016, GHG emissions stemming from the use of bio-fuels should be at least 35% lower compared to conventional fuels. GHG-emissions reductions should go further to 50% by 2017 and to 60% by 2018. Bio-fuels produced from crops grown on land converted from forest, from areas with high carbon storage and high biodiversity will not be counted toward the objective. The tightening of the life-cycle sustainability of bio-fuels will require a shift from first- to second-generation bio-fuels: the government's renewables action plan foresees that the share of second-generation bio-fuels in total bio-fuel use will rise above 20% by 2020 and to 40% by 2030 (Ministry of Economy, 2010). But achieving these goals will be challenging, given that Poland's bio-fuels industry produces almost exclusively first-generation bio-fuels.

The two major measures that help to achieve these bio-fuels goals are very similar to those applied in other European countries. First, a heavy penalty of more than PLN 15 (3 euros) per litre of bio-fuels not introduced is levied on fuel distributors that do not respect the annual targets. Second, a set of financial incentives are meant to encourage the production and consumption of bio-fuels, including exemption from the excise duty and the fuel charge and a tax reduction for bio-fuels producers. In addition, grants and low-interest loans from various funds are available for investment in bio-fuels production (Ministry of Economy, 2010; RE-Shaping, 2011). These instruments will help achieve the quantitative targets, but at a high cost. It would be more cost-efficient to target and/or tax the carbon content of fuels, rather than imposing volumetric production targets for bio-fuels because different bio-fuels have different GHG balances (International Transport Forum, 2008).

Improving energy-efficiency policies

Reflecting the EU's target of a 20% improvement in energy efficiency, *Energy Policy Of Poland Until 2030* sets two targets: i) a constant-energy-use economic growth path, which implies that energy-efficiency improvements would fully offset increased primary energy demand stemming from economic growth;[3] and ii) bringing Poland's energy intensity to the current EU15 level. Generally speaking, a single carbon price will enhance energy efficiency as a side effect of GHG emissions reduction. Therefore, energy-efficiency measures are best suited to compliment carbon prices if responsiveness to the carbon-price signal is considerably reduced in the presence of market failures such as credit-constrained households or asymmetric information. As such, they should be directly connected with CO_2 reduction. It is not fully clear how the energy-efficiency objectives are targeted at low-response sectors. More specifically, showing a business-as-usual scenario and the contribution of specific energy-efficiency measures to achieve the policy objectives would increase the credibility of the programme. A direct link to how efficiency measures would affect overall and sectoral GHG emissions would be very beneficial to clarify Poland's stance on climate-change-mitigation policies.

A number of ministries and agencies with diverging interests are in charge of the country's energy-efficiency strategy and its practical implementation, thereby posing challenges for coordination. While the overall national strategy is developed by the Ministry of Economy, the transport and tertiary (building) sectors are the purview of the Ministry of Infrastructure and regional and local governments, and the strategy's implications for climate change and municipal and industrial waste are dealt with by the Ministry of Environment. The Polish National Energy Conservation Agency (KAPE) is also involved in the strategy-making and implementation process. Financial support is provided by the National Fund for Environmental Protection and Water Management and regional funds (IEA, 2011a). A good example of the coordination problem is the different energy-performance criteria used for issuing energy certificates and for receiving financial support. This multi-layered institutional framework needs to be consolidated and coordinated or supervised by a single institution or ministry.

Energy-efficiency targets and white certificates

Poland is about to introduce a system of tradable white certificates. This is an important cross-cutting measure, which is expected by the government to have a major impact on improving energy efficiency in the economy. As in any other cap-and-trade system, the incentives ensure that cuts are carried out where they are the cheapest. According to the Energy Efficiency Law, voted in April 2011, energy (electricity, gas and heat) suppliers will have to improve efficiency via reducing losses in production, distribution, transmission and in the end-use sector. The law requires that claimed efficiency gains be subject to energy-savings audits, for which firms will be rewarded with white certificates, or, if they miss their targets, they will have to purchase white certificates or pay a substitution fee, much like the green-certificate system for renewables described above. The government has yet to announce details of the scheme, such as the total energy savings to be targeted, the amount of the substitution fee and how white certificates can be redeemed at the Energy Regulatory Office.

White certificates can be seen as a reasonable alternative to a carbon tax for "diffuse" energy consumption of households and small businesses, for which setting up a GHG emissions-trading system is too costly. The United Kingdom has used CO_2-weighted energy savings in the past, and CO_2-emissions reductions have been targeted there explicitly since 2008 (World Energy Council, 2010). Lessons from the experience of the five European countries – Belgium (Flanders), Denmark, France, Italy and the United Kingdom – operating white-certificate systems might prove useful for the design and operation of the Polish system (Table 2.10). First, energy savings need to be defined carefully. According to best practice, they should be accredited only for the installation of appliances with energy-efficiency levels in excess of the market average and only for the fraction representing energy savings above the market average and that was not supported by public funds. Second, to encourage innovation, apart from measures accredited independently for energy savings, energy suppliers should have the option to claim energy savings from innovative technologies, approved by public authorities on the basis of a small-scale demonstration, for example. Third, the regulatory set-up should decouple the energy distributors' revenues from the quantity of energy sold, because white certificates, aimed at reducing distributed energy, would create perverse incentives for energy distributors. Fourth, the ability to bank the certificates is essential for long-term investment. In addition, experience shows that energy-savings targets have been met easily, suggesting that objectives have not been ambitious enough or that the savings potential is substantial.

Table 2.10. **White certificate systems in Europe**

| | Period | Sectors covered | | Obligated companies | Nature of saving targets | Trading | Gross abatement cost (M EUR/TWh) |
		Residential (%)	Commercial (%)				
Belgium (Flanders)	2008	58	42	Electricity distributors	Annual final energy	No	44
Denmark	2008	42	50	Heat, electricity, gas and oil distributors	Annual final energy	Between distributors	30
Italy	2005-08	83	0	Electricity and gas distributors	Cumulative	Yes	8
France	2006-09	86.7	4.2	All energy suppliers	Lifetime final energy	Yes	3
United Kingdom	2005-08	100	0	Electricity and gas distributors	Lifetime final energy	Between suppliers	

Source: World Energy Council (2010) and OECD calculations.

Electricity production in Poland is among the least efficient in the OECD in terms of energy losses (Figure 2.12). Production losses, defined as the difference between gross electricity production and the electricity fed into the national grid (that is, the power plants' own needs) are the second highest in OECD after Estonia. Losses suffered in the

Figure 2.12. **Losses in the power sector, 2009**[1]

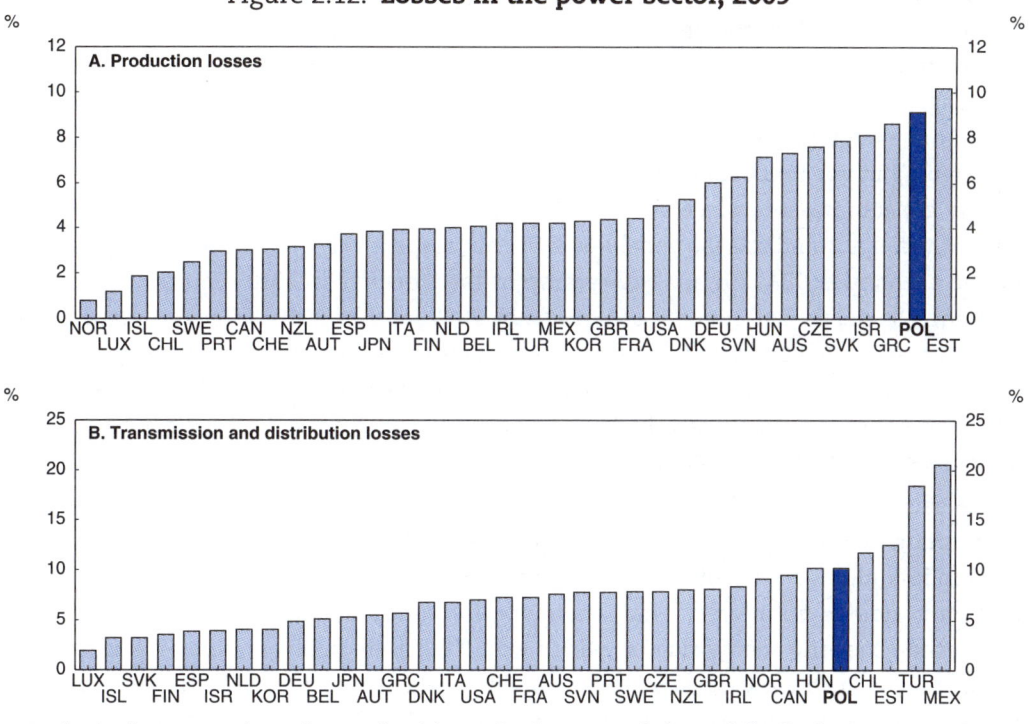

1. Production losses as a share of gross electricity production. Transmission and distribution losses as a share of electricity consumption.

Source: OECD calculations based on data obtained from the IEA.

StatLink http://dx.doi.org/10.1787/888932584908

transmission and distribution grid are also substantial. The government's objective to cut grid losses is commendable. It could be achieved via the modernisation of the existing transmission and distribution network and by encouraging small-scale power generation that could be linked directly to the distribution grid (Ministry of Economy, 2009). The government and the energy regulator have yet to propose tariff schemes to encourage investment in the national grid.

Transposing the mandatory labelling of energy efficiency of consumer products into Polish law, as required by the 2010 EU Directive on Energy Efficiency Labelling, will increase consumers' awareness and exploit the large potential for efficiency gains in consumer products. The Polish government could go one step further by requiring obligatory display of the over-the-lifetime environmental impact (including the carbon equivalent footprint) of consumer products, the production, distribution and waste management of which account for a large proportion of households' CO_2 emissions. This labelling could cover all products, imported and domestically produced. France's initiatives in this area may provide useful insights for practical implementation.

Energy efficiency in the residential, commercial and government sectors

Residential and commercial buildings cause 11% of Poland's global GHG emissions, which is higher than in most CEE countries. In addition, GHG emissions in this sector declined less between 1990 and 2009 than in the other countries (Table 2.3 above). This outcome is the result of a continuing use of coal for heating and hot water, coupled with low energy efficiency due to high heat losses because of poor thermal insulation and low efficiency of individual boilers (IEA, 2011a). Poland's energy strategy aims at cutting energy intensity by improving efficiency, which is expected to yield modest cuts in GHG emissions. These efforts are necessary to comply with the EU's Directive on the Energy Performance of Buildings, fully transposed to Polish Law in 2008. An important part of the directive is the minimum energy-performance standard required for new buildings and existing buildings undergoing major renovation. The existing ceiling of 90 to 120 kWh/m^2 annual primary energy consumption, in place since 1998, is not only high in comparison with French or Swedish energy standards (50 and 30-60 kWh/m^2, respectively), it is also not fully enforced by the authorities (IEA, 2011a). The revamp of the Directive in 2010 requires that all new buildings be nearly zero-energy structures by 2020 (and by 2018 for government-owned and -occupied new buildings), by designing them to produce sufficient energy to cover almost all their energy needs. Intermediate targets shall be set up by 2015 to secure the achievement of the 2020 target. Reducing new buildings' primary energy consumption to almost zero will be very challenging.

A second important measure attributable to the Directive is the system of energy-performance certificates for new and old private buildings that are sold or rented, and for all public buildings (in which the certificates have to be displayed prominently). The current system is not perfect. First, energy performance is shown on a continuous scale rather than showing energy classes, which would facilitate public understanding. And the certificates indicate only the share of renewable energy sources used by the buildings, not the overall standardised CO$_2$ emission levels. Finally, setting up a national register of energy certificates for buildings would be useful (Sowa, 2011).

The government provides financial support to energy-efficiency improvements in the building sector. The Thermo-Modernisation Fund, established in 1998, and transformed into the Thermo-Modernisation and Repair Fund in 2009, can cover up to 20% of a bank loan for investment in thermal renovation, but cannot exceed 16% of the total costs of investment. The support can be awarded to investment projects that reduce annual energy consumption by at least 10% if the heating system is modernised or by at least 25% in other cases (thermal insulation). Yet, the way the energy performance of the thermal investment projects is measured is different from the methodology used for the energy certificates. The two systems should be harmonised to ensure full transparency (Sowa, 2011). Furthermore, it would be preferable to support investment projects of credit-constrained households depending directly on their GHG emissions reduction.

Towards a more efficient organisation of the transport sector

GHG emissions in the transport sector almost doubled between 1990 and 2009, as the number of passenger cars per capita rose threefold (Figure 2.13). A further catch-up in the stock of cars and their heavier use, in line with rises in per capita income, is likely to result in a further increase in transport-related GHG emissions over the coming decades. Considering that per capita GHG emissions in transport are about half the level seen in more industrialised countries, they could potentially double over time. The government's strategy seeks to promote a shift towards sustainable transport systems. But the supporting policies are either too general (such as the preparation of urban plans for sustainable transport and the promotion of alternatives to road transport) and not backed by specific actions, or, while useful, are likely to have only a marginal impact. This includes the promotion of "eco driving", car-pooling, the checking of tyre pressure and lifestyle changes to rely less on cars (IEA, 2011a).

Figure 2.13. **Passenger cars per 1 000 inhabitants, 1991-2009**

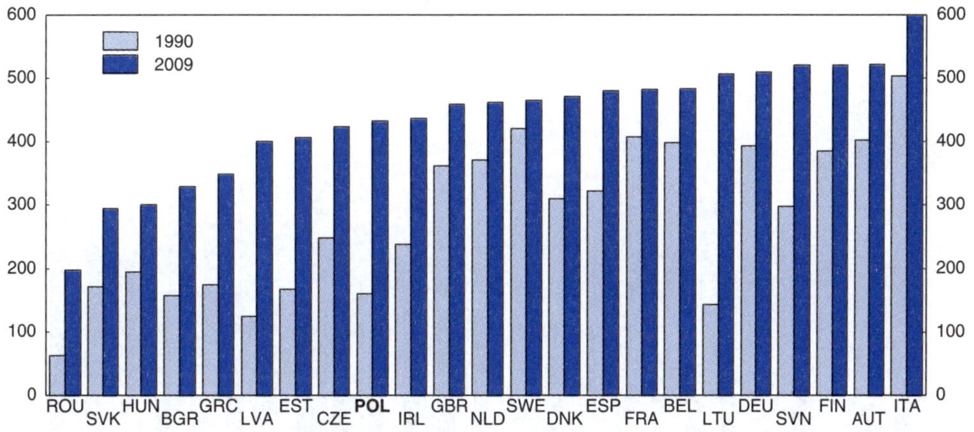

Source: Eurostat.

StatLink ᴬᴵˢᴾ http://dx.doi.org/10.1787/888932584927

Cutting GHG emissions in the transport sector is especially challenging, given that the demand for travel is very unlikely to decline in the future. Increasing the fuel efficiency of currently available engine technologies could smooth the transition period before a massive deployment of alternative low-carbon technologies. To date, it seems probable that cars fuelled by electricity stored in batteries or in other ways (wind-produced liquid hydrogen or other renewable energies) and capable of travelling considerable distances will pave the way to a low-carbon transport sector. If implicit or explicit carbon taxes give the right price signals, rational and fully informed consumers would opt for carbon-efficient cars. In the case of market failure, when myopic behaviour and asymmetric information prevent consumers from fully perceiving the lifecycle carbon savings, carbon emissions standards can be a useful tool to achieve higher fuel and carbon efficiency. In 2009, the European Union set emissions-performance standards with a view to reducing the average CO_2 emissions of the new car fleet to 130 grammes per km by 2015 and to 95 grammes per km by 2020. Some European countries have managed to cut the emissions of new cars substantially over the last decade, and Denmark, Portugal and France were in compliance with the 2015 target already in 2010. Poland, starting from a comparatively low average emissions level upon EU entry, has achieved little progress, like its Central and Eastern European peers, and was in the middle of the field in 2010 (Figure 2.14).

The virtual explosion of the number of cars per inhabitant came at a cost of the expansion of an ever ageing, polluting and fuel-consuming car fleet. The average age of Polish passenger cars is around14 years (against eight years in Western Europe), and almost 70% of cars are older than 10 years. In the aftermath of Poland's EU accession, the number of second-hand cars imported from the EU, mainly from Germany, skyrocketed from close to zero to almost a million per year, as the abolition of the import duty lowered the price of imported cars by 20 to 30%. Today, three-quarters of newly registered cars are imported used vehicles. In 2006, the government wanted to replace the existing one-off registration tax by one calculated on the basis of engine size and EU emissions standards, aimed at reducing emissions other than CO_2. While such a tax would have certainly halted the flood of imported second-hand cars, it was not implemented. Yet, in 2009 the registration fee of 3.1%, applied regardless of the car's age and engine size, was raised to 18.6% for cars with engines bigger than two litres.

Figure 2.14. **Average CO$_2$ emissions per km travelled from new passenger cars in Europe**

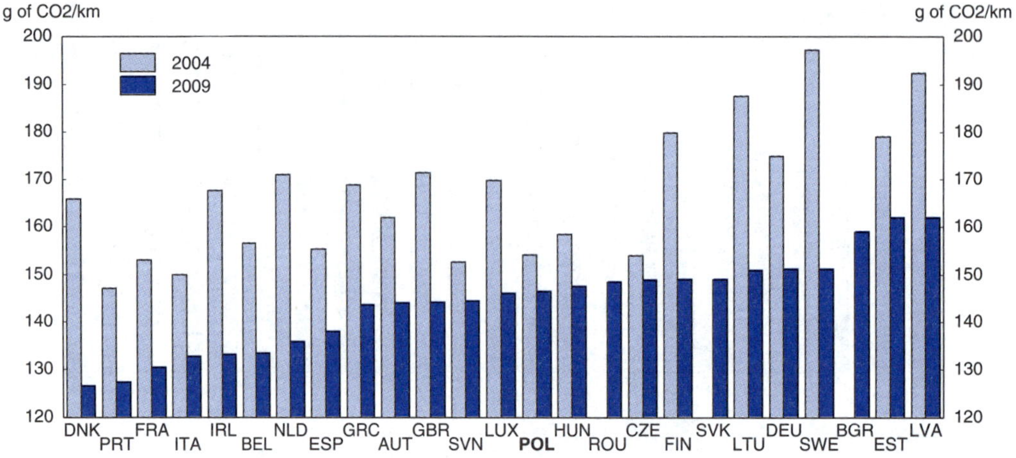

Source: Eurostat.

StatLink http://dx.doi.org/10.1787/888932584946

The European Commission (2005) argues that annual vehicle taxes should incorporate an element linked to CO$_2$ emissions and that car registration taxes should be phased out, as they can lead to double taxation for second-hand cars and thus impede the free movement of goods within the EU. Such a solution may be second best compared to taxes proportional to use. Polish passenger-car taxation, which comprises moderately high one-off registration taxes and fees applied to newly registered cars but no annual vehicle taxes, would certainly benefit from an overhaul, along the lines of the Commission proposal. The huge stock of ageing cars cannot be contained any more by a one-off registration tax, especially if not set based on the level of environmental externalities. Instead, a well designed annual vehicle tax could provide powerful incentives for the renewal of the car fleet. Elsewhere in Europe annual vehicle taxes based on CO$_2$ emissions, in some cases coupled with similar upfront fees and taxes, not rare in Europe, have led to a rapid decline in the average emissions of the overall car fleet, as large, old and heavily polluting vehicles were replaced by small, new and carbon-efficient cars (Table 2.11). To date, in Poland, taxes related to the purchase, registration, ownership and usage of passenger cars are not linked to carbon efficiency.

If Poland decides to introduce annual car taxes, they should, in addition to a CO$_2$ component, also have a penalty for local air pollution. Most Polish cars meet only Euro 1 and 2 fuel standards, which are much more lenient than Euro 4 or 5 with regard to air pollutants. For instance, a modern diesel car emits 14 times less particulate matter than older models meeting only Euro 1, CO and NO$_X$ emissions are also considerably lower. A penalty on CO$_2$ and other air pollutants, increasing over time, preferably in line with the actual social costs of the related negative externalities (climate change, health, and water and soil pollution) could engineer a shift towards newer, cleaner and more energy-efficient vehicles. It is crucial that diesel cars are not treated more favourably than petrol cars, as happens in many countries. Even if diesel cars account for only 20% of the Polish passenger car fleet, diesel represents about 70% of total fuel consumption, reflecting its extensive use in trucks, buses and agriculture.

Table 2.11. **CO$_2$-based car taxes in Europe, 2010**

	Upfront	% of car net price (2008)	Bonus-penalty	Annual	Annual company car tax
Austria	Fuel efficiency	10	<120g CO$_2$/km, +EUR 300 >160g CO$_2$/km, –EUR 25/g		
Belgium	Tax incentives for cars <115g CO$_2$/km	4	<125gCO$_2$/km, +EUR 1 000 >155gCO$_2$/km, –EUR 1 500	Discount of –15% for cars <150gCO$_2$/km	CO$_2$-based
Denmark	Fuel efficiency (P/D)	170		Fuel efficiency (petrol/diesel)	
Germany		0		Base tax based on engine power + CO$_2$ part EUR 2 per gCO2/km cars <120g/km exempted (<110g/km in 2012-13; 95g/km after 2014)	
Finland	Linear CO$_2$-based 12.2% <60g/km 48.8% >360g/km	42		CO$_2$-based starting in 2011 EUR 20 to EUR 605	
France		3.4	<110gCO$_2$/km >150gCO$_2$/km		CO$_2$-based
Ireland	Linear CO$_2$-based 14% <120g/km 36% >225g/km	36		CO$_2$-based EUR 104 to EUR 2100	
Latvia	CO$_2$-based LVL 0.3 per g/km <120g/km LVL 5 per g/km >350g/km	2			
Luxembourg		0		CO$_2$-based, exponentially increasing	
Netherlands	CO$_2$-based (P/D)	36			
Portugal	Engine size and CO$_2$-based	37			
Romania	Based on CO$_2$, cylinder capacity and Euro emission standards	3.5			
Spain	CO$_2$-based 0% <120g/km 14.75% >200g/km	9.75			
Sweden		0		CO$_2$-based + supplement for diesel cars	
United Kingdom	CO$_2$-based extra fee >165g/km	0		CO$_2$-based GBP 0 to GBP 405	

Source: ACEA (2010), *www.acea.be/images/uploads/files/20100420_CO2_tax_overview.pdf; Copenhagen Economics (2010).*

Company cars represent nearly half of new passenger cars in Poland, midway between Greece's 24% and 60% in Sweden and Germany. If the tax system encourages the private use of company cars over private cars, private-sector employees will drive bigger and more expensive cars than what they otherwise would be willing to buy, and they will add more mileage than they would do if they had to pay privately. The fact that personal income tax for company car use is based on the leasing cost of a comparable car and fuel costs for private use paid by the company are not subject to an explicit benefits tax results in an over-use of company cars for private purposes in Poland.[4] Car taxes should be changed to remove this distortion. In addition, the companies themselves should also be encouraged to rationalise the use of passenger cars by the introduction of environmental taxes similar to those to be applied for private cars.

Some of the new motorways under construction will be run by private companies. Investment costs will be recouped by tolls. At the same time, an electronic collection system for trucks (with a weight of over 3.5 tonnes) was launched in July 2011 on public motorways and major routes, replacing the existing vignette system for heavy-duty trucks (over 12.5 tonnes). The toll is a function of the distance travelled, and the vehicle's weight and Euro emissions standards. Light trucks pay 20% less than heavy trucks and the same as buses, and vehicles meeting Euro 5 standards are charged 50% less than those on Euro 2 (viaTOLL, 2011). While the principle of differentiating according to environmental performance is commendable, properly monetising external costs relating to air pollution would yield much wider differences. The electronic toll system, which lets vehicles pass through the gates without stopping, thus limiting emissions, is initially being run on about 1 600 kilometres of motorways, expressways and selected sections of national roads, but coverage will eventually be extended to 8 000 kilometres of roads under the supervision of national road administration.

The government has recently adopted a railway investment programme until 2013, possibly to be extended until 2015 (Ministry of Infrastructure, 2011). The programme foresees the modernisation of existing railroads aimed at the reduction of travel time and the improvement of passenger safety.

Nevertheless, the government's desire to encourage railroads as part of a sustainable transport mix may be inconsistent with the ongoing expansion of the country's motorway network. Helped massively by EU funds to double its length between 2004 and 2011, the country's 1 000 km long motorway network remains smaller than that of geographically much smaller countries like the Czech Republic or Hungary. The plan is to build a network by 2015 around three major axes, two connecting east and west Poland and the third running from the north to the Czech border. Facing fiscal constraints, the government decided to slow down the expansion of the road network for 2014-20. At the same time, because of savings from lower than expected contract prices and the slow absorption of EU funds in the railway sector, Poland asked the European Commission for permission to relocate funds from railroad projects to motorway construction. This could amplify under-investment in new railroad infrastructure. Part of the railroad network's problem is inefficient management. The pricing system allowing for operating- and possibly also capital-cost recovery, coupled with a truly independent sector regulator, and perhaps with more private sector involvement, is key to seeing railways as a real alternative to roads, both for passenger and freight transport. Indeed, the modal split is strongly biased in favour of roads: rail passenger transport accounts for only 6% of total inland passenger transport, and just 20% of freight is transported by rail.

Box 2.2. Recommendations pertaining to climate-change policies

Carbon tax

- Implicit and explicit carbon taxes should be equalised for sectors outside the EU-ETS and aligned to the EU-ETS prices with a view to achieving a unique carbon price for the whole economy, first by progressively eliminating exemptions from the excise duty for coal and gas for household use. Lump-sum cash compensation for the poor should be provided. Taxes on petrol and diesel should be adjusted to internalise negative global and local externalities.

Box 2.2. **Recommendations pertaining to climate-change policies** *(cont.)*

Electricity production and distribution

- The responsiveness to the price signal for investment in generation capacity should be reinforced by deepening the organised wholesale electricity market (power exchange), improving cross-border interconnections and potentially by privatising electricity generation capacity.

- A long-term national plan for grid development is needed to keep up with demand and allow new installed capacity to be connected. Price regulation should encourage private-sector investment in grid development. Increasing cross-border interconnection capacity should be a priority to spread the burden of EU-ETS over a larger region.

- Investment choices in new power-generation capacity should be backed by transparent cost-benefit analysis. Negative externalities should be accounted for in the tariffs. For nuclear energy, the approval of the estimation of costs of future decommissioning and long-term waste disposal should be insulated from political influence and the independence of the president of the nuclear energy agency should be strengthened by a fixed-term nomination going beyond political cycles and during which he or she cannot be removed. Strict safety and environmental standards should be imposed and enforced to minimise the tail risks of nuclear energy. For natural gas from shale formations, environmental risks should be continuously and effectively monitored, especially with respect to water pollution and methane leakage. For wind, the time needed to obtain a construction permit should be considerably reduced and a one-stop shop opened for contacts with public administration.

- Special attention should be paid to the lifecycle GHG balance of renewable resources, especially of biomass and bio-fuels. Binding sustainability criteria for the use of biomass, including energy crops and woodchip, should be set following the European Commission's proposal. The cost-efficiency advantage of uniform support to renewables via green certificates should be retained. Uncertainty for new investment should be mitigated by extending the time horizon of the scheme.

- A regulatory framework for smart grid deployment should be developed, which, combined with a deeper power exchange, will help implement real-time tariffs for end-users.

Energy efficiency

- The white-certificate scheme should be directly aimed at CO_2 reduction rather than energy savings. It should be targeted at sectors with low responsiveness to the carbon price signal.

- The systems of energy-performance certificates for buildings should be extended to cover CO_2 emissions and other environmental impacts. Certificates should be made more transparent by setting CO_2 classes. Financial support provided for energy-efficiency projects should depend on CO_2 performance. Stricter energy performance standards for new buildings should be properly enforced.

Transport sector

- Incentives in the railway sector for investment in network infrastructure need to be strengthened by private-sector involvement, a truly independent sector regulator and price regulation ensuring efficiency gains and cost recovery.

- An annual vehicle tax, calibrated to vehicles' environmental performance, should be introduced. Taxes should be extended to company cars.

Notes

1. Burning fossil energy releases particulate matter, nitrogen oxides, sulphur dioxide, ozone and volatile organic compounds into the atmosphere, damaging human health, degrading buildings and resulting in agricultural crop losses and harm to biodiversity and ecosystems through soil and water pollution. Further negative externalities include noise pollution, accidents not covered by private insurance and bottleneck and flow congestions resulting from the use of vehicles. Nevertheless, excise taxes might not be the most efficient way to deal with congestion, which could be taken care of more efficiently by road/congestion pricing. The total costs of local negative externalities vary a great deal depending on population density and time of day but also on the type of fuel used (diesel *versus* petrol) and the vehicle emission standard applied (Euro 1 *versus* Euro 5).

2. Environmental taxes are mainly aimed at correcting negative externalities. Using them beyond the level that would correct those externalities to raise tax revenues creates more distortion than an increase in a broad-based VAT.

3. EU regulation requires a 9% improvement in energy efficiency of the Polish economy by 2016.

4. See OECD (2011b) for the case of Israel.

Bibliography

Barth, V. (2008), "ALICE Electricity Sector Country Study: Poland", Carl von Ossietzky University, *mimeo.*

BP (2011), *BP Statistical Review of World Energy June 2011*, *www.bp.com/statisticalreview.*

Cathles, L.M., L. Brown, M. Taam and A. Hhunter (2012), A commentary on "The Greenhouse-Gas Footprint Of National Gas In Shale Formations" by R.W. Howearth, R. Santoro and Anthony Ingraffea, *Climate Change* (forthcoming) *http://drydensec.org/sites/default/files/rebuttal%20of%20Howarth%20fulltext.pdf*

COGENchallenge (2007), "Small-Scale CHP, Factsheet Poland", December.

Committee on Climate Change (2008), "Building A Low-Carbon Economy – The UK's Contribution To Tackling Climate Change", *The First Report Of The Committee On Climate Change*, December.

Copenhagen Economics (2010), "Company Car Taxation", *Working Paper*, No. 22/2010.

Energy Regulatory Office (2011a), *National Report To The European Commission, 2011*, July, Warsaw.

Energy Regulatory Office (2011b), "Polish Support Schemes For Renewable And Cogeneration Sources", Warsaw, *mimeo.*

Energy Regulatory Office (2011c), "Position Of The President Of Energy Regulatory Office On Necessary Requirements With Respect To Smart Metering Systems Implemented By DSO E Taking Into Consideration The Function Of The Objective And Proposed Support Mechanism In Context Of The Proposed Market Model", Warsaw, 31 May, *mimeo.*

Euroheat and Power (2011), *District Heating In Buildings*, Brussels.

European Commission (2005), "Proposal For A Council Directive Of 5 July 2005 On Passenger Car Related Taxes", 2005/261, Brussels.

European Commission (2008),"An EU Energy Security And Solidarity Action Plan: Energy Sources, Production Costs And Performance Of Technologies For Power Generation, Heating And Transport", *Commission Staff working document* accompanying the Communication from the Commission to the European Parliament, the Council, the European Economic and Social Committee and the Committee of the Regions, 13 November, Brussels.

European Commission (2010), "Commission Adopts Biomass Sustainability Report", IP/10/192, 25 February, Brussels.

European Commission (2011a), *A Roadmap For Moving To A Competitive Low Carbon Economy In 2050*, Brussels, 8.3.2011, COM(2011)112 final.

European Commission (2011b), "2009-2010 Report On Progress In Creating The Internal Gas And Electricity Market, Technical Annex", *Commission staff working paper*, 9 June, Brussels.

European Council (2011a), 4 February 2011 conclusions, Brussels, 8 March. *www.consilium.europa.eu/uedocs/cms_data/docs/pressdata/en/ec/119175.pdf.*

EWEA (2010), "Wind Barriers: Administrative And Grid Access Barriers To Wind Power", July.

The Guardian (2011),"Influential MEP Calls For Shale Gas Regulation", 30 June.

Grieshop, A.P., C.C.O. Reynolds, M. Kandlikar and H. Dowlatabadi (2009), "A Black-Carbon Mitigation Wedge", *Nature Geoscience*, 2 August.

Howarth, R.W., R. Santoro and A. Ingraffea (2011), "Methane And Greenhouse-Gas Footprint Of Natural Gas From Shale Formations: A Letter", *Climatic Change* (forthcoming), *www.sustainablefuture.cornell.edu/news/attachments/Howarth-EtAl-2011.pdf*.

International Energy Agency (2010), *Energy Technology Perspectives 2010: Scenarios and Strategies Until 2050*, Paris.

International Energy Agency (2011a), "Poland 2011 Review", *Energy Policies Of IEA Countries*, Paris.

International Energy Agency (2011b), "Are We Entering A Golden Age Of Gas? Special Report", *World Energy Outlook 2011*, Paris.

International Transport Forum (2008), "Bio-Fuels: Linking Support To Performance", *Joint Transport Research Centre, Discussion Paper*, No. 2008-7, Paris.

Kokkvoll Tveit, A. (2011), "Swedish Example Shows That Nuclear Waste Storage Could Be Far More Expensive Than Expected", Bellona, 16 August, *www.bellona.org/articles/articles_2011/waste_costs_sweden*.

Kolvits, K. (2008), "Wind Energy In Poland – Potential, Prospects And Pitfalls", joint seminar by demos Europa and the Danish Embassy, 19 November, Warsaw.

McKinsey (2009), *Assessment Of Greenhouse Gas Emissions Abatement Potential In Poland By 2030*, Warsaw.

Metcalf, G.E. (2009), "Tax Policies For Low-Carbon Technologies", *NBER Working Paper*, No. 15054.

Ministry of Economy (2009), *Energy Policy Of Poland Until 2030*, November, Warsaw.

Ministry of Economy (2010), *National Renewable Energy Action Plan*, Warsaw.

Ministry of Infrastructure (2011), *Multi-Annual Investment Programme In The Railway Sector Until 2013 (And 2015)*, Warsaw, *http://bip.transport.gov.pl/pl/bip/px_wpik_do_roku_2013_z_perspektywa_2015___po_konsultacjach_spolecznych.pdf*.

Mott MacDonald (2010), *UK Electricity Generation Costs Update*, Brighton.

NL Agency (2010), "Indirect Effects: Macro Monitoring And Land Use Planning", Ministry of Economic Affairs, Agriculture and Innovation, November, Utrecht.

OECD (2006), *The Political Economy Of Environmentally Related Taxes*, OECD Publishing, Paris.

OECD (2011a), *Economic Survey Of Sweden*, OECD Publishing, Paris.

OECD (2011b), *Economic Survey Of Israel*, OECD Publishing, Paris.

Ollagnier, J.M. (2010), "Réduire le coût de la transition vers une économie décarbonée", *Les Échos*, 17 August.

Perkins, S. (2011), "Green Growth And Transport", *International Transport Forum, Discussion Paper*, No. 2011-02, February.

Polish News Bulletin (2011a), "Renewable Energy Industry Calls For Changes In System", 24 August.

Polish News Bulletin (2011b), "EWEA Optimistic About Development Of Wind Energy In Poland", 12 July.

Polish News Bulletin (2011c), "Environmentalists Promoting Wind Farms", 14 July.

Polish News Bulletin (2011d), "Shale Gas From Poland In Two Years?", 10 June.

Polish News Bulletin (2011e), "Shale Gas Exploration Requires Legal Changes", 7 July.

Polish News Bulletin (2011f), "Electronic Tolls Will Be Launched On Time", 15 June.

Polish News Bulletin (2011g), "EC More Restrictive About CO_2", 1 August.

Reuters (2011), "EPA To Study Natgas Fracking In Five US States", 23 June.

RE-Shaping (2011), "Renewable Energy Policy Country Profiles", Intelligent Energy Europe, *www.reshaping-res-policy.eu*.

Shargal, M. (2010), *From Policy To Implementation: The Status Of Europe's Smart Metering Market*, Capgemini, *http://ddata.over-blog.com/xxxyyy/1/15/80/34/Energie/capgemini-smart-metering.pdf*.

Sowa, J. (2011), "Implementation Of The EPBD In Poland: Status In November 2010", Concerted Action, Energy Performance of Buildings.

Steenblik, R. (2007), "Subsidies: The Distorted Economics Of Bio-Fuels", *International Transport Forum,Joint Transport Research Centre, Discussion Paper*, No. 2007-3.

Suwala, W. (2010), "Lessons Learned From The Restructuring Of Poland's Coal Mining Industry", Global Subsidies Initiative (GSI) of the International Institute for Sustainable Development (IISD), Geneva.

US Energy Information Administration (2011), "*World Shale Gas Resources:An Initial Assessment Of 14 Regions Outside The United States*", April, Washington.

viaTOLL (2011), "Toll Rates", *www.viatoll.pl/en/heavy-vehicles/viatoll-system.*

World Bank (2011), *Transition To A Low-Emissions Economy In Poland*, February, *www.worldbank.org/pl/lowemissioneconomy.*

World Energy Council (2010), *Energy Efficiency: A Recipe For Success*, London.

APPENDIX 2.A1

Table 2.A1.1. **Per capita GHG emissions and their decomposition, 2009**

	GHG (tCO$_2$-eq) per capita for specific sectors				Energy sector		Electricity and heat prod		GDP
	Total	Non-energy	Energy	E&H	GHG/Energy production	Energy prod/ GDP	GHG/E&H production	E&H prod/ GDP	Per capita GDP (1 000 EUR)
Latvia	4.8	1.6	3.2	0.8	4 020	0.06	1 693	0.04	13
Turkey	4.9	1.2	3.7	1.3	9 994	0.03	5 478	0.02	11
Romania	6.1	2.0	4.0	1.8	3 020	0.12	4 917	0.03	11
Sweden	6.4	1.7	4.8	0.9	1 545	0.10	509	0.05	32
Lithuania	6.5	2.9	3.6	1.0	3 085	0.08	1 387	0.05	15
Croatia	6.5	1.7	4.8	1.0	5 433	0.05	3 202	0.02	16
Hungary	6.7	1.7	5.0	1.5	4 646	0.06	3 412	0.03	17
Switzerland	6.7	1.3	5.5	0.3	3 319	0.04	415	0.02	37
Portugal	7.0	2.0	5.0	1.6	10 612	0.02	3 723	0.02	21
Bulgaria	7.8	1.9	5.9	3.8	4 402	0.12	5 375	0.06	11
Spain	8.0	1.8	6.2	1.6	9 465	0.02	2 992	0.02	27
Slovakia	8.0	2.7	5.3	1.2	4 880	0.06	1 886	0.03	19
Ukraine	8.1	2.5	5.6	1.9	3 146	0.31	3 011	0.11	6
Italy	8.2	1.4	6.8	1.6	15 759	0.02	3 395	0.02	27
France	8.3	2.5	5.8	0.7	2 831	0.07	893	0.03	30
Belarus	9.1	3.4	5.7	3.1	13 606	0.04	3 294	0.08	12
United Kingdom	9.2	1.4	7.8	2.5	3 037	0.08	4 579	0.02	32
Slovenia	9.5	1.7	7.8	3.0	4 329	0.07	3 721	0.03	25
Japan	9.5	0.9	8.6	2.8	11 776	0.02	3 970	0.02	30
Austria	9.6	2.3	7.3	1.1	5 396	0.04	1 243	0.03	35
Poland	**9.9**	**1.8**	**8.1**	**4.2**	**4 600**	**0.10**	**7 842**	**0.03**	**17**
Norway	10.6	2.6	8.1	0.4	176	0.96	153	0.05	48
Greece	10.9	2.0	8.9	4.5	10 290	0.03	10 480	0.02	26
Germany	11.2	1.9	9.3	3.8	5 926	0.05	4 957	0.02	32
Denmark	11.3	2.3	8.9	3.9	2 066	0.13	3 585	0.03	32
Belgium	11.5	2.1	9.5	2.0	6 575	0.04	2 505	0.02	32
Netherlands	12.0	1.9	10.1	3.2	2 650	0.10	4 148	0.02	36
Finland	12.4	2.5	9.9	4.2	3 229	0.10	2 106	0.06	31
Estonia	12.6	1.8	10.7	7.7	3 412	0.20	6 829	0.07	16
Czech Republic	12.7	2.2	10.5	5.5	3 487	0.14	5 763	0.04	22
Ireland	14.0	4.7	9.3	2.8	28 601	0.01	5 301	0.01	36
Iceland	14.5	8.1	6.4	0.0	441	0.43	9	0.16	34
Russia	15.2	2.7	12.6	5.6	1 422	0.65	3 465	0.12	14
New Zealand	16.4	9.1	7.3	1.4	2 023	0.15	1 583	0.04	25
Canada	20.5	3.7	16.8	2.9	1 478	0.33	1 802	0.05	35
United States	21.5	2.8	18.7	7.1	3 405	0.13	5 843	0.03	42
Australia	25.0	5.9	19.1	9.5	1 348	0.41	9 762	0.03	34

Note: The energy production-to-GDP ratio is multiplied by 1 000 to fit in the table. E&H denotes Electricity and Heating.
Source: OECD calculations based on data obtained from UNFCCC.

Table 2.A1.2. **Implicit carbon prices based on excise taxes**

Euros/tonne, 2010Q4

	Petrol	Diesel	D/Petrol	LPG	Natural gas		Electricity		Light fuel oil		Coal
					HH	IND	HH	IND	HH	IND	
Netherlands	323	159	0.49	51	88	14	10	26	96	96	–
Turkey	322	175	0.55	152	0	6	16	7	143	–	0
United Kingdom	302	251	0.83		0	2	0	6	48	48	2
Norway	300	191	0.64	–	–	–	822	0	68	68	–
Greece	299	153	0.51	–	0	0	18	20	8	8	–
Germany	292	174	0.60	54	–	–	133	–	23	23	0
Finland	280	135	0.48	–	10	10	38	11	32	32	17
Belgium	274	146	0.53	0	12	5	76	46	7	7	0
France	271	159	0.59	35	6	8	156	100	21	21	0
Sweden	267	174	0.65		130	39	1 937	36	153	25	–
Portugal	260	135	0.52	33	0	0	0	0	79	–	0
Israel	259	191	0.74	–	–	–	0	0	191	–	1
Italy	252	157	0.62	74	–	–	72	98	149	149	0
Denmark	250	144	0.58	–	152	–	160	13	123	21	19
Switzerland	248	217	0.87	–	28	28	555	555	28	28	8
Ireland	242	166	0.69	–	15	0	0	0	33	18	0
Czech Republic	231	164	0.71	51	0	7	2	2	10	10	2
Slovak Republic	230	136	0.59	0	0	7	0	0	–	0	–
Korea	227	125	0.55	85	22	22	–	–	25	25	–
Slovenia	223	162	0.73	44	23	23	37	30	45	45	–
Japan	223	113	0.51	51	–	0	8	8	7	7	2
Austria	217	143	0.66	–	31	–	127	109	40	40	17
Luxembourg	206	115	0.56	32	–	–	–	–	4	8	0
Hungary	200	135	0.68	55	0	5	0	3	–	–	0
Spain	197	127	0.65	19	0	0	0	0	32	32	–
Lithuania	194	102	0.52	99	0	0	0	3	8	8	–
Estonia	189	146	0.77	41	12	9	14	13	41	41	–
Poland	**187**	**120**	**0.64**	**68**	**0**	**0**	**6**	**6**	**22**	**22**	**0**
Croatia	182	123	0.68	40	0	0	0	0	28	–	–
Latvia	161	120	0.75	75	–	–	0	0	16	16	–
Bulgaria	157	114	0.73	55	0	0	0	2	114	114	–
Romania	155	108	0.70	40	42	19	0	0	108	108	–
Chile	154	32	0.21	0	0	–	0	0	0	–	–
New Zealand	147	1	0.00	–	5	5	0	0	–	0	–
Australia	124	103	0.83	0	–	–	–	–	–	–	–
South Africa	121	92	0.76	–	–	–	–	–	–	–	–
Canada	106	55	0.52	–	0	0	–	–	13	8	–
United States	40	37	0.92	–	–	–	–	–	–	–	0
Mexico	0	0	–	–	0	0	0	0	0	0	0

Note: The implied carbon price is computed as the amount of the tax levied per litre times the amount (litres) of fuel that needs to be burnt to reach a CO_2 emission of one tonne of CO_2 eq. One litre of diesel (light fuel oil for households and industry), petrol and LPG (liquefied petroleum gas) is assumed to produce respectively 2.7, 2.24 and 1.7 kg of CO_2. It is assumed that 4 535 269 kcal of natural gas generates 1 tonne of CO_2 and that burning 1 kg of coal generates 2.93 kg of CO_2. HH and IND refer to households and industry, respectively.

Source: OECD calculations based on data obtained from International Energy Agency (2011), *Energy Prices And Taxes*, Paris.

ORGANISATION FOR ECONOMIC CO-OPERATION AND DEVELOPMENT

The OECD is a unique forum where governments work together to address the economic, social and environmental challenges of globalisation. The OECD is also at the forefront of efforts to understand and to help governments respond to new developments and concerns, such as corporate governance, the information economy and the challenges of an ageing population. The Organisation provides a setting where governments can compare policy experiences, seek answers to common problems, identify good practice and work to co-ordinate domestic and international policies.

The OECD member countries are: Australia, Austria, Belgium, Canada, Chile, the Czech Republic, Denmark, Estonia, Finland, France, Germany, Greece, Hungary, Iceland, Ireland, Israel, Italy, Japan, Korea, Luxembourg, Mexico, the Netherlands, New Zealand, Norway, Poland, Portugal, the Slovak Republic, Slovenia, Spain, Sweden, Switzerland, Turkey, the United Kingdom and the United States. The European Union takes part in the work of the OECD.

OECD Publishing disseminates widely the results of the Organisation's statistics gathering and research on economic, social and environmental issues, as well as the conventions, guidelines and standards agreed by its members.

OECD PUBLISHING, 2, rue André-Pascal, 75775 PARIS CEDEX 16
(10 2012 07 1 P) ISBN 978-92-64-12728-9 – No. 59957 2012-02